SOCIAL MEDIA MINING

The growth of social media over the last decade has revolutionized the way individuals interact and industries conduct business. Individuals produce data at an unprecedented rate by interacting, sharing, and consuming content through social media. Understanding and processing this new type of data to glean actionable patterns presents challenges and opportunities for interdisciplinary research, novel algorithms, and tool development.

Social Media Mining integrates social media, social network analysis, and data mining to provide a convenient and coherent platform for students, practitioners, researchers, and project managers to understand the basics and potentials of social media mining. It introduces the unique problems arising from social media data and presents fundamental concepts, emerging issues, and effective algorithms for network analysis and data mining.

Suitable for use in advanced undergraduate and beginning graduate courses as well as professional short courses, the text contains exercises of different degrees of difficulty that improve understanding and help apply concepts, principles, and methods in various scenarios of social media mining.

Reza Zafarani is a research associate of Computer Science and Engineering at Arizona State University. His research interests are in social media mining, machine learning, social network analysis, and social computing. His research emphasis is on user behavioral analysis at scale, and information integration and modeling across social media sites.

Mohammad Ali Abbasi is a research associate of Computer Science and Engineering at Arizona State University. His research interests are in data mining, machine learning, and social computing. In particular, his research is focused on user profiling, user credibility assessment, and real-world applications of social media.

Huan Liu is a professor of Computer Science and Engineering at Arizona State University where he has been recognized for excellence in teaching and research. His research interests are in data mining, machine learning, social computing, artificial intelligence, and investigating problems that arise in real-world data-intensive applications with high-dimensional data of disparate forms, such as social media.

SOCIAL MEDIA MINING

An Introduction

REZA ZAFARANI

Arizona State University, Tempe

MOHAMMAD ALI ABBASI

Arizona State University, Tempe

HUAN LIU

Arizona State University, Tempe

CAMBRIDGE
UNIVERSITY PRESS

CAMBRIDGE
UNIVERSITY PRESS

32 Avenue of the Americas, New York, NY 10013-2473, USA

Cambridge University Press is part of the University of Cambridge.

It furthers the University's mission by disseminating knowledge in the pursuit of
education, learning, and research at the highest international levels of excellence.

www.cambridge.org
Information on this title: www.cambridge.org/9781107018853

© Reza Zafarani, Mohammad Ali Abbasi, and Huan Liu 2014

First published 2014

Printed in the United States of America

A catalog record for this publication is available from the British Library.

Library of Congress Cataloging in Publication data
Zafarani, Reza, 1983–
Social media mining : an introduction / Reza Zafarani, Arizona State University, Tempe,
Mohammad Ali Abbasi, Arizona State University, Tempe, Huan Liu, Arizona State
University, Tempe.
pages   cm
Includes bibliographical references and index.
ISBN 978-1-107-01885-3 (hardback)
1. Data mining.   2. Social media – Research.   3. Behavioral assessment – Data processing.
4. Webometrics.   I. Abbasi, Mohammad Ali, 1975–   II. Liu, Huan, 1958–   III. Title.
QA76.9.D343Z34   2014
006.3'12–dc23   2013035271

ISBN 978-1-107-01885-3 Hardback

Additional resources for this publication at http://dmml.asu.edu/smm

To our families . . .

Contents

Preface

We live in an age of big data. With hundreds of millions of people spending countless hours on social media to share, communicate, connect, interact, and create user-generated data at an unprecedented rate, social media has become one unique source of big data. This novel source of rich data provides unparalleled opportunities and great potential for research and development. Unfortunately, more data does not necessarily beget more good, only more of the right (or relevant) data that enables us to glean gems. Social media data differs from traditional data we are familiar with in data mining. Thus, new computational methods are needed to mine the data. Social media data is noisy, free-format, of varying length, and multimedia. Furthermore, social relations among the entities, or social networks, form an inseparable part of social media data; hence, it is important that social theories and research methods be employed with statistical and data mining methods. It is therefore a propitious time for social media mining.

Social media mining is a rapidly growing new field. It is an interdisciplinary field at the crossroad of disparate disciplines deeply rooted in computer science and social sciences. There are an active community and a large body of literature about social media. The fast-growing interests and intensifying need to harness social media data require research and the development of tools for finding insights from big social media data. This book is one of the intellectual efforts to answer the novel challenges of social media. It is designed to enable students, researchers, and practitioners to acquire fundamental concepts and algorithms for social media mining.

Researchers in this emerging field are expected to have knowledge in different areas, such as data mining, machine learning, text mining, social network analysis, and information retrieval, and are often required to consult research papers to learn the state of the art of social media mining. To mitigate such a strenuous effort and help researchers get up to speed in a convenient way, we take advantage of our teaching and research of many years to survey, summarize, filter, categorize, and connect disparate research findings and fundamental concepts of social media mining. This book is our diligent attempt to provide an easy reference or entry point to help researchers quickly acquire a wide range of essentials of social media mining. Social media not only produces big user-generated data; it also has a huge potential for social science research, business development, and understanding human and group behavior. If you want to share a piece of information or a site on social media, you would like to grab precious attention from other equally eager users of social media; if you are curious to know what is hidden or who is influential in the complex world of social media, you might wonder how one can find this information in big and messy social media; if you hope to serve your customers better in social media, you certainly want to employ effective means to understand them better. These are just some scenarios in which social media mining can help. If one of these scenarios fits your need or you simply wish to learn something interesting in this emerging field of social media mining, this book is for you. We hope this book can be of benefit to you in accomplishing your goals of dealing with big data of social media.

Book Website and Resources

The book's website and further resources can be found at

`http://dmml.asu.edu/smm`

The website provides lecture slides, homework and exam problems, and sample projects, as well as pointers to useful material and resources that are publicly available and relevant to social media mining.

To Instructors

The book is designed for a one-semester course for senior undergraduate or graduate students. Though it is mainly written for students with a background in computer science, readers with a basic understanding of probability, statistics, and linear algebra will find it easily accessible. Some chapters can be skipped or assigned as a homework assignment for reviewing purposes if students have knowledge of a chapter. For example, if students have taken a data mining or machine learning course, they can skip Chapter 5. When time is limited, Chapters 6–8 should be discussed in depth, and Chapters 9 and 10 can be either discussed briefly or assigned as part of reading material for course projects.

Reza Zafarani
Mohammad Ali Abbasi
Huan Liu
Tempe, AZ
August 2013

Acknowledgments

In the past several years, enormous pioneering research has been performed by numerous researchers in the interdisciplinary fields of data mining, social computing, social network analysis, network science, computer science, and the social sciences. We are truly dwarfed by the depth, breadth, and extent of the literature, which not only made it possible for us to complete a text on this emerging topic – *social media mining* – but also made it a seemingly endless task. In the process, we have been fortunate in drawing inspiration and obtaining great support and help from many people to whom we are indebted.

We would like to express our tremendous gratitude to the current and former members of the Data Mining and Machine Learning laboratory at Arizona State University (ASU); in particular, Nitin Agrawal, Salem Alelyani, Geoffrey Barbier, William Cole, Zhuo Feng, Magdiel Galan-Oliveras, Huiji Gao, Pritam Gundecha, Xia (Ben) Hu, Isaac Jones, Shamanth Kumar, Fred Morstatter, Sai Thejasvee Moturu, Ashwin Rajadesingan, Suhas Ranganath, Jiliang Tang, Lei Tang, Xufei Wang, and Zheng Zhao. Without their impressive accomplishments and continuing strides in advancing research in data mining, machine learning, and social computing, this book would have not been possible. Their stimulating thoughts, creative ideas, friendly aggressiveness, willingness to extend the research frontier, and cool company during our struggling moments (Arizona could be scorchingly hot in some months), directly and indirectly, offered us encouragement, drive, passion, and ideas, as well as critiques in the process toward the completion of the book.

This book project stemmed from a course on social computing offered in 2008 at ASU. It was a seminar course that enjoyed active participation by graduate students and bright undergraduates with intelligent and provocative minds. Lively discussion and heated arguments were fixtures of the seminar course. Since then, it has become a regular course, evolving into a focused theme on *social media mining*. Teaching assistants, students, and guest speakers in these annual courses were of significant help to us in choosing topics to include, determining the depth and extent of each topic, and offering feedback on lecture materials such as homework problems, slides, course projects, and reading materials.

We would like to especially thank Denny Abraham Cheriyan, Nitin Ahuja, Amy Baldwin, Sai Prasanna Baskaran, Gaurav Pandey, Prerna Satija, Nitesh Kedia, Bernard Ma, Dhanyatha Manjunath, Girish Kumar Reddy Marthala, Apurv Patki, Greggory Scherer, Nikhil Sunkesula Bhaskar, Yajin Wang, and Ruozhou Yu for their detailed comments on the drafts of this book. In addition, we owe our gratitude to Daria Bazzi and Michael Meeder for their help in proofreading earlier versions of the book, Farzad Zafarani for preparing the book's website, Subbarao Kambhampati for reading an earlier draft and offering encouragement, and Rebecca Goolsby for continually challenging us in understanding social media and developing social computing tools for real-world applications of humanitarian assistance and disaster relief.

The idea of having this book published by Cambridge University Press began with a casual conversation with K. Selcuk Candan, a well-received Cambridge author. It was an enjoyable and pleasant process working with Cambridge University Press. We would like to thank Lauren Cowles, a senior editor of Mathematics and Computer Sciences at Cambridge, for her patience and kind support during the process, and the Cambridge team, David Jou and Joshua Penney, as well as Adrian Pereira and his colleagues at Aptara for their work on the production of the book.

Our research on social computing, data mining, and social network analysis has been, in part, supported by the Office of Naval Research, National Science Foundation, and Army Research Office.

We have truly enjoyed our collaboration in this arduous journey. We will certainly miss our weekly meetings and many missed deadlines.

1

Introduction

With the rise of *social media*, the web has become a vibrant and lively realm SOCIAL
in which billions of individuals all around the globe interact, share, post, MEDIA
and conduct numerous daily activities. Information is collected, curated, and
published by *citizen journalists* and simultaneously shared or consumed by CITIZEN
thousands of individuals, who give spontaneous feedback. Social media JOURNALISM
enables us to be connected and interact with each other anywhere and any-
time – allowing us to observe human behavior in an unprecedented scale
with a new lens. This social media lens provides us with golden opportunities to understand individuals at scale and to mine human behavioral
patterns otherwise impossible. As a byproduct, by understanding individuals better, we can design better computing systems tailored to individuals' needs that will serve them and society better. This new social media
world has no geographical boundaries and incessantly churns out oceans
of data. As a result, we are facing an exacerbated problem of big data –
"drowning in data, but thirsty for knowledge." Can data mining come to the
rescue?

Unfortunately, social media data is significantly different from the traditional data that we are familiar with in data mining. Apart from enormous
size, the mainly user-generated data is noisy and unstructured, with abun-
dant social relations such as friendships and followers-followees. This new
type of data mandates new computational data analysis approaches that can
combine social theories with statistical and data mining methods. The pressing demand for new techniques ushers in and entails a new interdisciplinary
field – social media mining.

1.1 What Is Social Media Mining

Social media shatters the boundaries between the real world and the virtual
world. We can now integrate social theories with computational methods
to study how individuals (also known as *social atoms*) interact and how SOCIAL ATOM

1

SOCIAL
MOLECULE

communities (i.e., *social molecules*) form. The uniqueness of social media data calls for novel data mining techniques that can effectively handle user-generated content with rich social relations. The study and development of these new techniques are under the purview of social media mining, an emerging discipline under the umbrella of data mining. **Social Media Mining** *is the process of representing, analyzing, and extracting actionable patterns from social media data.*

SOCIAL
MEDIA
MINING

Social Media Mining, introduces basic concepts and principal algorithms suitable for investigating massive social media data; it discusses theories and methodologies from different disciplines such as computer science, data mining, machine learning, social network analysis, network science, sociology, ethnography, statistics, optimization, and mathematics. It encompasses the tools to formally represent, measure, model, and mine meaningful patterns from large-scale social media data.

DATA
SCIENTIST

Social media mining cultivates a new kind of *data scientist* who is well versed in social and computational theories, specialized to analyze recalcitrant social media data, and skilled to help bridge the gap from what we know (social and computational theories) to what we want to know about the vast social media world with computational tools.

1.2 New Challenges for Mining

Social media mining is an emerging field where there are more problems than ready solutions. Equipped with interdisciplinary concepts and theories, fundamental principles, and state-of-the-art algorithms, we can stand on the shoulders of the giants and embark on solving challenging problems and developing novel data mining techniques and scalable computational algorithms. In general, social media can be considered a world of social atoms (i.e., individuals), entities (e.g., content, sites, networks, etc.), and interactions between individuals and entities. Social theories and social norms govern the interactions between individuals and entities. For effective social media mining, we collect information about individuals and entities, measure their interactions, and discover patterns to understand human behavior.

Mining social media data is the task of mining user-generated content with social relations. This data[1] presents novel challenges encountered in social media mining.

BIG DATA
PARADOX

Big Data Paradox. Social media data is undoubtedly big. However, when we zoom into individuals for whom, for example, we would like to make relevant recommendations, we often have little data for each specific individual. We have to exploit the characteristics of social media and use its multidimensional, multisource, and multisite data to aggregate information with sufficient statistics for effective mining.

Obtaining Sufficient Samples. One of the commonly used methods to collect data is via application programming interfaces (APIs) from social media sites. Only a limited amount of data can be obtained daily. Without knowing the population's distribution, how can we know that our samples are reliable representatives of the full data? Consequently, how can we ensure that our findings obtained from social media mining are any indication of true patterns that can benefit our research or business development?

OBTAINING
SUFFICIENT
SAMPLES

Noise Removal Fallacy. In classic data mining literature, a successful data mining exercise entails extensive data preprocessing and noise removal as "garbage in and garbage out." By its nature, social media data can contain a large portion of noisy data. For this data, we notice two important observations: (1) blindly removing noise can worsen the problem stated in the big data paradox because the removal can also eliminate valuable information, and (2) the definition of noise becomes complicated and relative because it is dependent on our task at hand.

NOISE
REMOVAL
FALLACY

Evaluation Dilemma. A standard procedure of evaluating patterns in data mining is to have some kind of ground truth. For example, a dataset can be divided into training and test sets. Only the training data is used in learning, and the test data serves as ground truth for testing. However, ground truth is often not available in social media mining. Evaluating patterns from social media mining poses a seemingly insurmountable challenge. On the other hand, without credible evaluation, how can we guarantee the validity of the patterns?

EVALUATION
DILEMMA

This book contains basic concepts and fundamental principles that will help readers contemplate and design solutions to address these challenges intrinsic to social media mining.

1.3 Book Overview and Reader's Guide

This book consists of three parts. Part I, *Essentials*, outlines ways to represent social media data and provides an understanding of fundamental elements of social media mining. Part II, *Communities and Interactions*, discusses how communities can be found in social media and how interactions occur and information propagates in social media. Part III, *Applications*, offers some novel illustrative applications of social media mining. Throughout the book, we use examples to explain how things work and to deepen the understanding of abstract concepts and profound algorithms. These examples show in a tangible way how theories are applied or ideas are materialized in discovering meaningful patterns in social media data.

Consider an online social networking site with millions of members in which members have the opportunity to befriend one another, send messages to each other, and post content on the site. Facebook, LinkedIn, and Twitter are exemplars of such sites. To make sense of data from these sites, we resort to social media mining to answer corresponding questions. In Part I: Essentials (Chapters 2–5), we learn to answer questions such as the following:

1. Who are the most important people in a social network?
2. How do people befriend others?
3. How can we find interesting patterns in user-generated content?

These essentials come into play in Part II: Communities and Interactions (Chapters 6 and 7) where we attempt to analyze how communities are formed, how they evolve, and how the qualities of detected communities are evaluated. We show ways in which information diffusion in social media can be studied. We aim to answer general questions such as the following:

1. How can we identify communities in a social network?
2. When someone posts an interesting article on a social network, how far can the article be transmitted in that network?

In Part III: Application (Chapters 8–10), we exemplify social media mining using real-world problems in dealing with social media: measuring influence, recommending in a social environment, and analyzing user behavior. We aim to answer these questions:

1. How can we measure the influence of individuals in a social network?
2. How can we recommend content or friends to individuals online?
3. How can we analyze the behavior of individuals online?

To provide an overall picture of the book content, we created a dependency graph among chapters (Fig. 1.1) in which arrows suggest dependencies between chapters. Based on the dependency graph, therefore, a reader can start with Chapter 2 (graph essentials), and it is recommended that he or she read Chapters 5 (data mining essentials) and 8 (influence and homophily) before Chapter 9 (recommendation in social media). We have

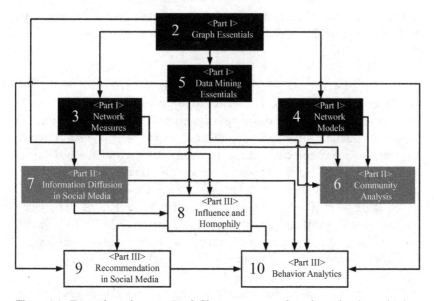

Figure 1.1. Dependency between Book Chapters. Arrows show dependencies and colors represent book parts.

also color-coded chapter boxes that are of the same level of importance and abstraction. The darkest chapters are the essentials of this book, and the lightest boxes are those chapters that are more applied and have materials that are built on the foundation of other chapters.

Who Should Read This Book?

A reader with a basic computer science background and knowledge of data structures, search, and graph algorithms will find this book easily accessible. Limited knowledge of linear algebra, calculus, probability, and statistics will help readers understand technical details with ease. Having a data mining or machine learning background is a plus, but not necessary.

The book is designed for senior undergraduate and graduate students. It is organized in such a way that it can be taught in one semester to students with a basic prior knowledge of statistics and linear algebra. It can also be used for a graduate seminar course by focusing on more advanced chapters with the supplement of detailed bibliographical notes. Moreover, the book can be used as a reference book for researchers, practitioners, and project managers of related fields who are interested in both learning the basics and tangible examples of this emerging field and understanding the potentials and opportunities that social media mining can offer.

1.4 Summary

As defined by Kaplan and Haenlein [2010], social media is the "group of internet-based applications that build on the ideological and techno-logical foundations of Web 2.0, and that allow the creation and exchange of user-generated content." There are many categories of social media including, but not limited to, social networking (Facebook or LinkedIn), microblogging (Twitter), photo sharing (Flickr, Photobucket, or Picasa), news aggregation (Google reader, StumbleUpon, or Feedburner), video sharing (YouTube, MetaCafe), livecasting (Ustream or Justin.TV), virtual worlds (Kaneva), social gaming (World of Warcraft), social search (Google, Bing, or Ask.com), and instant messaging (Google Talk, Skype, or Yahoo! messenger).

The first social media site was introduced by Geocities in 1994, which allowed users to create their own homepages. The first social networking site, SixDegree.com, was introduced in 1997. Since then, many other social media sites have been introduced, each providing service to millions of people. These individuals form a virtual world in which individuals (social atoms), entities (content, sites, etc.) and interactions (between individuals, between entities, between individuals and entities) coexist. Social norms and human behavior govern this virtual world. By understanding these social norms and models of human behavior and combining them with the observations and measurements of this virtual world, one can systematically analyze and mine social media.

Social media mining is the process of representing, analyzing, and extracting meaningful patterns from data in social media, resulting from social interactions. It is an interdisciplinary field encompassing techniques from computer science, data mining, machine learning, social network anal-ysis, network science, sociology, ethnography, statistics, optimization, and mathematics. Social media mining faces grand challenges such as the big data paradox, obtaining sufficient samples, the noise removal fallacy, and evaluation dilemma.

Social media mining represents the virtual world of social media in a computable way, measures it, and designs models that can help us under-stand its interactions. In addition, social media mining provides neces-sary tools to mine this world for interesting patterns, analyze information diffusion, study influence and homophily, provide effective recommendations, and analyze novel social behavior in social media.

1.5 Bibliographic Notes

For historical notes on social media sites and challenges in social media, refer to [Ellison et al., 2007; Lietsala and Sirkkunen, 2008; Kaplan and Haenlein, 2010; Kleinberg, 1998; Gundecha and Liu, 2012]. Kaplan and Haenlein [2010] provide a categorization of social media sites into collaborative projects, blogs, content communities, social networking sites, virtual game worlds, and virtual social worlds. Our definition of social media is a rather abstract one whose elements are social atoms (individuals), entities, and interactions. A more detailed abstraction can be found in the work of [Kietzmann et al., 2011]. They consider the seven building blocks of social media to be identity, conversation, sharing, presence, relationships, reputation, and groups. They argue that the amount of attention that sites give to these building blocks makes them different in nature. For instance, YouTube provides more functionality in terms of groups than LinkedIn.

Social media mining brings together techniques from many disciplines. General references that can accompany this book and help readers better understand the material in this book can be found in data mining and web mining [Han et al., 2006; Tang, Wang, and Liu, 2012; Friedman, Hastie, and Tibshirani, 2009; Liu, 2007; Chakrabarti, 2003], machine learning [Bishop, 2006], and pattern recognition [Duda, Hart, and Stork, 2012] texts, as well as network science and social network analysis [Easley and Kleinberg, 2010; Scott, 1988; Newman, 2010; Kadushin, 2012; Barrat, Barthelemy, and Vespignani, 2008] textbooks. For relevant references on optimization refer to [Boyd and Vandenberghe, 2004; Nocedal and Wright, 2006; Papadimitriou and Steiglitz, 1998; Nemhauser and Wolsey, 1988] and for algorithms to [Cormen et al., 2009; Kleinberg and Tardos, 2005]. For general references on social research methods consult [Bernard, 2012; Bryman, 2012]. Note that these are generic references and more specific references are provided at the end of each chapter. This book discusses non–multimedia data in social media. For multimedia data analysis refer to [Candan and Sapino, 2010].

Recent developments in social media mining can be found in journal articles in IEEE Transactions on Knowledge and Data Engineering (TKDE), ACM Transactions on Knowledge Discovery from Data (TKDD), ACM Transactions on Intelligent Systems and Technology (TIST), Social

Network Analysis and Mining (SNAM), Knowledge and Information Systems (KAIS), ACM Transactions on the Web (TWEB), Data Mining and Knowledge Discovery (DMKD), World Wide Web Journal, Social Networks, Internet Mathematics, IEEE Intelligent Systems, and SIGKDD Exploration. Conference papers can be found in proceedings of Knowledge Discovery and Data Mining (KDD), World Wide Web (WWW), Association for Computational Linguistics (ACL), Conference on Information and Knowledge Management (CIKM), International Conference on Data Mining (ICDM), Internet Measuring Conference (IMC), International Conference on Weblogs and Social Media (ICWSM), International Conference on Web Engineering (ICWE), Pacific-Asia Conference on Knowledge Discovery and Data Mining (PAKDD), The European Conference on Machine Learning and Principles and Practice of Knowledge Discovery in Data Basis (ECML/PKDD), Web Search and Data Mining (WSDM), International Joint Conferences on Artificial Intelligence (IJCAI), Association for the Advancement of Artificial Intelligence (AAAI), Recommender Systems (RecSys), Computer-Human Interaction (CHI), SIAM International Conference on Data Mining (SDM), Hypertext (HT), and Social Computing Behavioral-Cultural Modeling and Prediction (SBP) conferences.

1.6 Exercises

1. Discuss some methodologies that can address the grand challenges of social media.

2. What are the key characteristics of social media that differentiate it from other media? Please list at least two with a brief explanation.

3. What are the different types of social media? Name two, and provide a definition and an example for each type.

4. (a) Visit the websites in Table 1.1 (or find similar ones) and identify the types of activities that individuals can perform on each one.

   (b) Similar to questions posed in Section 1.3, design two questions that you find interesting to ask with respect to each site.

Table 1.1. *List of Websites*

Amazon	Flickr	Facebook	Twitter
BlogCatalog	MySpace	Last.fm	Pandora
LinkedIn	Reddit	Vimeo	Del.icio.us
StumbleUpon	Yelp	YouTube	Meetup

5. What marketing opportunities do you think exist in social media? Can you outline an example of such an opportunity in Twitter?

6. How does behavior of individuals change across sites? What behaviors remain consistent and what behaviors likely change? What are possible reasons behind these differences?

7. How does social media influence real-world behaviors of individuals? Identify a behavior that is due to the usage of, say, Twitter.

8. Outline how social media can help NGOs fulfill their missions better in performing tasks such as humanitarian assistance and disaster relief.

9. Identify at least three major side effects of information sharing on social media.

10. Rumors spread rapidly on social media. Can you think of some method to block the spread of rumors on social media?

Part I

Essentials

2

Graph Essentials

We live in a connected world in which networks are intertwined with our daily life. Networks of air and land transportation help us reach our destinations; critical infrastructure networks that distribute water and electricity are essential for our society and economy to function; and networks of communication help disseminate information at an unprecedented rate. Finally, our social interactions form *social networks* of friends, family, and colleagues. Social media attests to the growing body of these social networks in which individuals interact with one another through friendships, email, blogposts, buying similar products, and many other mechanisms.

Social media mining aims to make sense of these individuals embedded in networks. These connected networks can be conveniently represented using graphs. As an example, consider a set of individuals on a social networking site where we want to find the most influential individual. Each individual can be represented using a *node* (circle) and two individuals who know each other can be connected with an *edge* (line). In Figure 2.1, we show a set of seven individuals and their friendships. Consider a hypothetical social theory that states that "the more individuals you know, the more influential you are." This theory in our graph translates to the individual with the maximum *degree* (the number of edges connected to its corresponding node) being the most influential person. Therefore, in this network *Juan* is the most influential individual because he knows four others, which is more than anyone else. This simple scenario is an instance of many problems that arise in social media, which can be solved by modeling the problem as a graph. This chapter formally details the essentials required for using graphs and the fundamental algorithms required to explore these graphs in social media mining.

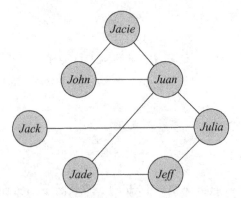

Figure 2.1. A Sample Graph. In this graph, individuals are represented with nodes (circles), and individuals who know each other are connected with edges (lines).

2.1 Graph Basics

In this section, we review some of the common notation used in graphs. Any graph contains both a set of objects, called *nodes*, and the connections between these nodes, called *edges*. Mathematically, a graph G is denoted as pair $G(V, E)$, where V represents the set of nodes and E represents the set of edges. We formally define nodes and edges next.

2.1.1 Nodes

All graphs have fundamental building blocks. One major part of any graph is the set of *nodes*. In a graph representing friendship, these nodes represent people, and any pair of connected people denotes the friendship between them. Depending on the context, these nodes are called *vertices* or *actors*. For example, in a web graph, nodes represent websites, and the connections between nodes indicate web-links between them. In a social setting, these nodes are called actors. The mathematical representation for a set of nodes is

VERTICES
AND ACTORS

$$V = \{v_1, v_2, \ldots, v_n\}, \tag{2.1}$$

where V is the set of nodes and v_i, $1 \leq i \leq n$, is a single node. $|V| = n$ is called the *size of the graph*. In Figure 2.1, $n = 7$.

2.1.2 Edges

Another important element of any graph is the set of *edges*. Edges connect nodes. In a social setting, where nodes represent social entities such as

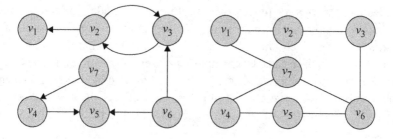

(a) Directed Graph   (b) Undirected Graph

Figure 2.2. A Directed Graph and an Undirected Graph. Circles represent nodes, and lines or arrows connecting nodes are edges.

people, edges indicate inter-node relationships and are therefore known as *relationships* or *(social) ties* . The edge set is usually represented using E,   RELATIONSHIPS AND TIES

$$E = \{e_1, e_2, \ldots, e_m\}, \tag{2.2}$$

where e_i, $1 \leq i \leq m$, is an edge and the size of the set is commonly shown as $m = |E|$. In Figure 2.1, lines connecting nodes represent the edges, so in this case, $m = 8$. Edges are also represented by their endpoints (nodes), so $e(v_1, v_2)$ (or (v_1, v_2)) defines an edge e between nodes v_1 and v_2. Edges can have directions, meaning one node is connected to another, but not vice versa. When edges are undirected, nodes are connected both ways. Note that in Figure 2.2(b), edges $e(v_1, v_2)$ and $e(v_2, v_1)$ are the same edges, because there is no direction in how nodes get connected. We call edges in this graph *undirected* edges and this kind of graph an *undirected graph*. Conversely, when edges have directions, $e(v_1, v_2)$ is not the same as $e(v_2, v_1)$. Graph 2.2(a) is a graph with *directed* edges; it is an example of a *directed graph*. Directed edges are represented using arrows. In a directed graph, an edge $e(v_i, v_j)$ is represented using an arrow that starts at v_i and ends at v_j. Edges can start and end at the same node; these edges are called *loops* or *self-links* and are represented as $e(v_i, v_i)$. For any node v_i, in an undirected graph, the set of nodes it is connected to via an edge is called its *neighborhood* and is represented as $N(v_i)$. In Figure 2.1, $N(Jade) = \{Jeff,$ NEIGHBORHOOD *Juan*}. In directed graphs, node v_i has incoming neighbors $N_{in}(v_i)$ (nodes that connect to v_i) and outgoing neighbors $N_{out}(v_i)$ (nodes that v_i connects to). In Figure 2.2(a), $N_{in}(v_2) = \{v_3\}$ and $N_{out}(v_2) = \{v_1, v_3\}$.

2.1.3 Degree and Degree Distribution

The number of edges connected to one node is the *degree* of that node. Degree of a node v_i is often denoted using d_i. In the case of directed edges, nodes have *in-degrees* (edges pointing toward the node) and *out-degrees* (edges pointing away from the node). These values are presented using d_i^{in} and d_i^{out}, respectively. In social media, degree represents the number of friends a given user has. For example, on Facebook, degree represents the user's number of friends, and on Twitter in-degree and out-degree represent the number of followers and followees, respectively. In any undirected graph, the summation of all node degrees is equal to twice the number of edges.

Theorem 2.1. *The summation of degrees in an undirected graph is twice the number of edges,*

$$\sum_i d_i = 2|E|. \tag{2.3}$$

Proof. Any edge has two endpoints; therefore, when calculating the degrees d_i and d_j for any connected nodes v_i and v_j, the edge between them contributes 1 to both d_i and d_j; hence, if the edge is removed, d_i and d_j become $d_i - 1$ and $d_j - 1$, and the summation $\sum_k d_k$ becomes $\sum_k d_k - 2$. Hence, by removal of all m edges, the degree summation becomes smaller by $2m$. However, we know that when all edges are removed the degree summation becomes zero; therefore, the degree summation is $2 \times m = 2|E|$. □

Lemma 2.1. *In an undirected graph, there are an even number of nodes having odd degree.*

Proof. The result can be derived from the previous theorem directly because the summation of degrees is even: $2|E|$. Therefore, when nodes with even degree are removed from this summation, the summation of nodes with odd degree should also be even; hence, there must exist an even number of nodes with odd degree. □

Lemma 2.2. *In any directed graph, the summation of in-degrees is equal to the summation of out-degrees,*

$$\sum_i d_i^{out} = \sum_j d_j^{in}. \tag{2.4}$$

Proof. The proof is left as an exercise. □

Degree Distribution

In very large graphs, distribution of node degrees (*degree distribution*) is an important attribute to consider. The degree distribution plays an important role in describing the network being studied. Any distribution can be described by its members. In our case, these are the degrees of all nodes in the graph. The degree distribution p_d (or $P(d)$, or $P(d_v = d)$) gives the probability that a randomly selected node v has degree d. Because p_d is a probability distribution $\sum_{d=0}^{\infty} p_d = 1$. In a graph with n nodes, p_d is defined as

$$p_d = \frac{n_d}{n},\tag{2.5}$$

where n_d is the number of nodes with degree d. An important, commonly performed procedure is to plot a histogram of the degree distribution, in which the x-axis represents the degree (d) and the y-axis represents either (1) the number of nodes having that degree (n_d) or (2) the fraction of nodes having that degree (p_d).

Example 2.1. *For the graph provided in Figure 2.1, the degree distribution p_d for $d = \{1, 2, 3, 4\}$ is*

$$p_1 = \tfrac{1}{7}, \quad p_2 = \tfrac{4}{7}, \quad p_3 = \tfrac{1}{7}, \quad p_4 = \tfrac{1}{7}.\tag{2.6}$$

Because we have four nodes have degree 2, and degrees 1, 3, and 4 are observed once.

Example 2.2. *On social networking sites, friendship relationships can be represented by a large graph. In this graph, nodes represent individuals and edges represent friendship relationships. We can compute the degrees and plot the degree distribution using a graph where the x-axis is the degree and the y-axis is the fraction of nodes with that degree.[1] The degree distribution plot for Facebook in May 2012 is shown in Figure 2.3. A general trend observable on social networking sites is that there exist many users with few connections and there exist a handful of users with very large numbers of friends. This is commonly called the power-law degree distribution.*

POWER-LAW
DISTRIBUTION

As previously discussed, any graph G can be represented as a pair $G(V, E)$, where V is the node set and E is the edge set. Since edges are between nodes, we have

$$E \subseteq V \times V.\tag{2.7}$$

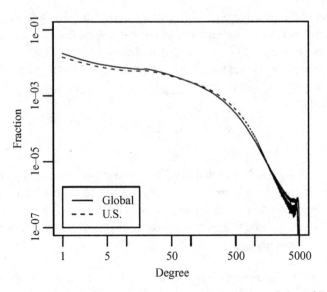

Figure 2.3. Degree Distribution for both the global and U.S. population of Facebook users (from Ugander et al. [2011]). There exist many users with few friends and a few users with many friends. This is due to a power-law degree distribution.

Graphs can also have *subgraphs*. For any graph $G(V, E)$, a graph $G'(V', E')$ is a *subgraph* of $G(V, E)$, if the following properties hold:

$$V' \subseteq V, \tag{2.8}$$

$$E' \subseteq (V' \times V') \cap E. \tag{2.9}$$

2.2 Graph Representation

We have demonstrated the visual representation of graphs. This representation, although clear to humans, cannot be used effectively by computers or manipulated using mathematical tools. We therefore seek representations that can store the node and edge sets in a way that (1) does not lose information, (2) can be manipulated easily by computers, and (3) can have mathematical methods applied easily.

Adjacency Matrix

A simple way of representing graphs is to use an *adjacency matrix* (also known as a *sociomatrix*). Figure 2.4 depicts an example of a graph and its corresponding adjacency matrix. A value of 1 in the adjacency matrix

SOCIOMATRIX

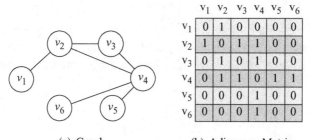

(a) Graph   (b) Adjacency Matrix

Figure 2.4. A Graph and Its Corresponding Adjacency Matrix.

indicates a connection between nodes v_i and v_j, and a 0 denotes no connection between the two nodes. When generalized, any real number can be used to show the strength of connections between two nodes. The adjacency matrix gives a natural mathematical representation for graphs. Note that in social networks, because of the relatively small number of interactions, many cells remain zero. This creates a large *sparse* matrix. In numerical analysis, a sparse matrix is one that is populated primarily with zeros.

In the adjacency matrix, diagonal entries represent *self-links* or *loops*. Adjacency matrices can be commonly formalized as

$$A_{i,j} = \begin{cases} 1 & \text{if } v_i \text{ is connected to } v_j, \\ 0 & \text{otherwise.} \end{cases} \qquad (2.10)$$

Adjacency List

In an *adjacency list*, every node is linked with a list of all the nodes that are connected to it. The list is often sorted based on node order or some other preference. For the graph shown in Figure 2.4, the corresponding adjacency list is shown in Table 2.1.

Table 2.1. *Adjacency List*

Node	Connected To
v_1	v_2
v_2	v_1, v_3, v_4
v_3	v_2, v_4
v_4	v_2, v_3, v_5, v_6
v_5	v_4
v_6	v_4

Edge List

Another simple and common approach to storing large graphs is to save all edges in the graph. This is known as the *edge list* representation. For the graph shown in Figure 2.4, we have the following edge list representation:

$$(v_1, v_2)$$

$$(v_2, v_3)$$

$$(v_2, v_4)$$

$$(v_3, v_4)$$

$$(v_4, v_5)$$

$$(v_4, v_6)$$

In this representation, each element is an edge and is represented as (v_i, v_j), denoting that node v_i is connected to node v_j. Since social media networks are sparse, both the adjacency list and edge list representations save significant space. This is because many zeros need to be stored when using adjacency matrices, but do not need to be stored in an adjacency or an edge list.

2.3 Types of Graphs

In general, there are many basic types of graphs. In this section we discuss several basic types of graphs.

Null Graph. A null graph is a graph where the node set is empty (there are no nodes). Obviously, since there are no nodes, there are also no edges. Formally,

$$G(V, E), \quad V = E = \emptyset. \tag{2.11}$$

Empty Graph. An empty or *edgeless* graph is one where the edge set is empty.

$$G(V, E), \quad E = \emptyset. \tag{2.12}$$

Note that the node set can be non-empty. A null graph is an empty graph but not vice versa.

Directed/Undirected/Mixed Graphs. Graphs that we have discussed thus far rarely had directed edges. As mentioned, graphs that only have directed edges are called *directed* graphs and ones that only have undirected ones are called *undirected* graphs. *Mixed* graphs have both directed and undirected edges. In directed graphs, we can have two edges between i and j (one from i to j and one from j to i), whereas in undirected graphs only one edge can exist. As a result, the adjacency matrix for directed graphs is not in general symmetric (i connected to j does not mean j is connected to i, i.e., $A_{i,j} \neq A_{j,i}$), whereas the adjacency matrix for undirected graphs is symmetric ($A = A^T$).

In social media, there are many directed and undirected networks. For instance, Facebook is an undirected network in which if *Jon* is a friend of *Mary*, then *Mary* is also a friend of *Jon*. Twitter is a directed network, where follower relationships are not bidirectional. One direction is called followers, and the other is denoted as following.

Simple Graphs and Multigraphs. In the example graphs that we have provided thus far, only one edge could exist between any pair of nodes. These graphs are denoted as *simple* graphs. *Multigraphs* are graphs where multiple edges between two nodes can exist. The adjacency matrix for multigraphs can include numbers larger than one, indicating multiple edges between nodes. Multigraphs are frequently observed in social media where two individuals can have different interactions with one another. They can be friends and, at the same time, colleagues, group members, or other relation. For each one of these relationships, a new edge can be added between the individuals, creating a multigraph.

Weighted Graphs. A weighted graph is one in which edges are associated with weights. For example, a graph could represent a map, where nodes are cities and edges are routes between them. The weight associated with each edge represents the distance between these cities. Formally, a weighted graph can be represented as $G(V, E, W)$, where W represents the weights associated with each edge, $|W| = |E|$. For an adjacency matrix representation, instead of 1/0 values, we can use the weight associated with the edge. This saves space by combining E and W into one adjacency matrix A, assuming that an edge exists between v_i and v_j if and only if $W_{ij} \neq 0$. Depending on the context, this weight can also be represented by w_{ij} or $w(i, j)$.

An example of a weighted graph is the web graph. A web graph is a way of representing how internet sites are connected on the web. In general, a web graph is a directed graph. Nodes represent sites and edge weights represent number of links between sites. Two sites can have multiple links pointing to each other, and individual sites can have loops (links pointing to themselves).

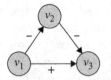

Figure 2.5. A Signed Graph Example.

SIGNED
EDGES AND
SIGNED
GRAPHS

A special case of a weighted graph is when we have binary weights $(0/1$ or $+/-)$ on edges. These edges are commonly called *signed edges*, and the weighted graph is called a *signed graph*. Signed edges can be employed to represent contradictory behavior. For instance, one can use signed edges to represent *friends* and *foes*. A positive $(+)$ edge between two nodes represents friendship, and a negative $(-)$ edge denotes that the endpoint nodes (individuals) are considered enemies. When edges are directed, one endpoint considers the other endpoint a friend or a foe, but not vice versa. When edges are undirected, endpoints are mutually friends or foes. In another setting, a $+$ edge can denote a higher *social status*, and a $-$ edge can represent lower *social status*. Social status is the rank assigned to one's position in society. For instance, a school principal can be connected via a directed $+$ edge to a student of the school because, in the school environment, the principal is considered to be of higher status. Figure 2.5 shows a *signed graph* consisting of nodes and the signed edges between them.

2.4 Connectivity in Graphs

Connectivity defines how nodes are connected via a sequence of edges in a graph. Before we define connectivity, some preliminary concepts need to be detailed.

Adjacent Nodes and Incident Edges. Two nodes v_1 and v_2 in graph $G(V, E)$ are *adjacent* when v_1 and v_2 are connected via an edge:

$$v_1 \text{ is adjacent to } v_2 \quad \equiv \quad e(v_1, v_2) \in E. \qquad (2.13)$$

Two edges $e_1(a, b)$ and $e_2(c, d)$ are *incident* when they share one endpoint (i.e., are connected via a node):

$$e_1(a, b) \text{ is incident to } e_2(c, d)$$

$$\equiv (a = c) \vee (a = d) \vee (b = c) \vee (b = d). \qquad (2.14)$$

Figure 2.6 depicts adjacent nodes and incident edges in a sample graph. In a directed graph, two edges are incident if the ending of one is the

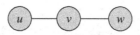

Figure 2.6. Adjacent Nodes and Incident Edges. In this graph u and v, as well as v and w, are adjacent nodes, and edges (u, v) and (v, w) are incident edges.

beginning of the other; that is, the edge directions must match for edges to be incident.

Traversing an Edge. An edge in a graph can be *traversed* when one starts at one of its end-nodes, moves along the edge, and stops at its other end-node. So, if an edge $e(a, b)$ connects nodes a and b, then visiting it can start at a and end at b. Alternatively, in an undirected graph we can start at b and end the visit at a.

Walk, Path, Trail, Tour, and Cycle. A walk is a sequence of incident edges traversed one after another. In other words, if in a walk one traverses edges $e_1(v_1, v_2), e_2(v_2, v_3), e_3(v_3, v_4), \ldots, e_n(v_n, v_{n+1})$, we have v_1 as the walk's starting node and v_{n+1} as the walk's ending node. When a walk does not end where it started ($v_1 \neq v_{n+1}$) then it is called an *open walk*. When a walk returns to where it was started ($v_1 = v_{n+1}$), it is called a *closed walk*. Similarly, a walk can be denoted as a sequence of nodes, $v_1, v_2, v_3, \ldots, v_n$. In this representation, the edges that are traversed are $e_1(v_1, v_2)$, $e_2(v_2, v_3), \ldots, e_{n-1}(v_{n-1}, v_n)$. The length of a walk is the number of edges traversed during the walk and in our case is $n - 1$. OPEN WALK AND CLOSED WALK

A *trail* is a walk where no edge is traversed more than once; therefore, all walk edges are distinct. A closed trail (one that ends where it started) is called a *tour* or *circuit*.

A walk where nodes and edges are distinct is called a *path*, and a closed path is called a *cycle*. The length of a path or cycle is the number of edges traversed in the path or cycle. In a directed graph, we have *directed paths* because traversal of edges is only allowed in the direction of the edges. In Figure 2.7, v_4, v_3, v_6, v_4, v_2 is a walk; v_4, v_3 is a path; v_4, v_3, v_6, v_4, v_2 is a trail; and v_4, v_3, v_6, v_4 is both a tour and a cycle.

A graph has a *Hamiltonian* cycle if it has a cycle such that all the nodes in the graph are visited. It has an *Eulerian* tour if all the edges are traversed only once. Examples of a Hamiltonian cycle and an Eulerian tour are provided in Figure 2.8.

One can perform a *random walk* on a weighted graph, where nodes are visited randomly. The weight of an edge, in this case, defines the probability of traversing it. For this to work correctly, we must make sure that for all RANDOM WALK

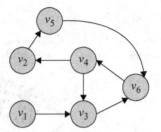

Figure 2.7. Walk, Path, Trail, Tour, and Cycle. In this figure, v_4, v_3, v_6, v_4, v_2 is a walk; v_4, v_3 is a path; v_4, v_3, v_6, v_4, v_2 is a trail; and v_4, v_3, v_6, v_4 is both a tour and a cycle.

edges that start at v_i we have

$$\sum_x w_{i,x} = 1, \forall i, j \ w_{i,j} \geq 0. \qquad (2.15)$$

The random walk procedure is outlined in Algorithm 2.1. The algorithm starts at a node v_0 and visits its adjacent nodes based on the transition probability (weight) assigned to edges connecting them. This procedure is performed for t steps (provided to the algorithm); therefore, a walk of length t is generated by the random walk.

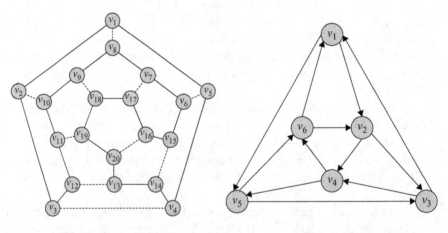

(a) Hamiltonian Cycle   (b) Eulerian Tour

Figure 2.8. Hamiltonian Cycle and Eulerian Tour. In a Hamiltonian cycle we start at one node, visit all other nodes only once, and return to our start node. In an Eulerian tour, we traverse all edges only once and return to our start point. In an Eulerian tour, we can visit a single node multiple times. In this figure, $v_1, v_5, v_3, v_1, v_2, v_4, v_6, v_2, v_3, v_4, v_5, v_6, v_1$ is an Eulerian tour.

Algorithm 2.1 Random Walk

Require: Initial Node v_0, Weighted Graph $G(V, E, W)$, Steps t
1: **return** Random Walk P
2: state $= 0$;
3: $v_t = v_0$;
4: $P = \{v_0\}$;
5: **while** state $< $ t **do**
6:     state $=$ state $+ 1$;
7:
8:     select a random node v_j adjacent to v_t with probability $w_{t,j}$;
9:     $v_t = v_j$;
10:    $P = P \cup \{v_j\}$;
11: **end while**
12: Return P

Connectivity. A node v_i is *connected* to node v_j (or v_j is *reachable* from v_i) if it is adjacent to it or there exists a *path* from v_i to v_j. A graph is *connected* if there exists a path between any pair of nodes in it. In a directed graph, the graph is *weakly connected* if there exists a path between any pair of nodes, without following the edge directions (i.e., directed edges are replaced with undirected edges). The graph is *strongly connected* if there exists a directed path (following edge directions) between any pair of nodes. Figure 2.9 shows examples of connected, disconnected, weakly connected, and strongly connected graphs.

Components. A component in an undirected graph is a subgraph such that, there exists a path between every pair of nodes inside the component. Figure 2.10(a) depicts an undirected graph with three components. A component in a directed graph is strongly connected if, for every pair

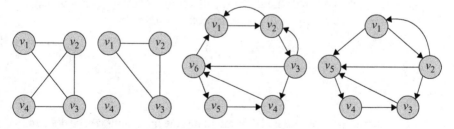

(a) Connected   (b) Disconnected   (c) Strongly connected   (d) Weakly connected

Figure 2.9. Connectivity in Graphs.

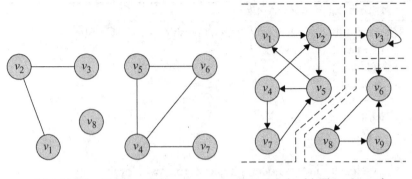

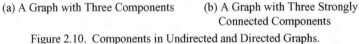

(a) A Graph with Three Components   (b) A Graph with Three Strongly
                                              Connected Components

Figure 2.10. Components in Undirected and Directed Graphs.

of nodes v and u, there exists a directed path from v to u and one from u to v. The component is weakly connected if replacing directed edges with undirected edges results in a connected component. A graph with three strongly connected components is shown in Figure 2.10(b).

Shortest Path. When a graph is connected, multiple paths can exist between any pair of nodes. Often, we are interested in the path that has the shortest length. This path is called the *shortest path*. Applications for shortest paths include GPS routing, where users are interested in the shortest path to their destination. In this chapter, we denote the length of the shortest path between nodes v_i and v_j as $l_{i,j}$. The concept of the neighborhood of a node v_i can be generalized using shortest paths. An *n-hop neighborhood* of node v_i is the set of nodes that are within n hops distance from node v_i. That is, their shortest path to v_i has length less than or equal to n.

Diameter. The *diameter* of a graph is defined as the length of the longest shortest path between any pair of nodes in the graph. It is defined only for connected graphs because the shortest path might not exist in disconnected graphs. Formally, for a graph G, the diameter is defined as

$$diameter_G = \max_{(v_i, v_j) \in V \times V} l_{i,j}. \qquad (2.16)$$

2.5 Special Graphs

Using general concepts defined thus far, many special graphs can be defined. These special graphs can be used to model different problems. We review some well-known special graphs and their properties in this section.

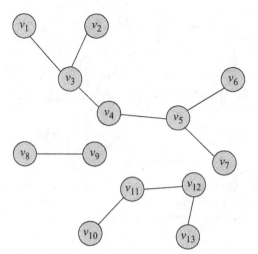

Figure 2.11. A Forest Containing Three Trees.

2.5.1 Trees and Forests

Trees are special cases of undirected graphs. A *tree* is a graph structure that has no cycle in it. In a tree, there is exactly one path between any pair of nodes. A graph consisting of set of disconnected trees is called a *forest*. A forest is shown in Figure 2.11.

In a tree with $|V|$ nodes, we have $|E| = |V| - 1$ edges. This can be proved by contradiction (see Exercises).

2.5.2 Special Subgraphs

Some subgraphs are frequently used because of their properties. Two such subgraphs are discussed here.

1. **Spanning Tree.** For any connected graph, the *spanning tree* is a subgraph and a tree that includes all the nodes of the graph. Obviously, when the original graph is not a tree, then its spanning tree includes all the nodes, but not all the edges. There may exist multiple spanning trees for a graph. For a weighted graph and one of its spanning trees, the weight of that spanning tree is the summation of the edge weights in the tree. Among the many spanning trees found for a weighted graph, the one with the minimum weight is called the *minimum spanning tree* (MST) .

   For example, consider a set of cities, where roads need to be built to connect them. We know the distance between each pair of cities. We

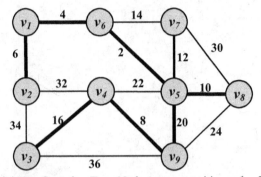

Figure 2.12. Minimum Spanning Tree. Nodes represent cities and values assigned to edges represent geographical distance between cities. Highlighted edges are roads that are built in a way that minimizes their total length.

can represent each city with a node and the distance between these nodes using an edge between them labeled with the distance. This graph-based view is shown in Figure 2.12. In this graph, nodes v_1, $v_2, \ldots, v_9$ represent cities, and the values attached to edges represent the distance between them. Note that edges only represent distances (potential roads!), and roads may not exist between these cities. Due to construction costs, the government needs to minimize the total mileage of roads built and, at the same time, needs to guarantee that there is a path (i.e., a set of roads) that connects every two cities. The minimum spanning tree is a solution to this problem. The edges in the MST represent roads that need to be built to connect all of the cities at the minimum length possible. Figure 2.2 highlights the minimum spanning tree.

2. **Steiner Tree.** The Steiner Tree problem is similar to the minimum spanning tree problem. Given a weighted graph $G(V, E, W)$ and a subset of nodes $V' \subseteq V$ (*terminal* nodes) , the Steiner tree problem aims to find a tree such that it spans all the V' nodes and the weight of the tree is minimized. Note that the problem is different from the MST problem because we do not need to span all nodes of the graph V, but only a subset of the nodes V'. A Steiner tree example is shown in Figure 2.13. In this example, $V' = \{v_2, v_4, v_7\}$.

TERMINAL
NODES

2.5.3 Complete Graphs

A complete graph is a graph where for a set of nodes V, all possible edges exist in the graph. In other words, all pairs of nodes are connected with

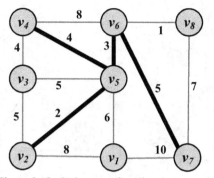

Figure 2.13. Steiner tree for $V' = \{v_2, v_4, v_7\}$.

an edge. Hence,

$$|E| = \binom{|V|}{2}. \tag{2.17}$$

Complete graphs with n nodes are often denoted as K_n. K_1, K_2, K_3, and K_4 are shown in Figure 2.14.

2.5.4 Planar Graphs

A graph that can be drawn in such a way that no two edges cross each other (other than the endpoints) is called *planar*. A graph that is not planar is denoted as *nonplanar*. Figure 2.15 shows an example of a planar graph and a nonplanar graph.

2.5.5 Bipartite Graphs

A bipartite graph $G(V, E)$ is a graph where the node set can be partitioned into two sets such that, for all edges, one endpoint is in one set and the other endpoint is in the other set. In other words, edges connect nodes in these two sets, but there exist no edges between nodes that belong to the same

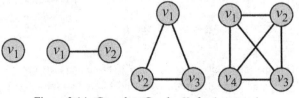

Figure 2.14. Complete Graphs K_i for $1 \le i \le 4$.

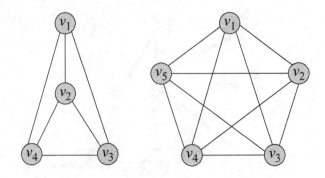

(a) Planar Graph   (b) Non-planar Graph
Figure 2.15. Planar and Nonplanar Graphs.

set. Formally,

$$V = V_L \cup V_R, \qquad (2.18)$$

$$V_L \cap V_R = \emptyset, \qquad (2.19)$$

$$E \subseteq V_L \times V_R. \qquad (2.20)$$

Figure 2.16(a) shows a sample bipartite graph. In this figure, $V_L = \{v_1, v_2\}$ and $V_R = \{v_3, v_4, v_5\}$.

In social media, *affiliation networks* are well-known examples of bipartite graphs. In these networks, nodes in one part (V_L or V_R) represent individuals, and nodes in the other part represent affiliations. If an individual

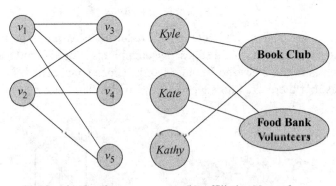

(a) Bipartite Graph   (b) Affiliation Network
Figure 2.16. Bipartite Graphs and Affiliation Networks.

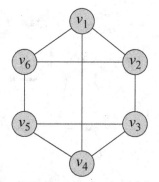

Figure 2.17. Regular Graph with $k = 3$.

is associated with an affiliation, an edge connects the corresponding nodes. A sample affiliation network is shown in Figure 2.16(b).

2.5.6 Regular Graphs

A *regular* graph is one in which all nodes have the same degree. A regular graph where all nodes have degree 2 is called a 2-regular graph. More generally, a graph where all nodes have degree k is called a k-regular graph. Regular graphs can be connected or disconnected. Complete graphs are examples of regular graphs, where all n nodes have degree $n - 1$ (i.e., $k = n - 1$). Cycles are also regular graphs, where $k = 2$. Another example for $k = 3$ is shown in Figure 2.17.

2.5.7 Bridges

Consider a graph with several connected components. Edges in this graph whose removal will increase the number of connected components are called *bridges*. As the name suggests, these edges act as bridges between connected components. The removal of these edges results in the disconnection of formerly connected components and hence an increase in the number of components. An example graph and all its bridges are depicted in Figure 2.18.

2.6 Graph Algorithms

In this section, we review some well-known algorithms for graphs, although they are only a small fraction of the plethora of algorithms related to graphs.

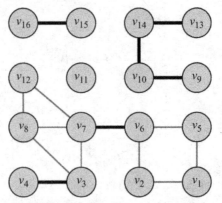

Figure 2.18. Bridges. Highlighted edges represent bridges; their removal will increase the number of components in the graph.

2.6.1 Graph/Tree Traversal

Among the most useful algorithms for graphs are the traversal algorithms for graphs, and special subgraphs, such as trees. Consider a social media site that has many users, and we are interested in surveying it and computing the average age of its users. The usual technique is to start from one user and employ some traversal technique to browse his friends and then these friends' friends and so on. The traversal technique guarantees that (1) all users are visited and (2) no user is visited more than once.

In this section, we discuss two traversal algorithms: *depth-first search (DFS)* and *breadth-first search (BFS)*.

Depth-First Search (DFS)

Depth-first search (DFS) starts from a node v_i, selects one of its neighbors $v_j \in N(v_i)$, and performs DFS on v_j before visiting other neighbors in $N(v_i)$. In other words, DFS explores as deep as possible in the graph using one neighbor before backtracking to other neighbors. Consider a node v_i that has neighbors v_j and v_k; that is, $v_j, v_k \in N(v_i)$. Let $v_{j(1)} \in N(v_j)$ and $v_{j(2)} \in N(v_j)$ denote neighbors of v_j such that $v_i \neq v_{j(1)} \neq v_{j(2)}$. Then for a depth-first search starting at v_i, that visits v_j next, nodes $v_{j(1)}$ and $v_{j(2)}$ are visited before visiting v_k. In other words, a deeper node $v_{j(1)}$ is preferred to a neighbor v_k that is closer to v_i. Depth-first search can be used both for trees and graphs, but is better visualized using trees. The DFS execution on a tree is shown in Figure 2.19(a).

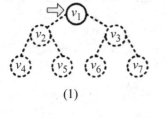

(1)

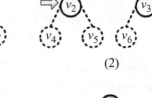

(2)

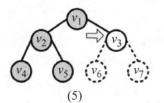

(3)

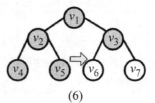

(4)

(5)

(6)

(a) Depth-First Search (DFS)

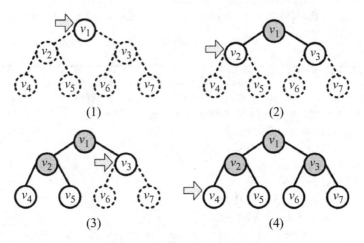

(1)

(2)

(3)

(4)

(b) Breadth-First Search (BFS)

Figure 2.19. Graph Traversal Example.

Algorithm 2.2 Depth-First Search (DFS)

Require: Initial node v, graph/tree $G(V, E)$, stack S
1: **return** An ordering on how nodes in G are visited
2: Push v into S;
3: *visitOrder* = 0;
4: **while** S not empty **do**
5:    *node* = pop from S;
6:    **if** *node* not visited **then**
7:       *visitOrder* = *visitOrder* +1;
8:       Mark *node* as visited with order *visitOrder*; //or print *node*
9:       Push all neighbors/children of *node* into S;
10:   **end if**
11: **end while**
12: Return all nodes with their visit order.

The DFS algorithm is provided in Algorithm 2.2. The algorithm uses a stack structure to visit nonvisited nodes in a depth-first fashion.

Breadth-First Search (BFS)

Breadth-first search (BFS) starts from a node, visits all its immediate neighbors first, and then moves to the second level by traversing their neighbors. Like DFS, the algorithm can be used both for trees and graphs and is provided in Algorithm 2.3.

Algorithm 2.3 Breadth-First Search (BFS)

Require: Initial node v, graph/tree $G(V, E)$, queue Q
1: **return** An ordering on how nodes are visited
2: Enqueue v into queue Q;
3: *visitOrder* = 0;
4: **while** Q not empty **do**
5:    *node* = dequeue from Q;
6:    **if** *node* not visited **then**
7:       *visitOrder* = *visitOrder* + 1;
8:       Mark *node* as visited with order *visitOrder*; //or print *node*
9:       Enqueue all neighbors/children of *node* into Q;
10:   **end if**
11: **end while**

The algorithm uses a queue data structure to achieve its goal of breadth traversal. Its execution on a tree is shown in Figure 2.19(b).

In social media, we can use BFS or DFS to traverse a social network: the algorithm choice depends on which nodes we are interested in visiting first. In social media, immediate neighbors (i.e., friends) are often more important to visit first; therefore, it is more common to use breadth-first search.

2.6.2 Shortest Path Algorithms

In many scenarios, we require algorithms that can compute the shortest path between two nodes in a graph. For instance, in the case of navigation, we have a weighted network of cities connected via roads, and we are interested in computing the shortest path from a source city to a destination city. In social media mining, we might be interested in determining how tightly connected a social network is by measuring its diameter. The diameter can be calculated by finding the longest shortest path between any two nodes in the graph.

Dijkstra's Algorithm

A well-established shortest path algorithm was developed in 1959 by Edsgerd Dijkstra. The algorithm is designed for weighted graphs with non-negative edges. The algorithm finds the shortest paths that start from a starting node s to all other nodes and the lengths of those paths.

The Dijkstra's algorithm is provided in Algorithm 2.4. As mentioned, the goal is to find the shortest paths and their lengths from a source node s to all other nodes in the graph. The *distance* array (Line 3) keeps track of the shortest path distance from s to other nodes. The algorithm starts by assuming that there is a shortest path of infinite length to any node, except s, and will update these distances as soon as a better distance (shorter path) is observed. The steps of the algorithm are as follows:

1. All nodes are initially unvisited. From the unvisited set of nodes, the one that has the minimum shortest path length is selected. We denote this node as *smallest* in the algorithm.
2. For this node, we check all its neighbors that are still unvisited. For each unvisited neighbor, we check if its current distance can be improved by considering the shortest path that goes through *smallest*.

Algorithm 2.4 Dijkstra's Shortest Path Algorithm

Require: Start node s, weighted graph/tree $G(V, E, W)$

1: **return** Shortest paths and distances from s to all other nodes.
2: **for** $v \in V$ **do**
3:     $distance[v] = \infty$;
4:     $predecessor[v] = -1$;
5: **end for**
6: $distance[s] = 0$;
7: $unvisited = V$;
8: **while** $unvisited \neq \emptyset$ **do**
9:     $smallest = \arg\min_{v \in unvisited} distance(v)$;
10:     **if** $distance(smallest) == \infty$ **then**
11:         break;
12:     **end if**
13:     $unvisited = unvisited \setminus \{smallest\}$;
14:     $currentDistance = distance(smallest)$;
15:     **for** adjacent node to $smallest$: $neighbor \in unvisited$ **do**
16:         $newPath = currentDistance + w(smallest, neighbor)$;
17:         **if** $newPath < distance(neighbor)$ **then**
18:             $distance(neighbor) = newPath$;
19:             $predecessor(neighbor) = smallest$;
20:         **end if**
21:     **end for**
22: **end while**
23: Return $distance[]$ and $predecessor[]$ arrays

This can be performed by comparing its current shortest path length ($distance(neighbor)$) to the path length that goes through *smallest* ($distance(smallest) + w(smallest, neighbor)$). This condition is checked in Line 17.

3. If the current shortest path can be improved, the path and its length are updated. The paths are saved based on predecessors in the path sequence. Since, for every node, we only need the predecessor to reconstruct a path recursively, the *predecessor* array keeps track of this.

4. A node is marked as visited after all its neighbors are processed and is no longer changed in terms of (1) the shortest path that ends with it and (2) its shortest path length.

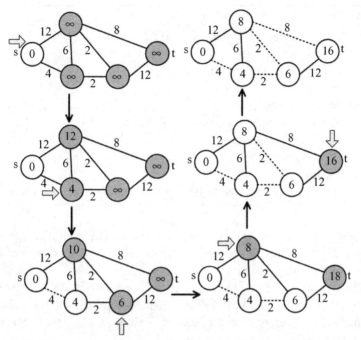

Figure 2.20. Dijkstra's Algorithm Execution Example. The shortest path between node *s* and *t* is calculated. The values inside nodes at each step show the best shortest path distance computed up to that step. An arrow denotes the node being analyzed.

To further clarify the process, an example of the Dijkstra's algorithm is provided.

Example 2.3. *Figure 2.20 provides an example of the Dijkstra's shortest path algorithm. We are interested in finding the shortest path between s and t. The shortest path is highlighted using dashed lines. In practice, shortest paths are saved using the predecessor array.*

2.6.3 Minimum Spanning Trees

A spanning tree of a connected undirected graph is a tree that includes all the nodes in the original graph and a subset of its edges. Spanning trees play important roles in many real-life applications. A cable company that wants to lay wires wishes not only to cover all areas (nodes) but also minimize the cost of wiring (summation of edges). In social media mining, consider a network of individuals who need to be provided with a piece of information. The information spreads via friends, and there is a cost associated with

---

Algorithm 2.5 Prim's Algorithm

Require: Connected weighted graph $G(V, E, W)$
  1: **return** Spanning tree $T(V_s, E_s)$
  2: $V_s = \{$a random node from $V\}$;
  3: $E_s = \{\}$;
  4: **while** $V \neq V_s$ **do**
  5:   $e(u, v) = argmin_{(u,v), u \in V_s, v \in V - V_s} w(u, v)$
  6:   $V_s = V_s \cup \{v\}$;
  7:   $E_s = E_s \cup e(u, v)$;
  8: **end while**
  9: Return tree $T(V_s, E_s)$ as the minimum spanning tree;

---

spreading information among every two nodes. The minimum spanning tree of this network will provide the minimum cost required to inform all individuals in this network.

There exist a variety of algorithms for finding minimum spanning trees. A famous algorithm for finding MSTs in a weighted graph is *Prim's algorithm* [Prim, 1957]. Interested readers can refer to the bibliographic notes for further references.

Prim's Algorithm

Prim's algorithm is provided in Algorithm 2.5. It starts by selecting a random node and adding it to the spanning tree. It then grows the spanning tree by selecting edges that have one endpoint in the existing spanning tree and one endpoint among the nodes that are not selected yet. Among the possible edges, the one with the minimum weight is added to the set (along with its endpoint). This process is iterated until the graph is fully spanned. An example of Prim's algorithm is provided in Figure 2.21.

2.6.4 Network Flow Algorithms

Consider a network of pipes that connect an infinite water source to a water sink. In these networks, given the capacity of these pipes, an interesting question is, What is the maximum flow that can be sent from the source to the sink?

Network flow algorithms aim to answer this question. This type of question arises in many different fields. At first glance, these problems do not seem to be related to network flow algorithms, but there are strong parallels.

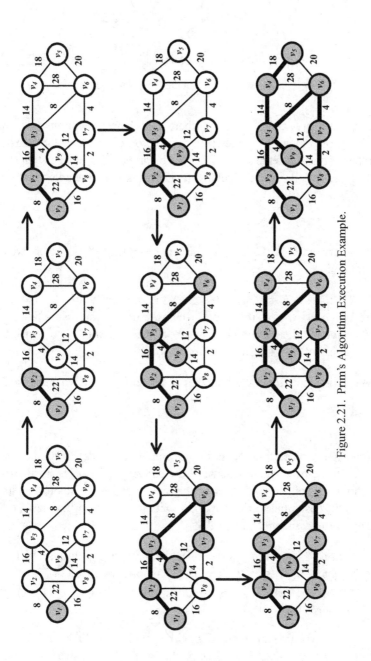

Figure 2.21. Prim's Algorithm Execution Example.

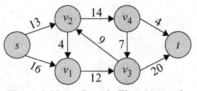

Figure 2.22. A Sample Flow Network.

For instance, in social media sites where users have daily limits (the capacity, here) of sending messages (the flow) to others, what is the maximum number of messages the network should be prepared to handle at any time? Before we delve into the details, let us formally define a flow network.

Flow Network

A flow network $G(V, E, C)^2$ is a directed weighted graph, where we have the following:

SOURCE AND SINK

- $\forall\ e(u, v) \in E, c(u, v) \geq 0$ defines the edge capacity.
- When $(u, v) \in E, (v, u) \notin E$ (opposite flow is impossible).
- s defines the *source* node and t defines the *sink* node. An infinite supply of flow is connected to the source.

A sample flow network, along with its capacities, is shown in Figure 2.22.

Flow

Given edges with certain capacities, we can fill these edges with the flow up to their capacities. This is known as the *capacity constraint*. Furthermore, we should guarantee that the flow that enters any node other than source s and sink t is equal to the flow that exits it so that no flow is lost (*flow conservation constraint*). Formally,

- $\forall(u, v) \in E, f(u, v) \geq 0$ defines the flow passing through that edge.
- $\forall(u, v) \in E, 0 \leq f(u, v) \leq c(u, v)$ (capacity constraint).
- $\forall v \in V, v \notin \{s, t\}, \sum_{k:(k,v)\in E} f(k, v) - \sum_{l:(v,l)\in E} f(v, l)$ (flow conservation constraint).

Commonly, to visualize an edge with capacity c and flow f, we use the notation f/c. A sample flow network with its flows and capacities is shown in Figure 2.23.

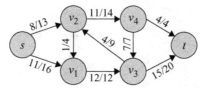

Figure 2.23. A Sample Flow Network with Flows and Capacities.

Flow Quantity

The flow quantity (or value of the flow) in any network is the amount of outgoing flow from the source minus the incoming flow to the source. Alternatively, one can compute this value by subtracting the outgoing flow from the sink from its incoming value:

$$flow = \sum_v f(s, v) - \sum_v f(v, s) = \sum_v f(v, t) - \sum_v f(t, v). \qquad (2.21)$$

Example 2.4. *The flow quantity for the example in Figure 2.23 is 19:*

$$flow = \sum_v f(s, v) - \sum_v f(v, s) = (11 + 8) - 0 = 19. \qquad (2.22)$$

Our goal is to find the flow assignments to each edge with the maximum flow quantity. This can be achieved by a maximum flow algorithm. A well-established one is the Ford-Fulkerson algorithm [Ford and Fulkerson, 1956].

Ford-Fulkerson Algorithm

The intuition behind this algorithm is as follows: Find a path from source to sink such that there is unused capacity for all edges in the path. Use that capacity (the minimum capacity unused among all edges on the path) to increase the flow. Iterate until no other path is available.

Before we formalize this, let us define some concepts.

Given a flow in network $G(V, E, C)$, we define another network $G_R(V, E_R, C_R)$, called the *residual* network. This network defines how much capacity remains in the original network. The residual network has an edge between nodes u and v if and only if either (u, v) or (v, u) exists in the original graph. If one of these two exists in the original network, we would have **two** edges in the residual network: one from (u, v) and one from (v, u). The intuition is that when there is no flow going through an edge in the original network, a flow of as much as the capacity of the edge remains

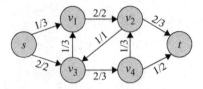

(a) Flow Network

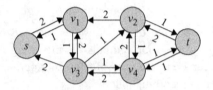

(b) Residual Network

Figure 2.24. A Flow Network and Its Residual.

in the residual. However, in the residual network, one has the ability to send flow in the opposite direction to cancel some amount of flow in the original network.

The *residual capacity* $c_R(u, v)$ for any edge (u, v) in the residual graph is

$$c_R(u, v) = \begin{cases} c(u, v) - f(u, v) & \text{if } (u, v) \in E \\ f(v, u) & \text{if } (u, v) \notin E \end{cases} \quad (2.23)$$

A flow network example and its resulted residual network are shown in Figure 2.24. In the residual network, edges that have zero residual capacity are not shown.

Augmentation and Augmenting Paths

In the residual graph, when edges are in the same direction as the original graph, their capacity shows how much more flow can be pushed along that edge in the original graph. When edges are in the opposite direction, their capacities show how much flow can be pushed back on the original graph edge. So, by finding a flow in the residual, we can *augment* the flow in the original graph. Any simple path from s to t in the residual graph is an *augmenting* path. Since all capacities in the residual are positive, these paths can augment flows in the original, thus increasing the flow. The amount of flow that can be pushed along this path is equal to the minimum capacity along the path, since the edge with that capacity limits the amount of flow

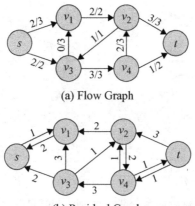

(a) Flow Graph

(b) Residual Graph

Figure 2.25. Augmenting Flow Graph.

being pushed.[3] Given flow $f(u, v)$ in the original graph and flow $f_R(u, v)$ WEAK LINK
and $f_R(v, u)$ in the residual graph, we can augment the flow as follows:

$$f_{augmented}(u, v) = f(u, v) + f_R(u, v) - f_R(v, u). \tag{2.24}$$

Example 2.5. *Consider the graph in Figure 2.24(b) and the augmenting
path s, v_1, v_3, v_4, v_2, t. It has a minimum capacity of 1 along the path, so
the flow quantity will be 1. We can augment the original graph with this
path. The new flow graph and its corresponding residual graph are shown
in Figure 2.25. In the new residual, no more augmenting paths can be found.*

The Ford-Fulkerson algorithm will find the maximum flow in a network,
but we skip the proof of optimality. Interested readers can refer to the
bibliographic notes for proof of optimality and further information. The
algorithm is provided in Algorithm 2.6.

Algorithm 2.6 Ford-Fulkerson Algorithm

Require: Connected weighted graph $G(V, E, W)$, Source s, Sink t
1: **return** A Maximum flow graph
2: $\forall (u, v) \in E, f(u, v) = 0$
3: **while** there exists an augmenting path p in the residual graph G_R **do**
4:     Augment flows by p
5: **end while**
6: Return flow value and flow graph;

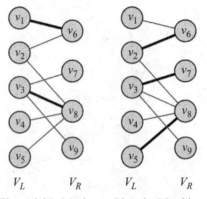

Figure 2.26. Maximum Bipartite Matching.

The algorithm searches for augmenting paths, if possible, in the residual and augments flows in the original flow network. Path finding can be achieved by any graph traversal algorithm, such as BFS.

2.6.5 Maximum Bipartite Matching

Suppose we are trying to solve the following problem in social media:

Given n products and m users such that some users are only interested in certain products, find the maximum number of products that can be bought by users.

The problem is graphically depicted in Figure 2.26. The nodes on the left represent products and the nodes on the right represent users. Edges represent the interest of users in products. Highlighted edges demonstrate MATCHING a *matching*, where products are matched with users. The figure on the left depicts a matching and the figure on the right depicts a *maximum matching*, where no more edges can be added to increase the size of the matching.

This problem can be reformulated as a bipartite graph problem. Given a bipartite graph, where V_L and V_R represent the left and right node sets ($V = V_L \cup V_R$), and E represents the edges, we define a *matching M*, $M \subset E$, such that each node in V appears in at most one edge in M. In other words, either the node is matched (appears in an edge $e \in M$) or not. A *maximum bipartite matching* M_{Max} is a matching such that, for any other matching M' in the graph, $|M_{\text{Max}}| \geq |M'|$.

Here we solve the maximum bipartite matching problem using the previously discussed Ford-Fulkerson maximum flow technique. The problem can

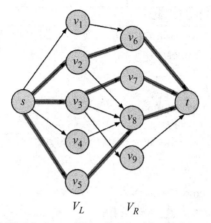

Figure 2.27. Maximum Bipartite Matching Using Max Flow.

be easily solved by creating a flow graph $G(V', E', C)$ from our bipartite graph $G(V, E)$, as follows:

- Set $V' = V \cup \{s\} \cup \{t\}$.
- Connect all nodes in V_L to s and all nodes in V_R to t,

$$E' = E \cup \{(s, v)|v \in V_L\} \cup \{(v, t)|v \in V_R\}. \qquad (2.25)$$

- Set $c(u, v) = 1, \forall(u, v) \in E'$.

This procedure is graphically shown in Figure 2.27. By solving the max flow for this flow graph, the maximum matching is obtained, since the maximum number of edges need to be used between V_L and V_R for the flow to become maximum.[4]

2.6.6 Bridge Detection

As discussed in Section 2.5.7, *bridges* or *cut edges* are edges whose CUT-EDGES removal makes formerly connected components disconnected. Here we list a simple algorithm for detecting bridges. This algorithm is computationally expensive, but quite intuitive. More efficient algorithms have been described for the same task.

Since we know that, by removing bridges, formerly connected components become disconnected, one simple algorithm is to remove edges one by one and test if the connected components become disconnected. This algorithm is outlined in Algorithm 2.7.

Algorithm 2.7 Bridge Detection Algorithm

Require: Connected graph $G(V, E)$

  1: **return** Bridge Edges
  2: *bridgeSet* = {}
  3: **for** $e(u, v) \in E$ **do**
  4:     G' = Remove e from G
  5:     Disconnected = False;
  6:     **if** BFS in G' starting at u does not visit v **then**
  7:         Disconnected = True;
  8:     **end if**
  9:     **if** Disconnected **then**
10:       *bridgeSet* = *bridgeSet* ∪ {*e*}
11:     **end if**
12: **end for**
13: Return *bridgeSet*

The disconnectedness of a component whose edge $e(u, v)$ is removed can be analyzed by means of any graph traversal algorithm (e.g., BFS or DFS). Starting at node u, we traverse the graph using BFS and, if node v cannot be visited (Line 6), the component has been disconnected and edge e is a bridge (Line 10).

2.7 Summary

This chapter covered the fundamentals of graphs, starting with a presentation of the fundamental building blocks required for graphs: first nodes and edges, and then properties of graphs such as degree and degree distribution. Any graph must be represented using some data structure for computability. This chapter covered three well-established techniques: adjacency matrix, adjacency list, and edge list. Due to the sparsity of social networks, both adjacency list and edge list are more efficient and save significant space when compared to adjacency matrix. We then described various types of graphs: null and empty graphs, directed/undirected/mixed graphs, simple/multigraphs, and weighted graphs. Signed graphs are examples of weighted graphs that can be used to represent contradictory behavior.

We discussed connectivity in graphs and concepts such as paths, walks, trails, tours, and cycles. Components are connected subgraphs. We discussed strongly and weakly connected components. Given the connectivity of a graph, one is able to compute the shortest paths between different nodes. The longest shortest path in the graph is known as the diameter. Special graphs can be formed based on the way nodes are connected and the degree distributions. In complete graphs, all nodes are connected to all other nodes, and in regular graphs, all nodes have an equal degree. A tree is a graph with no cycle. We discussed two special trees: the spanning tree and the Steiner tree. Bipartite graphs can be partitioned into two sets of nodes, with edges between these sets and no edges inside these sets. Affiliation networks are examples of bipartite graphs. Bridges are single-point-of-failure edges that can make previously connected graphs disconnected.

In the section on graph algorithms, we covered a variety of useful techniques. Traversal algorithms provide an ordering of the nodes of a graph. These algorithms are particularly useful in checking whether a graph is connected or in generating paths. Shortest path algorithms find paths with the shortest length between a pair of nodes; Dijkstra's algorithm is an example. Spanning tree algorithms provide subgraphs that span all the nodes and select edges that sum up to a minimum value; Prim's algorithm is an example. The Ford-Fulkerson algorithm, is one of the maximum flow algorithms. It finds the maximum flow in a weighted capacity graph. Maximum bipartite matching is an application of maximum flow that solves a bipartite matching problem. Finally, we provided a simple solution for bridge detection.

2.8 Bibliographic Notes

The algorithms detailed in this chapter are from three well-known fields: graph theory, network science, and social network analysis. Interested readers can get better insight regarding the topics in this chapter by referring to general references in graph theory [Bondy and Murty, 1976; West, 2001; Diestel, 2005], algorithms and algorithm design [Kleinberg and Tardos, 2005; Cormen et al., 2009], network science [Newman, 2010], and social network analysis [Wasserman and Faust, 1994].

Other algorithms not discussed in this chapter include graph coloring [Jensen and Toft, 1994], (quasi) clique detection [Abello, Resende, and Sudarsky, 2002], graph isomorphism [McKay, 1980], topological sort algorithms [Cormen et al., 2009], and the traveling salesman problem (TSP) [Cormen et al., 2009], among others. In graph coloring, one aims to color elements of the graph such as nodes and edges such that certain constraints are satisfied. For instance, in node coloring the goal is to color nodes such that adjacent nodes have different colors. Cliques are complete subgraphs. Unfortunately, solving many problems related to cliques, such as finding a

clique that has more that a given number of nodes, is NP-complete. In clique
detection, the goal is to solve similar clique problems efficiently or provide
approximate solutions. In graph isomorphism, given two graphs G and G',
our goal is to find a mapping f from nodes of G to G' such that for any
two nodes of G that are connected, their mapped nodes in G' are connected
as well. In topological sort algorithms, a linear ordering of nodes is found
in a directed graph such that for any directed edge (u, v) in the graph, node
u comes before node v in the ordering. In the traveling salesman problem
(TSP), we are provided cities and pairwise distances between them. In graph
theory terms, we are given a weighted graph where nodes represent cities
and edge weights represent distances between cities. The problem is to find
the shortest walk that visits all cities and returns to the origin city.

Other noteworthy shortest path algorithms such as the A^* [Hart, Nilsson,
and Raphael, 2003], the Bellman-Ford [Bellman and Ford, 1956], and all-
pair shortest path algorithms such as Floyd-Warshall's [Floyd, 1962] are
employed extensively in other literature.

In spanning tree computation, the Kruskal Algorithm [Kruskal, 1956]
or Boruvka [Motwani and Raghavan, 1995] are also well-established
algorithms.

General references for flow algorithms, other algorithms not discussed
in this chapter such as the Push-Relabel algorithm, and their optimality can
be found in [Cormen et al., 2009; Ahuja et al., 1993].

2.9 Exercises

Graph Basics

1. Given a directed graph $G(V, E)$ and its adjacency matrix A, we propose
   two methods to make G undirected,

$$A'_{ij} = \min(1, A_{ij} + A_{ji}), \tag{2.26}$$

$$A'_{ij} = A_{ij} \times A_{ji}, \tag{2.27}$$

   where $A'_{i,j}$ is the (i, j) entry of the undirected adjacency matrix. Discuss
   the advantages and disadvantages of each method.

Graph Representation

2. Is it possible to have the following degrees in a graph with 7 nodes?

$$\{4, 4, 4, 3, 5, 7, 2\}. \tag{2.28}$$

3. Given the following adjacency matrix, compute the adjacency list and the edge list.

$$A = \begin{bmatrix} 0 & 1 & 1 & 0 & 0 & 0 & 0 & 0 & 0 \\ 1 & 0 & 1 & 0 & 0 & 0 & 0 & 0 & 0 \\ 1 & 1 & 0 & 1 & 1 & 0 & 0 & 0 & 0 \\ 0 & 0 & 1 & 0 & 1 & 1 & 1 & 0 & 0 \\ 0 & 0 & 1 & 1 & 0 & 1 & 1 & 0 & 0 \\ 0 & 0 & 0 & 1 & 1 & 0 & 1 & 1 & 0 \\ 0 & 0 & 0 & 1 & 1 & 1 & 0 & 1 & 0 \\ 0 & 0 & 0 & 0 & 0 & 1 & 1 & 0 & 1 \\ 0 & 0 & 0 & 0 & 0 & 0 & 0 & 1 & 0 \end{bmatrix} \tag{2.29}$$

Special Graphs

4. Prove that $|E| = |V| - 1$ in trees.

Graph/Network Algorithms

5. Consider the tree shown in Figure 2.28. Traverse the graph using both BFS and DFS and list the order in which nodes are visited in each algorithm.

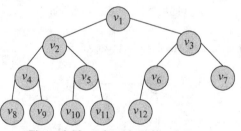

Figure 2.28. A Sample (Binary) Tree.

6. For a tree and a node v, under what condition is v visited sooner by BFS than DFS? Provide details.

7. For a real-world social network, is BFS or DFS more desirable? Provide details.

8. Compute the shortest path between any pair of nodes using Dijkstra's algorithm for the graph in Figure 2.29.

9. Detail why edges with negative weights are not desirable for computing shortest paths using Dijkstra's algorithm.

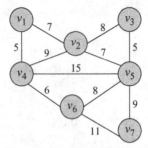

Figure 2.29. Weighted Graph.

10. Compute the minimal spanning tree using Prim's algorithm in the graph provided in Figure 2.30.

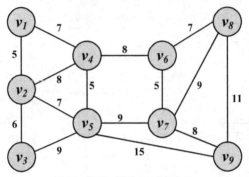

Figure 2.30. Weighted Graph.

11. Compute the maximum flow in Figure 2.31.

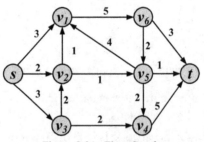

Figure 2.31. Flow Graph.

12. Given a flow network, you are allowed to change one edge's capacity. Can this increase the flow? How can we find the correct edge to change?

13. How many bridges are in a bipartite graph? Provide details.

3

Network Measures

In February 2012, Kobe Bryant, the American basketball star, joined Chinese microblogging site Sina Weibo. Within a few hours, more than 100,000 followers joined his page, anxiously waiting for his first microblogging post on the site. The media considered the tremendous number of followers Kobe Bryant received as an indication of his popularity in China. In this case, the number of followers *measured* Bryant's popularity among Chinese social media users. In social media, we often face similar tasks in which measuring different structural properties of a social media network can help us better understand individuals embedded in it. Corresponding measures need to be designed for these tasks. This chapter discusses measures for social media networks.

When mining social media, a graph representation is often used. This graph shows friendships or user interactions in a social media network. Given this graph, some of the questions we aim to answer are as follows:

- Who are the central figures (influential individuals) in the network?
- What interaction patterns are common in friends?
- Who are the *like-minded* users and how can we find these similar individuals?

To answer these and similar questions, one first needs to define *measures* for quantifying centrality, level of interactions, and similarity, among other qualities. These measures take as input a graph representation of a social interaction, such as friendships (adjacency matrix), from which the measure value is computed.

To answer our first question about finding central figures, we define measures for *centrality*. By using these measures, we can identify various types of central nodes in a network. To answer the other two questions, we define corresponding measures that can quantify interaction patterns and help find like-minded users. We discuss centrality next.

3.1 Centrality

Centrality defines how important a node is within a network.

3.1.1 Degree Centrality

In real-world interactions, we often consider people with many connections to be important. Degree centrality transfers the same idea into a measure. The degree centrality measure ranks nodes with more connections higher in terms of centrality. The degree centrality C_d for node v_i in an undirected graph is

$$C_d(v_i) = d_i, \tag{3.1}$$

where d_i is the degree (number of adjacent edges) of node v_i. In directed graphs, we can either use the in-degree, the out-degree, or the combination as the degree centrality value:

$$C_d(v_i) = d_i^{\text{in}} \qquad \text{(prestige)}, \tag{3.2}$$

$$C_d(v_i) = d_i^{\text{out}} \qquad \text{(gregariousness)}, \tag{3.3}$$

$$C_d(v_i) = d_i^{\text{in}} + d_i^{\text{out}}. \tag{3.4}$$

PROMINENCE
OR
PRESTIGE

When using in-degrees, degree centrality measures how popular a node is and its value shows *prominence* or *prestige*. When using out-degrees, it measures the *gregariousness* of a node. When we combine in-degrees and out-degrees, we are basically ignoring edge directions. In fact, when edge directions are removed, Equation 3.4 is equivalent to Equation 3.1, which measures degree centrality for undirected graphs.

The degree centrality measure does not allow for centrality values to be compared across networks (e.g., Facebook and Twitter). To overcome this problem, we can normalize the degree centrality values.

Normalizing Degree Centrality

Simple normalization methods include normalizing by the maximum possible degree,

$$C_d^{\text{norm}}(v_i) = \frac{d_i}{n - 1}, \tag{3.5}$$

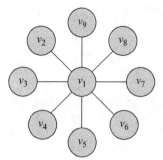

Figure 3.1. Degree Centrality Example.

where n is the number of nodes. We can also normalize by the maximum degree,

$$C_d^{\max}(v_i) = \frac{d_i}{\max_j d_j}.$$ (3.6)

Finally, we can normalize by the degree sum,

$$C_d^{\text{sum}}(v_i) = \frac{d_i}{\sum_j d_j} = \frac{d_i}{2|E|} = \frac{d_i}{2m}.$$ (3.7)

Example 3.1. *Figure 3.1 shows a sample graph. In this graph, degree centrality for node v_1 is $C_d(v_1) = d_1 = 8$, and for all others, it is $C_d(v_j) = d_j = 1, j \neq 1$.*

3.1.2 Eigenvector Centrality

In degree centrality, we consider nodes with more connections to be more important. However, in real-world scenarios, having more friends does not by itself guarantee that someone is important: *having more important friends* provides a stronger signal.

Eigenvector centrality tries to generalize degree centrality by incorporating the importance of the neighbors (or incoming neighbors in directed graphs). It is defined for both directed and undirected graphs. To keep track of neighbors, we can use the adjacency matrix A of a graph. Let $c_e(v_i)$ denote the eigenvector centrality of node v_i. We want the centrality of v_i to be a function of its neighbors' centralities. We posit that it is proportional to the summation of their centralities,

$$c_e(v_i) = \frac{1}{\lambda} \sum_{j=1}^{n} A_{j,i} c_e(v_j), \tag{3.8}$$

where λ is some fixed constant. Assuming $\mathbf{C}_e = (C_e(v_1), C_e(v_2), \ldots,$ $C_e(v_n))^T$ is the centrality vectors for all nodes, we can rewrite Equation 3.8 as

$$\lambda \mathbf{C}_e = A^T \mathbf{C}_e. \tag{3.9}$$

This basically means that $\mathbf{C}_e$ is an eigenvector of adjacency matrix A^T (or A in undirected networks, since $A = A^T$) and λ is the corresponding eigenvalue. A matrix can have many eigenvalues and, in turn, many corresponding eigenvectors. Hence, this raises the question: which eigenvalue–eigenvector pair should we select? We often prefer centrality values to be positive for convenient comparison of centrality values across nodes. Thus, we can choose an eigenvalue such that the eigenvector components are positive.[1] This brings us to the *Perron-Frobenius* theorem.

PERRON-FROBENIUS THEOREM

Theorem 3.1 (Perron-Frobenius Theorem). *Let $A \in \mathbb{R}^{n \times n}$ represent the adjacency matrix for a [strongly] connected graph or $A : A_{i,j} > 0$ (i.e. a positive n by n matrix). There exists a positive real number (Perron-Frobenius eigenvalue) λ_{max}, such that λ_{max} is an eigenvalue of A and any other eigenvalue of A is strictly smaller than λ_{max}. Furthermore, there exists a corresponding eigenvector $v = (v_1, v_2, \ldots, v_n)$ of A with eigenvalue λ_{max} such that $\forall v_i > 0$.*

Therefore, to have positive centrality values, we can compute the eigenvalues of A and then select the largest eigenvalue. The corresponding eigenvector is $\mathbf{C}_e$. Based on the Perron-Frobenius theorem, all the components of $\mathbf{C}_e$ will be positive, and this vector corresponds to eigenvector centralities for the graph.

Example 3.2. *For the graph shown in Figure 3.2(a), the adjacency matrix is*

$$A = \begin{bmatrix} 0 & 1 & 0 \\ 1 & 0 & 1 \\ 0 & 1 & 0 \end{bmatrix}. \tag{3.10}$$

Based on Equation 3.9, we need to solve $\lambda \mathbf{C}_e = A\mathbf{C}_e$, or

$$(A - \lambda I)\mathbf{C}_e = 0. \tag{3.11}$$

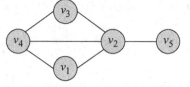

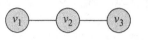

(a) A three node graph   (b) A five node graph

Figure 3.2. Eigenvector Centrality Example.

Assuming $\mathbf{C}_e = [u_1\ u_2\ u_3]^T$,

$$\begin{bmatrix} 0 - \lambda & 1 & 0 \\ 1 & 0 - \lambda & 1 \\ 0 & 1 & 0 - \lambda \end{bmatrix} \begin{bmatrix} u_1 \\ u_2 \\ u_3 \end{bmatrix} = \begin{bmatrix} 0 \\ 0 \\ 0 \end{bmatrix}. \tag{3.12}$$

Since $\mathbf{C}_e \neq [0\ 0\ 0]^T$, *the characteristic equation is*

$$det(A - \lambda I) = \begin{vmatrix} 0 - \lambda & 1 & 0 \\ 1 & 0 - \lambda & 1 \\ 0 & 1 & 0 - \lambda \end{vmatrix} = 0, \tag{3.13}$$

or equivalently,

$$(-\lambda)(\lambda^2 - 1) - 1(-\lambda) = 2\lambda - \lambda^3 = \lambda(2 - \lambda^2) = 0. \tag{3.14}$$

So the eigenvalues are $(-\sqrt{2}, 0, +\sqrt{2})$. *We select the largest eigenvalue:* $\sqrt{2}$. *We compute the corresponding eigenvector:*

$$\begin{bmatrix} 0 - \sqrt{2} & 1 & 0 \\ 1 & 0 - \sqrt{2} & 1 \\ 0 & 1 & 0 - \sqrt{2} \end{bmatrix} \begin{bmatrix} u_1 \\ u_2 \\ u_3 \end{bmatrix} = \begin{bmatrix} 0 \\ 0 \\ 0 \end{bmatrix}. \tag{3.15}$$

Assuming $\mathbf{C}_e$ *vector has norm 1, its solution is*

$$\mathbf{C}_e = \begin{bmatrix} u_1 \\ u_2 \\ u_3 \end{bmatrix} = \begin{bmatrix} 1/2 \\ \sqrt{2}/2 \\ 1/2 \end{bmatrix}, \tag{3.16}$$

which denotes that node v_2 *is the most central node and nodes* v_1 *and* v_3 *have equal centrality values.*

Example 3.3. *For the graph shown in Figure 3.2(b), the adjacency matrix is as follows:*

$$A = \begin{bmatrix} 0 & 1 & 0 & 1 & 0 \\ 1 & 0 & 1 & 1 & 1 \\ 0 & 1 & 0 & 1 & 0 \\ 1 & 1 & 1 & 0 & 0 \\ 0 & 1 & 0 & 0 & 0 \end{bmatrix}. \qquad (3.17)$$

The eigenvalues of A are $(-1.74, -1.27, 0.00, +0.33, +2.68)$. For eigenvector centrality, the largest eigenvalue is selected: 2.68. The corresponding eigenvector is the eigenvector centrality vector and is

$$\mathbf{C}_e = \begin{bmatrix} 0.4119 \\ 0.5825 \\ 0.4119 \\ 0.5237 \\ 0.2169 \end{bmatrix}. \qquad (3.18)$$

Based on eigenvector centrality, node v_2 is the most central node.

3.1.3 Katz Centrality

A major problem with eigenvector centrality arises when it considers directed graphs (see Problem 1 in the Exercises). Centrality is only passed on when we have (outgoing) edges, and in special cases such as when a node is in a directed acyclic graph, centrality becomes zero, even though the node can have many edges connected to it. In this case, the problem can be rectified by adding a bias term to the centrality value. The bias term β is added to the centrality values for all nodes no matter how they are situated in the network (i.e., irrespective of the network topology). The resulting centrality measure is called the *Katz centrality* and is formulated as

$$C_{\text{Katz}}(v_i) = \alpha \sum_{j=1}^{n} A_{j,i} C_{\text{Katz}}(v_j) + \beta. \qquad (3.19)$$

The first term is similar to eigenvector centrality, and its effect is controlled by constant α. The second term β, is the bias term that avoids zero centrality values. We can rewrite Equation 3.19 in a vector form,

$$\mathbf{C}_{\text{Katz}} = \alpha A^T \mathbf{C}_{\text{Katz}} + \beta \mathbf{1}, \qquad (3.20)$$

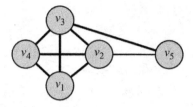

Figure 3.3. Katz Centrality Example.

where **1** is a vector of all 1's. Taking the first term to the left hand side and factoring C_{Katz},

$$\mathbf{C}_{\text{Katz}} = \beta(\mathbf{I} - \alpha A^T)^{-1} \cdot \mathbf{1}. \tag{3.21}$$

Since we are inverting a matrix here, not all α values are acceptable. When $\alpha = 0$, the eigenvector centrality part is removed, and all nodes get the same centrality value β. However, once α gets larger, the effect of β is reduced, and when $\det(\mathbf{I} - \alpha A^T) = 0$, the matrix $\mathbf{I} - \alpha A^T$ becomes non-invertible and the centrality values diverge. The $\det(\mathbf{I} - \alpha A^T)$ first becomes 0 when $\alpha = 1/\lambda$, where λ is the largest eigenvalue[2] of A^T. In practice, $\alpha < 1/\lambda$ is selected so that centralities are computed correctly.

DIVERGENCE IN CENTRALITY COMPUTATION

Example 3.4. *For the graph shown in Figure 3.3, the adjacency matrix is as follows:*

$$A = \begin{bmatrix} 0 & 1 & 1 & 1 & 0 \\ 1 & 0 & 1 & 1 & 1 \\ 1 & 1 & 0 & 1 & 1 \\ 1 & 1 & 1 & 0 & 0 \\ 0 & 1 & 1 & 0 & 0 \end{bmatrix} = A^T. \tag{3.22}$$

The eigenvalues of A are $(-1.68, -1.0, -1.0, +0.35, +3.32)$. The largest eigenvalue of A is $\lambda = 3.32$. We assume $\alpha = 0.25 < 1/\lambda$ and $\beta = 0.2$. Then, Katz centralities are

$$\mathbf{C}_{Katz} = \beta(\mathbf{I} - \alpha A^T)^{-1} \cdot \mathbf{1} = \begin{bmatrix} 1.14 \\ 1.31 \\ 1.31 \\ 1.14 \\ 0.85 \end{bmatrix}. \tag{3.23}$$

Thus, nodes v_2, and v_3 have the highest Katz centralities.

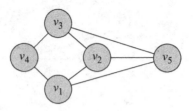

Figure 3.4. PageRank Example.

3.1.4 PageRank

Similar to eigenvector centrality, Katz centrality encounters some challenges. A challenge that happens in directed graphs is that, once a node
becomes an authority (high centrality), it passes **all** its centrality along **all**
of its out-links. This is less desirable, because not everyone known by a
well known person is well known. To mitigate this problem, one can divide
the value of passed centrality by the number of outgoing links (out-degree)
from that node such that each connected neighbor gets a fraction of the
source node's centrality:

$$C_p(v_i) = \alpha \sum_{j=1}^{n} A_{j,i} \frac{C_p(v_j)}{d_j^{\text{out}}} + \beta. \qquad (3.24)$$

This equation is only defined when d_j^{out} is nonzero. Thus, assuming
that all nodes have positive out-degrees $(d_j^{\text{out}} > 0)^3$, Equation 3.24 can be
reformulated in matrix format,

$$\mathbf{C}_p = \alpha A^T D^{-1} \mathbf{C}_p + \beta \mathbf{1}, \qquad (3.25)$$

which we can reorganize,

$$\mathbf{C}_p = \beta (\mathbf{I} - \alpha A^T D^{-1})^{-1} \cdot \mathbf{1}, \qquad (3.26)$$

where $D = diag(d_1^{\text{out}}, d_2^{\text{out}}, \ldots, d_n^{\text{out}})$ is a diagonal matrix of degrees. The
centrality measure is known as the *PageRank* centrality measure and is
PAGERANK   used by the Google search engine as a measure for ordering webpages.
AND GOOGLE   Webpages and their links represent an enormous web-graph. PageRank
WEB SEARCH   defines a centrality measure for the nodes (webpages) in this web-graph.
When a user queries Google, webpages that match the query and have higher
PageRank values are shown first. Similar to Katz centrality, in practice,

$\alpha < \frac{1}{\lambda}$ is selected, where λ is the largest eigenvalue of $A^T D^{-1}$. In undirected graphs, the largest eigenvalue of $A^T D^{-1}$ is $\lambda = 1$; therefore, $\alpha < 1$.

Example 3.5. *For the graph shown in Figure 3.4, the adjacency matrix is as follows,*

$$A = \begin{bmatrix} 0 & 1 & 0 & 1 & 1 \\ 1 & 0 & 1 & 0 & 1 \\ 0 & 1 & 0 & 1 & 1 \\ 1 & 0 & 1 & 0 & 0 \\ 1 & 1 & 1 & 0 & 0 \end{bmatrix}. \tag{3.27}$$

We assume $\alpha = 0.95 < 1$ and $\beta = 0.1$. Then, PageRank values are

$$\mathbf{C}_p = \beta(\mathbf{I} - \alpha A^T D^{-1})^{-1} \cdot \mathbf{1} = \begin{bmatrix} 2.14 \\ 2.13 \\ 2.14 \\ 1.45 \\ 2.13 \end{bmatrix}. \tag{3.28}$$

Hence, nodes v_1 and v_3 have the highest PageRank values.

3.1.5 Betweenness Centrality

Another way of looking at centrality is by considering how important nodes are in connecting other nodes. One approach, for a node v_i, is to compute the number of shortest paths between other nodes that pass through v_i,

$$C_b(v_i) = \sum_{s \neq t \neq v_i} \frac{\sigma_{st}(v_i)}{\sigma_{st}}, \tag{3.29}$$

where σ_{st} is the number of shortest paths from node s to t (also known as *information pathways*), and $\sigma_{st}(v_i)$ is the number of shortest paths from s to t that pass through v_i. In other words, we are measuring how central v_i's role is in connecting any pair of nodes s and t. This measure is called *betweenness centrality*.

Betweenness centrality needs to be normalized to be comparable across networks. To normalize betweenness centrality, one needs to compute the maximum value it takes. Betweenness centrality takes its maximum value when node v_i is on all shortest paths from s to t for any pair (s, t); that is, $\forall (s, t)$, $s \neq t \neq v_i$, $\frac{\sigma_{st}(v_i)}{\sigma_{st}} = 1$. For instance, in Figure 3.1, node v_1 is on the shortest path between all other pairs of nodes. Thus, the maximum value is

$$C_b(v_i) = \sum_{s \neq t \neq v_i} \frac{\sigma_{st}(v_i)}{\sigma_{st}} = \sum_{s \neq t \neq v_i} 1 = 2\binom{n-1}{2} = (n-1)(n-2).$$
(3.30)

The betweenness can be divided by its maximum value to obtain the normalized betweenness,

$$C_b^{\text{norm}}(v_i) = \frac{C_b(v_i)}{2\binom{n-1}{2}}.$$
(3.31)

Computing Betweenness

In betweenness centrality (Equation 3.29), we compute shortest paths between all pairs of nodes to compute the betweenness value. If an algorithm such as Dijkstra's is employed, it needs to be run for all nodes, because Dijkstra's algorithm will compute shortest paths from a single node to all other nodes. So, to compute all-pairs shortest paths, Dijkstra's algorithm needs to be run $|V| - 1$ times (with the exception of the node for which centrality is being computed). More effective algorithms such as the Brandes' algorithm [Brandes, 2001] have been designed. Interested readers can refer to the bibliographic notes for further references.

Example 3.6. *For Figure 3.1, the (normalized) betweenness centrality of node v_1 is*

$$C_b(v_1) = 2\binom{8}{2},$$
(3.32)

$$C_b^{\text{norm}}(v_1) = 1.$$
(3.33)

Since all the paths that go through any pair $(s,t), s \neq t \neq v_1$ pass through node v_1, the centrality is $2\binom{8}{2}$. Similarly, the betweenness centrality for any other node in this graph is 0.

Example 3.7. *Figure 3.5 depicts a sample graph. In this graph, the betweenness centrality for node v_1 is 0, since no shortest path passes through it.*

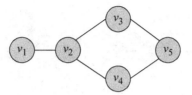

Figure 3.5. Betweenness Centrality Example.

For other nodes, we have

$$C_b(v_2) = 2 \times (\underbrace{(1/1)}_{s=v_1,t=v_3} + \underbrace{(1/1)}_{s=v_1,t=v_4} + \underbrace{(2/2)}_{s=v_1,t=v_5} + \underbrace{(1/2)}_{s=v_3,t=v_4} + \underbrace{0}_{s=v_3,t=v_5} + \underbrace{0}_{s=v_4,t=v_5})$$

$$= 2 \times 3.5 = 7, \tag{3.34}$$

$$C_b(v_3) = 2 \times (\underbrace{0}_{s=v_1,t=v_2} + \underbrace{0}_{s=v_1,t=v_4} + \underbrace{(1/2)}_{s=v_1,t=v_5} + \underbrace{0}_{s=v_2,t=v_4} + \underbrace{(1/2)}_{s=v_2,t=v_5} + \underbrace{0}_{s=v_4,t=v_5})$$

$$= 2 \times 1.0 = 2, \tag{3.35}$$

$$C_b(v_4) = C_b(v_3) = 2 \times 1.0 = 2, \tag{3.36}$$

$$C_b(v_5) = 2 \times (\underbrace{0}_{s=v_1,t=v_2} + \underbrace{0}_{s=v_1,t=v_3} + \underbrace{0}_{s=v_1,t=v_4} + \underbrace{0}_{s=v_2,t=v_3} + \underbrace{0}_{s=v_2,t=v_4} + \underbrace{(1/2)}_{s=v_3,t=v_4})$$

$$= 2 \times 0.5 = 1, \tag{3.37}$$

where centralities are multiplied by 2 because in an undirected graph
$$\sum_{s \neq t \neq v_i} \frac{\sigma_{st}(v_i)}{\sigma_{st}} = 2 \sum_{s \neq t \neq v_i, s < t} \frac{\sigma_{st}(v_i)}{\sigma_{st}}.$$

3.1.6 Closeness Centrality

In closeness centrality, the intuition is that the more central nodes are, the more quickly they can reach other nodes. Formally, these nodes should have a smaller average shortest path length to other nodes. Closeness centrality is defined as

$$C_c(v_i) = \frac{1}{\bar{l}_{v_i}}, \tag{3.38}$$

where $\bar{l}_{v_i} = \frac{1}{n-1} \sum_{v_j \neq v_i} l_{i,j}$ is node v_i's average shortest path length to other nodes. The smaller the average shortest path length, the higher the centrality for the node.

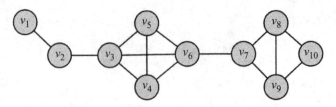

Figure 3.6. Example for All Centrality Measures.

Example 3.8. *For nodes in Figure 3.5, the closeness centralities are as follows:*

$$C_c(v_1) = 1 / ((1 + 2 + 2 + 3)/4) = 0.5, \qquad (3.39)$$

$$C_c(v_2) = 1 / ((1 + 1 + 1 + 2)/4) = 0.8, \qquad (3.40)$$

$$C_c(v_3) = C_b(v_4) = 1 / ((1 + 1 + 2 + 2)/4) = 0.66, \qquad (3.41)$$

$$C_c(v_5) = 1 / ((1 + 1 + 2 + 3)/4) = 0.57. \qquad (3.42)$$

Hence, node v_2 has the highest closeness centrality.

The centrality measures discussed thus far have different views on what a central node is. Thus, a central node for one measure may be deemed unimportant by other measures.

Example 3.9. *Consider the graph in Figure 3.6. For this graph, we compute the top three central nodes based on degree, eigenvector, Katz, PageRank, betweenness, and closeness centrality methods. These nodes are listed in Table 3.1.*

As shown in the table, there is a high degree of similarity between most central nodes for the first four measures, which utilize eigenvectors or degrees: degree centrality, eigenvector centrality, Katz centrality, and

Table 3.1. *A Comparison between Centrality Methods*

	First Node	Second Node	Third Node
Degree Centrality	v_3 or v_6	v_6 or v_3	$v \in \{v_4, v_5, v_7, v_8, v_9\}$
Eigenvector Centrality	v_6	v_3	v_4 or v_5
Katz Centrality: $\alpha = \beta = 0.3$	v_6	v_3	v_4 or v_5
PageRank: $\alpha = \beta = 0.3$	v_3	v_6	v_2
Betweenness Centrality	v_6	v_7	v_3
Closeness Centrality	v_6	v_3 or v_7	v_7 or v_3

PageRank. Betweenness centrality also generates similar results to close-ness centrality because both use the shortest paths to find most central nodes.

3.1.7 Group Centrality

All centrality measures defined so far measure centrality for a single node. These measures can be generalized for a group of nodes. In this section, we discuss how degree centrality, closeness centrality, and betweenness centrality can be generalized for a group of nodes. Let S denote the set of nodes to be measured for centrality. Let $V - S$ denote the set of nodes not in the group.

Group Degree Centrality

Group degree centrality is defined as the number of nodes from outside the group that are connected to group members. Formally,

$$C_d^{\text{group}}(S) = |\{v_i \in V - S | v_i \text{ is connected to } v_j \in S\}|. \tag{3.43}$$

Similar to degree centrality, we can define connections in terms of out-degrees or in-degrees in directed graphs. We can also normalize this value. In the best case, group members are connected to all other nonmembers. Thus, the maximum value of $C_d^{\text{group}}(S)$ is $|V - S|$. So dividing group degree centrality value by $|V - S|$ normalizes it.

Group Betweenness Centrality

Similar to betweeness centrality, we can define group betweenness centrality as

$$C_b^{\text{group}}(S) = \sum_{s \neq t, s \notin S, t \notin S} \frac{\sigma_{st}(S)}{\sigma_{st}}, \tag{3.44}$$

where $\sigma_{st}(S)$ denotes the number of shortest paths between s and t that pass through members of S. In the best case, all shortest paths between s and t pass through members of S, and therefore, the maximum value for $C_b^{\text{group}}(S)$ is $2\binom{|V-S|}{2}$. Similar to betweenness centrality, we can normalize group betweenness centrality by dividing it by the maximum value.

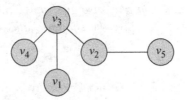

Figure 3.7. Group Centrality Example.

Group Closeness Centrality

Closeness centrality for groups can be defined as

$$C_c^{\text{group}}(S) = \frac{1}{\bar{l}_S^{\text{group}}}, \tag{3.45}$$

where $\bar{l}_S^{\text{group}} = \frac{1}{|V-S|} \sum_{v_j \notin S} l_{S,v_j}$ and l_{S,v_j} is the length of the shortest path between a group S and a nonmember $v_j \in V - S$. This length can be defined in multiple ways. One approach is to find the closest member in S to v_j:

$$l_{S,v_j} = \min_{v_i \in S} l_{v_i,v_j}. \tag{3.46}$$

One can also use the maximum distance or the average distance to compute this value.

Example 3.10. *Consider the graph in Figure 3.7. Let $S = \{v_2, v_3\}$. Group degree centrality for S is*

$$C_d^{\text{group}}(S) = 3, \tag{3.47}$$

since members of the group are connected to all other three members in $V - S = \{v_1, v_4, v_5\}$. The normalized value is 1, since $3/|V - S| = 1$. Group betweenness centrality is 6, since for $2\binom{3}{2}$ shortest paths between any two members of $V - S$, the path has to pass through members of S. The normalized group betweenness is 1, since $6/(2\binom{|V-S|}{2}) = 1$. Finally, group closeness centrality – assuming the distance from nonmembers to members of S is computed using the minimum function – is also 1, since any member of $V - S$ is connected to a member of S directly.

3.2 Transitivity and Reciprocity

Often we need to observe a specific behavior in a social media network. One such behavior is linking behavior. Linking behavior determines how links (edges) are formed in a social graph. In this section, we discuss two

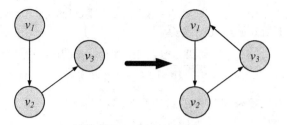

Figure 3.8. Transitive Linking.

well-known measures, *transitivity* and *reciprocity*, for analyzing this behavior. Both measures are commonly used in directed networks, and *transitivity* can also be applied to undirected networks.

3.2.1 Transitivity

In transitivity, we analyze the linking behavior to determine whether it demonstrates a transitive behavior. In mathematics, for a transitive relation R, $aRb \wedge bRc \rightarrow aRc$. The *transitive linking* behavior can be described as follows.

Transitive Linking

Let v_1, v_2, v_3 denote three nodes. When edges (v_1, v_2) and (v_2, v_3) are formed, if (v_3, v_1) is also formed, then we have observed a transitive linking behavior (*transitivity*). This is shown in Figure 3.8.

In a less formal setting,

Transitivity is when a friend of my friend is my friend.

As shown in the definition, a transitive behavior needs at least three edges. These three edges, along with the participating nodes, create a triangle. Higher transitivity in a graph results in a denser graph, which in turn is closer to a complete graph. Thus, we can determine how close graphs are to the complete graph by measuring transitivity. This can be performed by measuring the *[global] clustering coefficient* and *local clustering coefficient*. The former is computed for the network, whereas the latter is computed for a node.

Clustering Coefficient

The clustering coefficient analyzes transitivity in an undirected graph. Since transitivity is observed when triangles are formed, we can measure it by counting paths of length 2 (edges (v_1, v_2) and (v_2, v_3)) and checking whether the third edge (v_3, v_1) exists (i.e., the path is closed). Thus, clustering coefficient C is defined as

$$C = \frac{|\text{Closed Paths of Length 2}|}{|\text{Paths of Length 2}|}. \tag{3.48}$$

Alternatively, we can count triangles

$$C = \frac{(\text{Number of Triangles}) \times 6}{|\text{Paths of Length 2}|}. \tag{3.49}$$

Since every triangle has six closed paths of length 2, we can rewrite Equation 3.49 as

$$C = \frac{(\text{Number of Triangles}) \times 3}{\text{Number of Connected Triples of Nodes}}. \tag{3.50}$$

In this equation, a triple is an ordered set of three nodes, connected by two (i.e., open triple) or three (closed triple) edges. Two triples are different when

- their nodes are different, or
- their nodes are the same, but the triples are missing different edges.

For example, triples $v_i v_j v_k$ and $v_j v_k v_i$ are different, since the first triple is missing edge $e(v_k, v_i)$ and the second triple is missing edge $e(v_i, v_j)$, even though they have the same members. Following the same argument, triples $v_i v_j v_k$ and $v_k v_j v_i$ are the same, because both are missing edge $e(v_k, v_i)$ and have the same members. Since triangles have three edges, one edge can be missed in each triple; therefore, three different triples can be formed from one triangle. The number of triangles are therefore multiplied by a factor of 3 in the numerator of Equation 3.50. Note that the clustering coefficient is computed for the whole network.

Example 3.11. *For the graph in Figure 3.9, the clustering coefficient is*

$$C = \frac{(\text{Number of Triangles}) \times 3}{\text{Number of Connected Triples of Nodes}}$$

$$= \frac{2 \times 3}{2 \times 3 + \underbrace{2}_{v_2 v_1 v_4, v_2 v_3 v_4}} = 0.75. \tag{3.51}$$

The clustering coefficient can also be computed locally. The following subsection discusses how it can be computed for a single node.

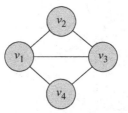

Figure 3.9. A Global Clustering Coefficient Example.

Local Clustering Coefficient

The local clustering coefficient measures transitivity at the node level. Commonly used for undirected graphs, it estimates how strongly neighbors of a node v (nodes adjacent to v) are themselves connected. The coefficient is defined as

$$C(v_i) = \frac{\text{Number of Pairs of Neighbors of } v_i \text{ That Are Connected}}{\text{Number of Pairs of Neighbors of } v_i}.$$

(3.52)

In an undirected graph, the denominator can be rewritten as $\binom{d_i}{2} = d_i(d_i - 1)/2$, since there are d_i neighbors for node v_i.

Example 3.12. *Figure 3.10 shows how the local clustering coefficient changes for node v_1. Thin lines depict v_1's connections to its neighbors. Dashed lines denote possible connections among neighbors, and solid lines denote current connections among neighbors. Note that when none of the neighbors are connected, the local clustering coefficient is zero, and when all the neighbors are connected, it becomes maximum, $C(v_i) = 1$.*

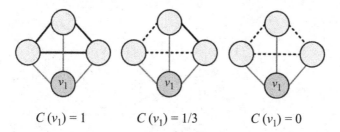

$$C(v_1) = 1 \qquad C(v_1) = 1/3 \qquad C(v_1) = 0$$

Figure 3.10. Change in Local Clustering Coefficient for Different Graphs. Thin lines depict connections to neighbors. Solid lines indicate connected neighbors, and dashed lines are the missing connections among neighbors.

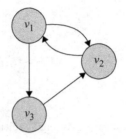

Figure 3.11. A Graph with Reciprocal Edges.

3.2.2 Reciprocity

Reciprocity is a simplified version of transitivity, because it considers closed loops of length 2, which can only happen in directed graphs. Formally, if node v is connected to node u, u by connecting to v exhibits reciprocity. On microblogging site Tumblr, for example, these nodes are known as "mutual followers." Informally, reciprocity is

If you become my friend, I'll be yours.

Figure 3.11 shows an example where two nodes (v_1 and v_2) in the graph demonstrate reciprocal behavior.

Reciprocity counts the number of reciprocal pairs in the graph. Any directed graph can have a maximum of $|E|/2$ pairs. This happens when all edges are reciprocal. Thus, this value can be used as a normalization factor. Reciprocity can be computed using the adjacency matrix A:

$$
\begin{aligned}
R &= \frac{\sum_{i,j,i<j} A_{i,j} A_{j,i}}{|E|/2}, \\
&= \frac{2}{|E|} \sum_{i,j,i<j} A_{i,j} A_{j,i}, \\
&= \frac{2}{|E|} \times \frac{1}{2} \mathrm{Tr}(A^2), \\
&= \frac{1}{|E|} \mathrm{Tr}(A^2), \\
&= \frac{1}{m} \mathrm{Tr}(A^2), \quad\quad (3.53)
\end{aligned}
$$

where $\text{Tr}(A) = A_{1,1} + A_{2,2} + \cdots + A_{n,n} = \sum_{i=1}^{n} A_{i,i}$ and m is the number of edges in the network. Note that the maximum value for $\sum_{i,j} A_{i,j} A_{j,i}$ is m when all directed edges are reciprocated.

Example 3.13. *For the graph shown in Figure 3.11, the adjacency matrix is*

$$A = \begin{bmatrix} 0 & 1 & 1 \\ 1 & 0 & 0 \\ 0 & 1 & 0 \end{bmatrix}. \tag{3.54}$$

Its reciprocity is

$$R = \frac{1}{m}\text{Tr}(A^2) = \frac{1}{4}\text{Tr}\left(\begin{bmatrix} 1 & 1 & 0 \\ 0 & 1 & 1 \\ 1 & 0 & 0 \end{bmatrix}\right) = \frac{2}{4} = \frac{1}{2}. \tag{3.55}$$

3.3 Balance and Status

A signed graph can represent the relationships of nodes in a social network, such as friends or foes. For example, a positive edge from node v_1 to v_2 denotes that v_1 considers v_2 as a friend and a negative edge denotes that v_1 assumes v_2 is an enemy. Similarly, we can utilize signed graphs to represent the social status of individuals. A positive edge connecting node v_1 to v_2 can also denote that v_1 considers v_2's status higher than its own in the society. Both cases represent interactions that individuals exhibit about their relationships. In real-world scenarios, we expect some level of consistency with respect to these interactions. For instance, it is more plausible for a friend of one's friend to be a friend than to be an enemy. In signed graphs, this consistency translates to observing triads with three positive edges (i.e., all friends) more frequently than ones with two positive edges and one negative edge (i.e., a friend's friend is an enemy). Assume we observe a signed graph that represents friends/foes or social status. Can we measure the consistency of attitudes that individual have toward one another?

To measure consistency in an individual's attitude, one needs to utilize theories from social sciences to define what is a consistent attitude. In this section, we discuss two theories, *social balance* and *social status*, that can help determine consistency in observed signed networks. Social balance theory is used when edges represent friends/foes, and social status theory is employed when they represent status.

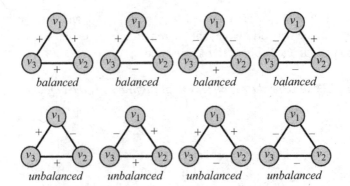

Figure 3.12. Sample Graphs for Social Balance Theory. In balanced triangles, there are an even number of negative edges.

Social Balance Theory

STRUCTURAL
BALANCE
THEORY

This theory, also known as *structural balance theory*, discusses consistency in friend/foe relationships among individuals. Informally, social balance theory says friend/foe relationships are consistent when

The friend of my friend is my friend,
The friend of my enemy is my enemy,
The enemy of my enemy is my friend,
The enemy of my friend is my enemy.

BALANCED
AND
UNBALANCED
TRIANGLES

We demonstrate a graph representation of social balance theory in Figure 3.12. In this figure, positive edges demonstrate friendships and negative ones demonstrate enemies. Triangles that are consistent based on this theory are denoted as *balanced* and triangles that are inconsistent as *unbalanced*. Let w_{ij} denote the value of the edge between nodes v_i and v_j. Then, for a triangle of nodes v_i, v_j, and v_k, it is consistent based on social balance theory; that is, it is balanced if and only if

$$w_{ij} w_{jk} w_{ki} \geq 0. \tag{3.56}$$

This is assuming that, for positive edges, $w_{ij} = 1$, and for negative edges, $w_{ij} = -1$. We observe that, for all balanced triangles in Figure 3.12, the value $w_{ij} w_{jk} w_{ki}$ is positive, and for all unbalanced triangles, it is negative. Social balance can also be generalized to subgraphs other than triangles. In general, for any cycle, if the product of edge values becomes positive, then the cycle is socially balanced.

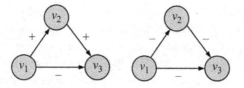

Figure 3.13. Sample Graphs for Social Status Theory. The left-hand graph is an unbalanced configuration, and the right-hand graph is a balanced configuration.

Social Status Theory

Social status theory measures how consistent individuals are in assigning status to their neighbors. It can be summarized as follows:

If X has a higher status than Y and Y has a higher status than Z, then X should have a higher status than Z.

We show this theory using two graphs in Figure 3.13. In this figure, nodes represent individuals. Positive and negative signs show higher or lower status depending on the arrow direction. A directed positive edge from node X to node Y shows that Y has a higher status than X, and a negative one shows the reverse. In the figure on the left, v_2 has a higher status than v_1 and v_3 has a higher status than v_2, so based on status theory, v_3 should have a higher status than v_1; however, we see that v_1 has a higher status in our configuration.[4] Based on social status theory, this is implausible, and thus this configuration is *unbalanced*. The graph on the right shows a balanced configuration with respect to social status theory.

In the example provided in Figure 3.13, social status is defined for the most general example: a set of three connected nodes (a triad). However, social status can be generalized to other graphs. For instance, in a cycle of n nodes, where $n - 1$ consecutive edges are positive and the last edge is negative, social status theory considers the cycle balanced.

Note that the identical configuration can be considered balanced by social balance theory and unbalanced based on social status theory (see Exercises).

3.4 Similarity

In this section, we review measures used to compute similarity between two nodes in a network. In social media, these nodes can represent individuals in a friendship network or products that are related. The similarity between these connected individuals can be computed either based on the network in which they are embedded (i.e., *network similarity*) or based on the similarity of the content they generate (i.e., *content similarity*). We discuss content similarity in Chapter 5. In this section, we demonstrate ways to compute similarity between two nodes using network information regarding the nodes and edges connecting them. When using network information, the similarity between two nodes can be computed by measuring their *structural equivalence* or their *regular equivalence*.

3.4.1 Structural Equivalence

To compute structural equivalence, we look at the neighborhood shared by two nodes; the size of this neighborhood defines how similar two nodes are. For instance, two brothers have in common sisters, mother, father, grandparents, and so on. This shows that they are similar, whereas two random male or female individuals do not have much in common and are not similar.

The similarity measures detailed in this section are based on the overlap between the neighborhoods of the nodes. Let $N(v_i)$ and $N(v_j)$ be the neighbors of nodes v_i and v_j, respectively. In this case, a measure of node similarity can be defined as follows:

$$\sigma(v_i, v_j) = |N(v_i) \cap N(v_j)|. \tag{3.57}$$

For large networks, this value can increase rapidly, because nodes may share many neighbors. Generally, similarity is attributed to a value that is bounded and is usually in the range [0, 1]. Various normalization procedures can take place such as the Jaccard similarity or the cosine similarity:

JACCARD
SIMILARITY
AND COSINE
SIMILARITY

$$\sigma_{\text{Jaccard}}(v_i, v_j) = \frac{|N(v_i) \cap N(v_j)|}{|N(v_i) \cup N(v_j)|}, \tag{3.58}$$

$$\sigma_{\text{Cosine}}(v_i, v_j) = \frac{|N(v_i) \cap N(v_j)|}{\sqrt{|N(v_i)||N(v_j)|}}. \tag{3.59}$$

In general, the definition of neighborhood $N(v_i)$ excludes the node itself (v_i). This leads to problems with the aforementioned similarities because nodes that are connected and do not share a neighbor will be assigned zero similarity. This can be rectified by assuming nodes to be included in their neighborhoods.

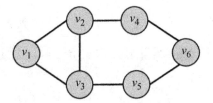

Figure 3.14. Sample Graph for Computing Similarity.

Example 3.14. *Consider the graph in Figure 3.14. The similarity values between nodes v_2 and v_5 are*

$$\sigma_{\text{Jaccard}}(v_2, v_5) = \frac{|\{v_1, v_3, v_4\} \cap \{v_3, v_6\}|}{|\{v_1, v_3, v_4, v_6\}|} = 0.25, \qquad (3.60)$$

$$\sigma_{\text{Cosine}}(v_2, v_5) = \frac{|\{v_1, v_3, v_4\} \cap \{v_3, v_6\}|}{\sqrt{|\{v_1, v_3, v_4\}||\{v_3, v_6\}|}} = 0.40. \qquad (3.61)$$

A more interesting way of measuring the similarity between v_i and v_j is to compare $\sigma(v_i, v_j)$ with the expected value of $\sigma(v_i, v_j)$ when nodes pick their neighbors at random. The more distant these two values are, the more significant the similarity observed between v_i and v_j ($\sigma(v_i, v_j)$) is. For nodes v_i and v_j with degrees d_i and d_j, this expectation is $\frac{d_i d_j}{n}$, where n is the number of nodes. This is because there is a $\frac{d_i}{n}$ chance of becoming v_i's neighbor and, since v_j selects d_j neighbors, the expected overlap is $\frac{d_i d_j}{n}$. We can rewrite $\sigma(v_i, v_j)$ as

$$\sigma(v_i, v_j) = |N(v_i) \cap N(v_j)| = \sum_k A_{i,k} A_{j,k}. \qquad (3.62)$$

Hence, a similarity measure can be defined by subtracting the random expectation $\frac{d_i d_j}{n}$ from Equation 3.62:

$$
\begin{aligned}
\sigma_{\text{significance}}(v_i, v_j) &= \sum_k A_{i,k} A_{j,k} - \frac{d_i d_j}{n} \\
&= \sum_k A_{i,k} A_{j,k} - n \frac{1}{n} \sum_k A_{i,k} \frac{1}{n} \sum_k A_{j,k} \\
&= \sum_k A_{i,k} A_{j,k} - n \bar{A}_i \bar{A}_j \\
&= \sum_k (A_{i,k} A_{j,k} - \bar{A}_i \bar{A}_j)
\end{aligned}
$$

$$= \sum_k (A_{i,k} A_{j,k} - \bar{A}_i \bar{A}_j - \bar{A}_i \bar{A}_j + \bar{A}_i \bar{A}_j)$$

$$= \sum_k (A_{i,k} A_{j,k} - A_{i,k} \bar{A}_j - \bar{A}_i A_{j,k} + \bar{A}_i \bar{A}_j)$$

$$= \sum_k (A_{i,k} - \bar{A}_i)(A_{j,k} - \bar{A}_j), \tag{3.63}$$

where $\bar{A}_i = \frac{1}{n} \sum_k A_{i,k}$. The term $\sum_k (A_{i,k} - \bar{A}_i)(A_{j,k} - \bar{A}_j)$ is basically the covariance between A_i and A_j. The covariance can be normalized by the multiplication of variances,

$$\sigma_{\text{pearson}}(v_i, v_j) = \frac{\sigma_{\text{significance}}(v_i, v_j)}{\sqrt{\sum_k (A_{i,k} - \bar{A}_i)^2} \sqrt{\sum_k (A_{j,k} - \bar{A}_j)^2}}$$

$$= \frac{\sum_k (A_{i,k} - \bar{A}_i)(A_{j,k} - \bar{A}_j),}{\sqrt{\sum_k (A_{i,k} - \bar{A}_i)^2} \sqrt{\sum_k (A_{j,k} - \bar{A}_j)^2}}, \tag{3.64}$$

PEARSON CORRELATION

which is called the *Pearson correlation coefficient*. Its value, unlike the other two measures, is in the range $[-1, 1]$. A positive correlation value denotes that when v_i befriends an individual v_k, v_j is also likely to befriend v_k. A negative value denotes the opposite (i.e., when v_i befriends v_k, it is unlikely for v_j to befriend v_k). A zero value denotes that there is no linear relationship between the befriending behavior of v_i and v_j.

3.4.2 Regular Equivalence

In regular equivalence, unlike structural equivalence, we do not look at the neighborhoods shared between individuals, but at how neighborhoods themselves are similar. For instance, athletes are similar not because they know each other in person, but because they know similar individuals, such as coaches, trainers, and other players. The same argument holds for any other profession or industry in which individuals might not know each other in person, but are in contact with very similar individuals. Regular equivalence assesses similarity by comparing the similarity of neighbors and not by their overlap.

One way of formalizing this is to consider nodes v_i and v_j similar when they have many similar neighbors v_k and v_l. This concept is shown in Figure 3.15(a). Formally,

$$\sigma_{\text{regular}}(v_i, v_j) = \alpha \sum_{k,l} A_{i,k} A_{j,l} \sigma_{\text{regular}}(v_k, v_l). \tag{3.65}$$

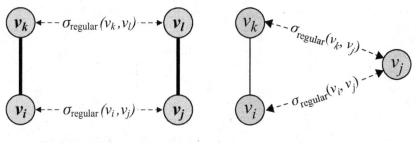

(a) Original Formulation   (b) Relaxed Formulation

Figure 3.15. Regular Equivalence. Solid lines denote edges, and dashed lines denote similarities between nodes. In regular equivalence, similarity between nodes v_i and v_j is replaced by similarity between (a) their neighbors v_k and v_l or between (b) neighbor v_k and node v_j.

Unfortunately, this formulation is self-referential because solving for i and j requires solving for k and l, solving for k and l requires solving for their neighbors, and so on. So, we relax this formulation and assume that node v_i is similar to node v_j when v_j is similar to v_i's neighbors v_k. This is shown in Figure 3.15(b). Formally,

$$\sigma_{\text{regular}}(v_i, v_j) = \alpha \sum_k A_{i,k} \sigma_{\text{regular}}(v_k, v_j). \tag{3.66}$$

In vector format, we have

$$\sigma_{\text{regular}} = \alpha A \sigma_{\text{regular}}. \tag{3.67}$$

A node is highly similar to itself. To make sure that our formulation guarantees this, we can add an identity matrix to this vector format. Adding an identity matrix will add 1 to all diagonal entries, which represent self-similarities $\sigma_{\text{regular}}(v_i, v_i)$:

$$\sigma_{\text{regular}} = \alpha A \sigma_{\text{regular}} + \mathbf{I}. \tag{3.68}$$

By rearranging, we get

$$\sigma_{\text{regular}} = (\mathbf{I} - \alpha A)^{-1}, \tag{3.69}$$

which we can use to find the regular equivalence similarity.

Note the similarity between Equation 3.69 and that of Katz centrality (Equation 3.21). As with Katz centrality, we must be careful how we choose α for convergence. A common practice is to select an α such that $\alpha < 1/\lambda$, where λ is the largest eigenvalue of A.

Example 3.15. *For the graph depicted in Figure 3.14, the adjacency matrix is*

$$
A = \begin{bmatrix}
0 & 1 & 1 & 0 & 0 & 0 \\
1 & 0 & 1 & 1 & 0 & 0 \\
1 & 1 & 0 & 0 & 1 & 0 \\
0 & 1 & 0 & 0 & 0 & 1 \\
0 & 0 & 0 & 1 & 1 & 0
\end{bmatrix}. \tag{3.70}
$$

The largest eigenvalue of A is 2.43. We set $\alpha = 0.4 < 1/2.43$, and we compute $(I - 0.4A)^{-1}$, which is the similarity matrix,

$$
\sigma_{\text{regular}} = (I - 0.4A)^{-1} = \begin{bmatrix}
1.43 & 0.73 & 0.73 & 0.26 & 0.26 & 0.16 \\
0.73 & 1.63 & 0.80 & 0.56 & 0.32 & 0.26 \\
0.73 & 0.80 & 1.63 & 0.32 & 0.56 & 0.26 \\
0.26 & 0.56 & 0.32 & 1.31 & 0.23 & 0.46 \\
0.26 & 0.32 & 0.56 & 0.23 & 1.31 & 0.46 \\
0.16 & 0.26 & 0.26 & 0.46 & 0.46 & 1.27
\end{bmatrix}. \tag{3.71}
$$

Any row or column of this matrix shows the similarity of a node to other nodes. We can see that node v_1 is the most similar (other than itself) to nodes v_2 and v_3. Furthermore, nodes v_2 and v_3 have the highest similarity in this graph.

3.5 Summary

In this chapter, we discussed measures for a social media network. Centrality measures attempt to find the most central node within a graph. Degree centrality assumes that the node with the maximum degree is the most central individual. In directed graphs, prestige and gregariousness are variants of degree centrality. Eigenvector centrality generalizes degree centrality and considers individuals who know many important nodes as central. Based on the Perron-Frobenius theorem, eigenvector centrality is determined by computing the eigenvector of the adjacency matrix. Katz centrality solves some of the problems with eigenvector centrality in directed graphs by adding a bias term. PageRank centrality defines a normalized version of Katz centrality. The Google search engine uses PageRank as a measure to rank webpages. Betweenness centrality assumes that central nodes act as hubs connecting other nodes, and closeness centrality implements the intuition that central nodes are close to all other nodes. Node centrality measures can be generalized to a group of nodes using group degree centrality, group betweenness centrality, and group closeness centrality.

Linking between nodes (e.g., befriending in social media) is the most commonly observed phenomenon in social media. Linking behavior is analyzed in terms of its transitivity and its reciprocity. Transitivity is "when a friend of my friend is my friend." The transitivity of linking behavior is analyzed by means of the clustering coefficient. The global clustering coefficient analyzes transitivity within a network, and the local clustering coefficient performs that for a node. Transitivity is commonly considered for closed triads of edges. For loops of length 2, the problem is simplified and is called reciprocity. In other words, reciprocity is when "if you become my friend, I'll be yours."

To analyze if relationships are consistent in social media, we used various social theories to validate outcomes. Social balance and social status are two such theories.

Finally, we analyzed node similarity measures. In structural equivalence, two nodes are considered similar when they share neighborhoods. We discussed cosine similarity and Jaccard similarity in structural equivalence. In regular equivalence, nodes are similar when their neighborhoods are similar.

3.6 Bibliographic Notes

General reviews of different measures in graphs, networks, the web, and social media can be found in [Newman, 2010; Witten, Frank, and Hall, 2011; Tan et al., 2005; Han et al., 2006; Wasserman and Faust, 1994].

A more detailed description of the PageRank algorithm can be found in [Page et al., 1999; Liu, 2007]. In practice, to compute the PageRank values, the *power iteration method* is used. Given a matrix A, this method produces an eigenvalue λ and an eigenvector v of A. In the case of PageRank, eigenvalue λ is set to 1. The iterative algorithm starts with an initial eigenvector v_0 and then, v_{k+1} is computed from v_k as follows,

$$v_{k+1} = Av_k. \tag{3.72}$$

The iterative process is continued until $v_k \approx v_{k+1}$ (i.e., convergence occurs). Other similar techniques to PageRank for computing influential nodes in a webgraph, such as the HITS [Kleinberg, 1998] algorithm, can be found in [Chakrabarti, 2003; Kosala and Blockeel, 2000]. Unlike PageRank, the HITS algorithm[5] considers two types of nodes: authority nodes and hub nodes. An authority is a webpage that has many in-links. A hub is a page with many out-links. Authority pages have in-links from many hubs. In other words, hubs represent webpages that contain many useful links to authorities and authorities are influential nodes in the webgraph. HITS employs an iterative approach to compute authority and hub scores for all nodes in the graph. Nodes with high authority scores are classified as authorities and nodes with high hub scores as hubs. Webpage with high authority scores or hub scores can be recommended to users in a web search engine.

Betweenness algorithms can be improved using all-pair shortest paths algorithms [Warshall, 1962] or algorithms optimized for computing betweenness, such as the Brandes' algorithm discussed in [Brandes, 2001; Tang and Liu, 2010].

A review of node similarity and normalization procedures is provided in [Leicht, Holme, and Newman, 2005]. Jaccard similarity was introduced in [Jaccard, 1901] and cosine similarity is introduced by Salton and McGill [1986].

REGE [White, 1980, 1984] and CATREGE [Stephen and Martin, 1993] are well-known algorithms for computing regular equivalence.

3.7 Exercises

Centrality

1. Come up with an example of a directed connected graph in which eigenvector centrality becomes zero for some nodes. Describe when this happens.
2. Does β have any effect on the order of centralities? In other words, if for one value of β the centrality value of node v_i is greater than that of v_j, is it possible to change β in a way such that v_j's centrality becomes larger than that of v_i's?
3. In PageRank, what α values can we select to guarantee that centrality values are calculated correctly (i.e., values do not diverge)?
4. Calculate PageRank values for this graph when

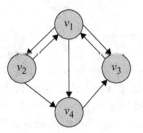

- $\alpha = 1, \beta = 0$
- $\alpha = 0.85, \beta = 1$
- $\alpha = 0, \beta = 1$

Discuss the effects of different values of α and β for this particular problem.

5. Consider a full n-tree. This is a tree in which every node other than the leaves has n children. Calculate the betweenness centrality for the root node, internal nodes, and leaves.

6. Show an example where the eigenvector centrality of all nodes in the graph is the same while betweenness centrality gives different values for different nodes.

Transitivity and Reciprocity

7. In a directed graph $G(V, E)$,
   - Let p be the probability that any node v_i is connected to any node v_j. What is the expected reciprocity of this graph?
   - Let m and n be the number of edges and number of nodes, respectively. What is the maximum reciprocity? What is the minimum?

8. Given all graphs $\{G(V, E)|s.t., |E| = m, |V| = n\}$,
   (a) When $m = 15$ and $n = 10$, find a graph with a minimum average clustering coefficient (one is enough).
   (b) Can you come up with an algorithm to find such a graph for any m and n?

Balance and Status

9. Find all conflicting directed triad configurations for social balance and social status. A conflicting configuration is an assignment of positive/negative edge signs for which one theory considers the triad balanced and the other considers it unbalanced.

Similarity

10. In Figure 3.6,
    - Compute node similarity using Jaccard and cosine similarity for nodes v_5 and v_4.
    - Find the most similar node to v_7 using regular equivalence.

4

Network Models

In May 2011, Facebook had 721 million users, represented by a graph of 721 million nodes. A Facebook user at the time had an average of 190 friends; that is, all Facebook users, taken into account, had a total of 68.5 billion friendships (i.e., edges). What are the principal underlying processes that help initiate these friendships? More importantly, how can these seemingly independent friendships form this complex friendship network?

In social media, many social networks contain millions of nodes and billions of edges. These complex networks have billions of friendships, the reasons for existence of most of which are obscure. Humbled by the complexity of these networks and the difficulty of independently analyzing each one of these friendships, we can design models that generate, on a smaller scale, graphs similar to real-world networks. On the assumption that these models simulate properties observed in real-world networks well, the analysis of real-world networks boils down to a cost-efficient measuring of different properties of simulated networks. In addition, these models

- allow for a better understanding of phenomena observed in real-world networks by providing concrete mathematical explanations and
- allow for controlled experiments on synthetic networks when real-world networks are not available.

We discuss three principal network models in this chapter: the *random graph model*, the *small-world model*, and the *preferential attachment model*. These models are designed to accurately model properties observed in real-world networks. Before we delve into the details of these models, we discuss their properties.

4.1 Properties of Real-World Networks

Real-world networks share common characteristics. When designing network models, we aim to devise models that can accurately describe these networks by mimicking these common characteristics. To determine these characteristics, a common practice is to identify their attributes and show that measurements for these attributes are consistent across networks. In particular, three network attributes exhibit consistent measurements across real-world networks: *degree distribution, clustering coefficient*, and *average path length*. As we recall, degree distribution denotes how node degrees are distributed across a network. The clustering coefficient measures transitivity of a network. Finally, average path length denotes the average distance (shortest path length) between pairs of nodes. We discuss how these three attributes behave in real-world networks next.

4.1.1 Degree Distribution

Consider the distribution of wealth among individuals. Most individuals have an average amount of capital, whereas a few are considered extremely wealthy. In fact, we observe exponentially more individuals with an average amount of capital than wealthier ones. Similarly, consider the population of cities. A few metropolitan areas are densely populated, whereas other cities have an average population size. In social media, we observe the same phenomenon regularly when measuring *popularity* or *interestingness* for entities. For instance,

- Many sites are visited less than a thousand times a month, whereas a few are visited more than a million times daily.
- Most social media users are active on a few sites, whereas a few individuals are active on hundreds of sites.
- There are exponentially more modestly priced products for sale compared to expensive ones.
- There exist many individuals with a few friends and a handful of users with thousands of friends.

The last observation is directly related to node degrees in social media. The degree of a node in social media often denotes the number of friends an individual has. Thus, the distribution of the number of friends denotes the degree distribution of the network. It turns out that in all provided observations, the distribution of values follows a *power-law distribution*. For instance, let k denote the degree of a node (i.e., the number of friends an individual has). Let p_k denote the fraction of individuals with degree k (i.e., $\frac{\text{frequency of observing } k}{|V|}$). Then, in the power-law distribution

POWER-LAW DISTRIBUTION

$$p_k = ak^{-b}, \tag{4.1}$$

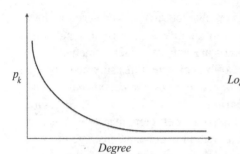

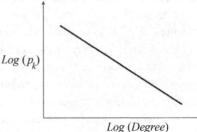

(a) Power-Law Degree Distribution   (b) Log-Log Plot of Power-Law
                                             Degree Distribution

Figure 4.1. Power-Law Degree Distribution and Its Log-Log Plot.

where b is the power-law exponent and a is the power-law intercept. A power-law degree distribution is shown in Figure 4.1(a).

Taking the logarithm from both sides of Equation 4.1, we get

$$\ln p_k = -b \ln k + \ln a. \qquad (4.2)$$

Equation 4.2 shows that the log-log plot of a power-law distribution is a straight line with slope $-b$ and intercept $\ln a$ (see Figure 4.1(b)). This also reveals a methodology for checking whether a network exhibits a power-law distribution.[1] We can do the following:

- Pick a popularity measure and compute it for the whole network. For instance, we can take the number of friends in a social network as a measure. We denote the measured value as k.
- Compute p_k, the fraction of individuals having popularity k.
- Plot a log-log graph, where the x-axis represents $\ln k$ and the y-axis represents $\ln p_k$.
- If a power-law distribution exists, we should observe a straight line in the plot.

Figure 4.2 depicts some log-log graphs for the number of friends on real-world networks. In all networks, a linear trend is observed denoting a power-law degree distribution.

SCALE-FREE NETWORKS   Networks exhibiting power-law degree distribution are often called *scale-free* networks. Since the majority of social networks are scale-free, we are interested in models that can generate synthetic networks with a power-law degree distribution.

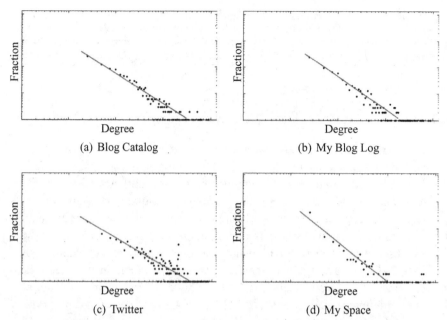

Figure 4.2. Log-Log Plots for Power-Law Degree Distribution in Social Media Networks. In these figures, the x-axis represents the logarithm of the degree, and the y-axis represents the logarithm of the fraction of individuals with that degree (i.e., $\log(p_k)$). The line demonstrates the linear trend observed in log-log plots of power-law distributions.

4.1.2 Clustering Coefficient

In real-world social networks, friendships are highly transitive. In other words, friends of an individual are often friends with one another. These friendships form triads of friendships that are frequently observed in social networks. These triads result in networks with high average [local] clustering coefficients. In May 2011, Facebook had an average clustering coefficient of 0.5 for individuals who had two friends; their degree was 2 [Ugander et al., 2011]. This indicates that for 50% of all users with two friends, their two friends were also friends with each other. Table 4.1 provides the average clustering coefficient for several real-world social networks and the web.

Table 4.1. *Average Local Clustering Coefficient in Real-World Networks (from [Broder et al., 2000; Ugander et al., 2011; Mislove et al., 2007])*

Web	Facebook	Flickr	LiveJournal	Orkut	YouTube
0.081	0.14 (with 100 friends)	0.31	0.33	0.17	0.13

Table 4.2. *Average Path Length in Real-World Networks (from [Broder et al., 2000; Ugander et al., 2011; Mislove et al., 2007])*

Web	Facebook	Flickr	LiveJournal	Orkut	YouTube
16.12	4.7	5.67	5.88	4.25	5.10

4.1.3 Average Path Length

In real-world networks, any two members of the network are usually connected via short paths. In other words, the average path length is small. This

SMALL-WORLD
AND SIX
DEGREES OF
SEPARATION

is known as the *small-world* phenomenon. In the well-known *small-world experiment* conducted in the 1960s by Stanley Milgram, Milgram conjectured that people around the world are connected to one another via a path of at most six individuals (i.e., *the six degrees of separation*). Similarly, we observe small average path lengths in social networks. For example, in May 2011, the average path length between individuals in the Facebook graph was 4.7. This average was 4.3 for individuals in the United States at the same time [Ugander et al., 2011]. Table 4.2 provides the average path length for real-world social networks and the web.

These three properties – power-law degree distribution, high clustering coefficient, and small average path length are consistently observed in real-world networks. We design models based on simple assumptions on how friendships are formed, hoping that these models generate scale-free networks, with high clustering coefficient and small average path lengths. We start with the simplest network model, the random graph model.

4.2 Random Graphs

We start with the most basic *assumption* on how friendships can be formed:

Edges (i.e., friendships) between nodes (i.e., individuals) are formed randomly.

The random graph model follows this basic assumption. In reality friendships in real-world networks are far from random. By assuming random friendships, we simplify the process of friendship formation in real-world networks, hoping that these random friendships ultimately create networks that exhibit common characteristics observed in real-world networks.

Formally, we can assume that for a graph with a *fixed* number of nodes n, any of the $\binom{n}{2}$ edges can be formed independently, with probability p.

$G(n, p)$

This graph is called a *random graph* and we denote it as the $G(n, p)$ model. This model was first proposed independently by Edgar Gilbert [1959] and

Solomonoff and Rapoport [1951]. Another way of randomly generating graphs is to assume that both the number of nodes n and the number of edges m are fixed. However, we need to determine which m edges are selected from the set of $\binom{n}{2}$ possible edges. Let Ω denote the set of graphs with n nodes and m edges. To generate a random graph, we can uniformly select one of the graphs in Ω. The number of graphs with n nodes and m edges (i.e., $|\Omega|$) is

$$|\Omega| = \binom{\binom{n}{2}}{m}. \tag{4.3}$$

The uniform random graph selection probability is $\frac{1}{|\Omega|}$. One can think of the probability of uniformly selecting a graph as an analog to p, the probability of selecting an edge in $G(n, p)$.

The second model was introduced by Paul Erdős and Alfred Rényi [1959] and is denoted as the $G(n, m)$ model. In the limit, both models act similarly. $G(n, m)$ The expected number of edges in $G(n, p)$ is $\binom{n}{2} p$. Now, if we set $\binom{n}{2} p = m$, in the limit, both models act the same because they contain the same number of edges. Note that the $G(n, m)$ model contains a fixed number of edges; however, the second model $G(n, p)$ is *likely* to contain none or all possible edges.

Mathematically, the $G(n, p)$ model is almost always simpler to analyze; hence the rest of this section deals with properties of this model. Note that there exist many graphs with n nodes and m edges (i.e., generated by $G(n, m)$). The same argument holds for $G(n, p)$, and many graphs can be generated by the model. Therefore, when measuring properties in random graphs, the measures are calculated over all graphs that can be generated by the model and then averaged. This is particularly useful when we are interested in the average, and not specific, behavior of large graphs.

In $G(n, p)$, the number of edges is not fixed; therefore, we first examine some mathematical properties regarding the expected number of edges that are connected to a node, the expected number of edges observed in the graph, and the likelihood of observing m edges in a random graph generated by the $G(n, p)$ process.

Proposition 4.1. *The expected number of edges connected to a node (expected degree) in $G(n, p)$ is $(n - 1)p$.*

Proof. A node can be connected to at most $n - 1$ nodes (via $n - 1$ edges). All edges are selected independently with probability p. Therefore, on average $(n - 1)p$ of them are selected. The expected degree is often denoted using notation c or k in the literature. Since we frequently use k to denote degree values, we use c to denote the expected degree of a random graph,

$$c = (n - 1)p, \tag{4.4}$$

or equivalently,

$$p = \frac{c}{n - 1}. \tag{4.5}$$

$\square$

Proposition 4.2. *The expected number of edges in $G(n, p)$ is $\binom{n}{2} p$.*

Proof. Following the same line of argument, because edges are selected independently and we have a maximum of $\binom{n}{2}$ edges, the expected number of edges is $\binom{n}{2} p$. $\square$

Proposition 4.3. *In a graph generated by $G(n, p)$ model, the probability of observing m edges is*

$$P(|E| = m) = \binom{\binom{n}{2}}{m} p^m (1 - p)^{\binom{n}{2} - m}, \tag{4.6}$$

which is a binomial distribution.

Proof. m edges are selected from the $\binom{n}{2}$ possible edges. These edges are formed with probability p^m, and other edges are not formed (to guarantee the existence of only m edges) with probability $(1 - p)^{\binom{n}{2} - m}$. $\square$

Given these basic propositions, we next analyze how random graphs evolve as we add edges to them.

4.2.1 Evolution of Random Graphs

In random graphs, when nodes form connections, after some time a large fraction of nodes get connected (i.e., there is a path between any pair of them). This large fraction forms a *connected component*, commonly called the *largest connected component* or the *giant component*. We can tune the behavior of the random graph model by selecting the appropriate p value. In $G(n, p)$, when $p = 0$, the size of the largest connected component is 0 (no two pairs are connected), and when $p = 1$, the size is n (all pairs are connected). Table 4.3 provides the size of the largest connected component (*slc* values in the table) for random graphs with 10 nodes and different p values.

GIANT
COMPONENT

Table 4.3. *Evolution of Random Graphs. Here, p is the random graph generation probability, c is the average degree, ds is the diameter size, slc is the size of the largest component, and l is the average path length. The highlighted column denotes phase transition in the random graph*

p	0.0	0.055	0.11	1.0
c	0.0	0.8	≈ 1	9.0
ds	0	2	6	1
slc	0	4	7	10
l	0.0	1.5	2.66	1.0

The table also provides information on the average degree c, the diameter size ds, the size of the largest component slc, and the average path length l of the random graph.

As shown, in Table 4.3, as p gets larger, the graph gets denser. When p is very small, the following is found:

1. No giant component is observed in the graph.
2. Small isolated connected components are formed.
3. The diameter is small because all nodes are in isolated components, in which they are connected to a handful of other nodes.

As p gets larger, the following occurs:

1. A giant component starts to appear.
2. Isolated components become connected.
3. The diameter values increase.

At this point, nodes are connected to each other via long paths (see $p = 0.11$ in Table 4.3). As p continues to get larger, the random graph properties change again. For larger values, the diameter starts shrinking as nodes get connected to each other via different paths (that are likely to be shorter). The point where diameter value starts to shrink in a random graph is called *phase transition*. At the point of *phase transition*, the following two phenomena are observed:

PHASE
TRANSITION

1. The giant component, which *just* started to appear, starts to grow.
2. The diameter, which *just* reached its maximum value, starts decreasing.

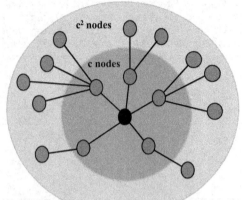

Figure 4.3. Nodes Visited by Moving n-hops away in a Random Graph. c denotes the expected node degree.

It is proven that in random graphs phase transition occurs when $c = 1$; that is, $p = 1/(n - 1)$.

Proposition 4.4. *In random graphs, phase transition happens at* $c = 1$.

Proof. (Sketch) Consider a random graph with expected node degree c, where $c = p(n - 1)$. In this graph, consider any **connected** set of nodes S and consider the complement set $\bar{S} = V - S$. For the sake of our proof, we assume that $|S| \ll |\bar{S}|$. Given any node v in S, if we move one hop (edge) away from v, we visit approximately c nodes. Following the same argument, if we move one hop away from nodes in S, we visit approximately $|S|c$ nodes. Assuming $|S|$ is small, the nodes in S only visit nodes in $\bar{S}$, and when moving one hop away from S, the set of nodes "guaranteed to be connected" gets larger by a factor c (see Figure 4.3). The connected set of visited nodes gets c^2 times larger when moving two hops and so on. Now, in the limit, if we want this component of visited nodes to become the largest connected component, then after traveling n hops, we must have

$$c^n \geq 1 \text{ or equivalently } c \geq 1. \tag{4.7}$$

Otherwise (i.e., $c < 1$), the number of visited nodes dies out exponentially. Hence, phase transition happens at $c = 1$.[2]   □

Note that this proof sketch provides an intuitive approach to understand the proposition. Interested readers can refer to the bibliographic notes for a concrete proof.

So far we have discussed the generation and evolution of random graphs; however, we also need to analyze how random graphs perform in terms of mimicking properties exhibited by real-world networks. It turns out that random graphs can model average path length in a real-world network accurately, but fail to generate a realistic degree distribution or clustering coefficient. We discuss these properties next.

4.2.2 Properties of Random Graphs

Degree Distribution

When computing degree distribution, we estimate the probability of observing $P(d_v = d)$ for node v.

Proposition 4.5. *For a graph generated by $G(n, p)$, node v has degree d, $d \leq n - 1$, with probability*

$$P(d_v = d) = \binom{n-1}{d} p^d (1-p)^{n-1-d}, \qquad (4.8)$$

which is again a binomial degree distribution.

Proof. The proof is left to the reader.[3] $\qquad \square$

This assumes that n is fixed. We can generalize this result by computing the degree distribution of random graphs in the limit (i.e., $n \to \infty$). In this case, using Equation 4.4 and the fact that $\lim_{x \to 0} \ln(1 + x) = x$, we can compute the limit for each term of Equation 4.8:

$$\lim_{n \to \infty} (1 - p)^{n-1-d} = \lim_{n \to \infty} e^{\ln(1-p)^{n-1-d}} = \lim_{n \to \infty} e^{(n-1-d)\ln(1-p)}$$

$$= \lim_{n \to \infty} e^{(n-1-d)\ln(1-\frac{c}{n-1})} = \lim_{n \to \infty} e^{-(n-1-d)\frac{c}{n-1}} = e^{-c}.$$

$$(4.9)$$

We also have

$$\lim_{n \to \infty} \binom{n-1}{d} = \lim_{n \to \infty} \frac{(n-1)!}{(n-1-d)!\, d!}$$

$$= \lim_{n \to \infty} \frac{((n-1) \times (n-2) \times \cdots (n-d))(n-1-d)!}{(n-1-d)!\, d!}$$

$$= \lim_{n \to \infty} \frac{((n-1) \times (n-2) \times \cdots (n-d))}{d!}$$

$$\approx \frac{(n-1)^d}{d!}. \qquad (4.10)$$

We can compute the degree distribution of random graphs in the limit by substituting Equations 4.10, 4.9, and 4.4 in Equation 4.8,

$$\lim_{n \to \infty} P(d_v = d) = \lim_{n \to \infty} \binom{n-1}{d} p^d (1-p)^{n-1-d}$$

$$= \frac{(n-1)^d}{d!} \left(\frac{c}{n-1}\right)^d e^{-c} = e^{-c} \frac{c^d}{d!}, \qquad (4.11)$$

which is basically the *Poisson distribution* with mean c. Thus, in the limit, random graphs generate Poisson degree distribution, which differs from the power-law degree distribution observed in real-world networks.

Clustering Coefficient

Proposition 4.6. *In a random graph generated by $G(n, p)$, the expected local clustering coefficient for node v is p.*

Proof. The local clustering coefficient for node v is

$$C(v) = \frac{\text{number of connected pairs of } v\text{'s neighbors}}{\text{number of pairs of } v\text{'s neighbors}}. \qquad (4.12)$$

However, v can have different degrees depending on the edges that are formed randomly. Thus, we can compute the expected value for $C(v)$:

$$\mathbf{E}(C(v)) = \sum_{d=0}^{n-1} \mathbf{E}(C(v)|d_v = d)\, P(d_v = d). \qquad (4.13)$$

The first term is basically the local clustering coefficient of a node given its degree. For a random graph, we have

$$\mathbf{E}(C(v)|d_v = d) = \frac{\text{number of connected pairs of } v\text{'s } d \text{ neighbors}}{\text{number of pairs of } v\text{'s } d \text{ neighbors}}$$

$$= \frac{p\binom{d}{2}}{\binom{d}{2}} = p. \tag{4.14}$$

Substituting Equation 4.14 in Equation 4.13, we get

$$\mathbf{E}(C(v)) = p \sum_{d=0}^{d=n-1} P(d_v = d) = p, \tag{4.15}$$

where we have used the fact that all probability distributions sum up to 1. $\qquad\square$

Proposition 4.7. *The global clustering coefficient of a random graph generated by $G(n, p)$ is p.*

Proof. The global clustering coefficient of a graph defines the probability of two neighbors of the same node being connected. In random graphs, for any two nodes, this probability is the same and is equal to the generation probability p that determines the probability of two nodes getting connected. Note that in random graphs, the expected local clustering coefficient is equivalent to the global clustering coefficient. $\qquad\square$

In random graphs, the clustering coefficient is equal to the probability p; therefore, by appropriately selecting p, we can generate networks with a high clustering coefficient. Note that selecting a large p is undesirable because doing so will generate a very dense graph, which is unrealistic, as in the real-world, networks are often sparse. Thus, random graphs are considered generally incapable of generating networks with high clustering coefficients without compromising other required properties.

Average Path Length

Proposition 4.8. *The average path length l in a random graph is*

$$l \approx \frac{\ln |V|}{\ln c}, \tag{4.16}$$

Proof. (Sketch) The proof is similar to the proof provided in determining when phase transition happens (see Section 4.2.1). Let $\mathcal{D}$ denote the expected diameter size in the random graph. Starting with any node in a

Table 4.4. *A Comparison between Real-World Networks and Simulated Random Graphs. In this table, C denotes the average clustering coefficient. The last two columns show the average path length and the clustering coefficient for the random graph simulated for the real-world network. Note that average path lengths are modeled properly, whereas the clustering coefficient is underestimated*

| Network | Original Network | | | | Simulated Random Graph | |
	Size	Average Degree	Average Path Length	C	Average Path Length	C
Film Actors	225,226	61	3.65	0.79	2.99	0.00027
Medline Coauthorship	1,520,251	18.1	4.6	0.56	4.91	1.8×10^{-4}
E. Coli	282	7.35	2.9	0.32	3.04	0.026
C. Elegans	282	14	2.65	0.28	2.25	0.05

random graph and its expected degree c, one can visit approximately c nodes by traveling one edge, c^2 nodes by traveling two edges, and $c^{\mathcal{D}}$ nodes by traveling "diameter" number of edges. After this step, almost all nodes should be visited. In this case, we have

$$c^{\mathcal{D}} \approx |V|. \qquad (4.17)$$

In random graphs, the expected diameter size tends to the average path length l in the limit. This we provide without proof. Interested readers can refer to the bibliographic notes for pointers to concrete proofs. Using this fact, we have

$$c^{\mathcal{D}} \approx c^l \approx |V|. \qquad (4.18)$$

Taking the logarithm from both sides we get $l \approx \frac{\ln|V|}{\ln c}$. Therefore, the average path length in a random graph is equal to $\frac{\ln|V|}{\ln c}$.   □

4.2.3 Modeling Real-World Networks with Random Graphs

Given a real-world network, we can simulate it using a random graph model. We can compute the average degree c in the given network. From c, the connection probability p can be computed ($p = \frac{c}{n-1}$). Using p and the number of nodes in the given network n, a random graph model $G(n, p)$ can be simulated. Table 4.4 demonstrates the simulation results for various real-world networks. As observed in the table, random graphs perform well in modeling the average path lengths; however, when considering the transitivity, the random graph model drastically underestimates the clustering coefficient.

To tackle this issue, we study the small-world model.

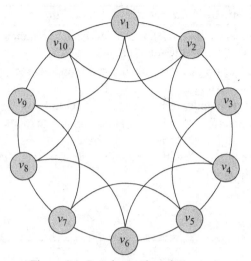

Figure 4.4. Regular Lattice of Degree 4.

4.3 Small-World Model

The assumption behind the random graph model is that connections in real-world networks are formed at random. Although unrealistic, random graphs can model average path lengths in real-world networks properly, but underestimate the clustering coefficient. To mitigate this problem, Duncan J. Watts and Steven Strogatz in 1997 proposed the small-world model.

In real-world interactions, many individuals have a limited and often at least, a fixed number of connections. Individuals connect with their parents, brothers, sisters, grandparents, and teachers, among others. Thus, instead of assuming random connections, as we did in random graph models, one can assume an *egalitarian* model in real-world networks, where people have the same number of neighbors (friends). This again is unrealistic; however, it models more accurately the clustering coefficient of real-world networks. In graph theory terms, this assumption is equivalent to embedding individuals in a *regular network*. A regular (ring) lattice is a special case of regular networks where there exists a certain pattern for how **ordered** nodes are connected to one another. In particular, in a regular lattice of degree c, nodes are connected to their previous $c/2$ and following $c/2$ neighbors. Formally, for node set $V = \{v_1, v_2, v_3, \ldots, v_n\}$, an edge exists between node v_i and v_j if and only if

REGULAR RING LATTICE

$$0 < |i - j| \leq c/2. \tag{4.19}$$

A regular lattice of degree 4 is shown in Figure 4.4.

Algorithm 4.1 Small-World Generation Algorithm

Require: Number of nodes $|V|$, mean degree c, parameter β
 1: **return** A small-world graph $G(V, E)$
 2: $G = $ A regular ring lattice with $|V|$ nodes and degree c
 3: **for** node v_i (starting from v_1), and all edges $e(v_i, v_j), i < j$ **do**
 4:     $v_k = $ Select a node from V uniformly at random.
 5:     **if** rewiring $e(v_i, v_j)$ to $e(v_i, v_k)$ does not create loops in the graph or multiple edges between v_i and v_k **then**
 6:         rewire $e(v_i, v_j)$ with probability β: $E = E - \{e(v_i, v_j)\}$, $E = E \cup \{e(v_i, v_k)\}$;
 7:     **end if**
 8: **end for**
 9: Return $G(V, E)$

The regular lattice can model transitivity well; however, the average path length is too high. Moreover, the clustering coefficient takes the value

$$\frac{3(c - 2)}{4(c - 1)} \approx \frac{3}{4}, \tag{4.20}$$

which is fixed and not tunable to clustering coefficient values found in real-world networks. To overcome these problems, the proposed small-world model dynamically lies between the regular lattice and the random network.

In the small-world model, we assume a parameter β that controls randomness in the model. The model starts with a regular lattice and starts adding random edges based on β. The $0 \leq \beta \leq 1$ controls how random the model is. When β is 0, the model is basically a regular lattice, and when $\beta = 1$, the model becomes a random graph.

The procedure for generating small-world networks is outlined in Algorithm 4.1. The procedure creates new edges by a process called *rewiring*. Rewiring replaces an existing edge between nodes v_i and v_j with a nonexisting edge between v_i and v_k with probability β. In other words, an edge is disconnected from one of its endpoints v_j and connected to a new endpoint v_k. Node v_k is selected uniformly.

The network generated using this procedure has some interesting properties. Depending on the β value, it can have a high clustering coefficient and also short average path lengths. The degree distribution, however, still does not match that of real-world networks.

4.3.1 Properties of the Small-World Model

Degree Distribution

The degree distribution for the small-world model is as follows:

$$P(d_v = d) = \sum_{n=0}^{\min(d-c/2,c/2)} \binom{c/2}{n} (1 - \beta)^n \beta^{c/2-n} \frac{(\beta c/2)^{d-c/2-n}}{(d - c/2 - n)} e^{-\beta c/2},$$

(4.21)

where $P(d_v = d)$ is the probability of observing degree d for node v. We provide this equation without proof due to techniques beyond the scope of this book (see Bibliographic Notes). Note that the degree distribution is quite similar to the Poisson degree distribution observed in random graphs (Section 4.2.2). In practice, in the graph generated by the small-world model, most nodes have similar degrees due to the underlying lattice. In contrast, in real-world networks, degrees are distributed based on a power-law distribution, where most nodes have small degrees and a few have large degrees.

Clustering Coefficient

The clustering coefficient for a regular lattice is $\frac{3(c-2)}{4(c-1)}$ and for a random graph model is $p = \frac{c}{n-1}$. The clustering coefficient for a small-world network is a value between these two, depending on β. Commonly, the clustering coefficient for a regular lattice is represented using $C(0)$, and the clustering coefficient for a small-world model with $\beta = p$ is represented as $C(p)$. The relation between the two values can be computed analytically; it has been proven that

$$C(p) \approx (1 - p)^3 C(0).$$

(4.22)

The intuition behind this relation is that because the clustering coefficient enumerates the number of closed triads in a graph, we are interested in triads that are still left connected after the rewiring process. For a triad to stay connected, all three edges must not be rewired with probability $(1 - p)$. Since the process is performed independently for each edge, the probability of observing triads is $(1 - p)^3$ times the probability of observing them in a regular lattice. Note that we also need to take into account new triads that are formed by the rewiring process; however, that probability is nominal and hence negligible. The graph in Figure 4.5 depicts the value of $\frac{C(p)}{C(0)}$ for different values of p.

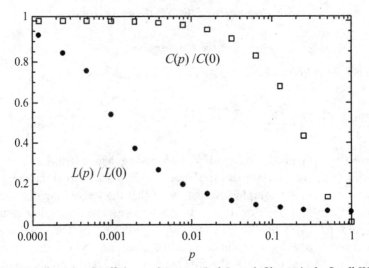

Figure 4.5. Clustering Coefficient and Average Path Length Change in the Small-World Model (from [Watts and Strogatz, 1997]). In this figure, $C(p)/C(0)$ denotes the clustering coefficient of a small-world model, with $\beta = p$, over the regular lattice. Similarly, $L(p)/L(0)$ denotes the average path length of a small-world model over the regular lattice. Since models with a high clustering coefficient and small average path length are desired, β values in range $0.01 \leq \beta = p \leq 0.1$ are preferred.

As shown in the figure, the value for $C(p)$ stays high until p reaches 0.1 (10% rewired) and then decreases rapidly to a value around zero. Since a high clustering coefficient is required in generated graphs, $\beta \leq 0.1$ is preferred.

Average Path Length

The same procedure can be done for the average path length. The average path length in a regular lattice is

$$\frac{n}{2c}. \tag{4.23}$$

We denote this value as $L(0)$. The average path length in a random graph is $\frac{\ln n}{\ln c}$. We denote $L(p)$ as the average path length for a small-world model where $\beta - p$. Unlike $C(p)$, no analytical formula for comparing $L(p)$ to $L(0)$ exists; however, the relation can be computed empirically for different values of p. Similar to $C(p)$, we plot $\frac{L(p)}{L(0)}$ in Figure 4.5. As shown in the figure, the average path length decays sooner than the clustering coefficient and becomes stable when around 1% of edges are rewired. Since we require small average path lengths in the generated graphs, $\beta \geq 0.01$ is preferred.

Table 4.5. *A Comparison between Real-World Networks and Simulated Graphs Using the Small-World Model. In this table C denotes the average clustering coefficient. The last two columns show the average path length and the clustering coefficient for the small-world graph simulated for the real-world network. Both average path lengths and clustering coefficients are modeled properly*

		Original Network			Simulated Graph	
Network	Size	Average Degree	Average Path Length	C	Average Path Length	C
Film Actors	225,226	61	3.65	0.79	4.2	0.73
Medline Coauthorship	1,520,251	18.1	4.6	0.56	5.1	0.52
E. Coli	282	7.35	2.9	0.32	4.46	0.31
C. Elegans	282	14	2.65	0.28	3.49	0.37

4.3.2 Modeling Real-World Networks with the Small-World Model

A desirable model for a real-world network should generate graphs with high clustering coefficients and short average path lengths. As shown in Figure 4.5, for $0.01 \leq \beta \leq 0.10$, the small-world network generated is acceptable, in which the average path length is small and the clustering coefficient is still high. Given a real-world network in which average degree c and clustering coefficient C are given, we set $C(p) = C$ and determine β using Equation 4.22. Given β, c, and n (size of the real-world network), we can simulate the small-world model.

Table 4.5 demonstrates the simulation results for various real-world networks. As observed in the table, the small-world model generates a realistic clustering coefficient and small average path length. Note that the small-world model is still incapable of generating a realistic degree distribution in the simulated graph. To generate scale-free networks (i.e., with a power-law degree distribution), we introduce the preferential attachment model next.

4.4 Preferential Attachment Model

There exist a variety of scale-free network-modeling algorithms. A well-established one is the model proposed by Barabási and Albert [1999]. The model is called *preferential attachment* or sometimes the Barábasi-Albert (BA) model and is as follows:

When new nodes are added to networks, they are more likely to connect to existing nodes that many others have connected to.

This connection likelihood is proportional to the degree of the node that the new node is aiming to connect to. In other words, a *rich-get-richer* phenomenon or *aristocrat network* is observed where the higher the

---

Algorithm 4.2 Preferential Attachment

Require: Graph $G(V_0, E_0)$, where $|V_0| = m_0$ and $d_v \geq 1 \,\forall\, v \in V_0$, number of expected connections $m \leq m_0$, time to run the algorithm t

1: **return** A scale-free network
2: //Initial graph with m_0 nodes with degrees at least 1
3: $G(V, E) = G(V_0, E_0)$;
4: **for** 1 to t **do**
5:     $V = V \cup \{v_i\}$; // add new node v_i
6:     **while** $d_i \neq m$ **do**
7:         Connect v_i to a random node $v_j \in V$, $i \neq j$ (i.e., $E = E \cup \{e(v_i, v_j)\}$)
            with probability $P(v_j) = \frac{d_j}{\sum_k d_k}$.
8:     **end while**
9: **end for**
10: Return $G(V, E)$

---

node's degree, the higher the probability of new nodes getting connected to it. Unlike random graphs in which we assume friendships are formed randomly, in the preferential attachment model we assume that individuals are more likely to befriend gregarious others. The model's algorithm is provided in Algorithm 4.2.

The algorithm starts with a graph containing a small set of nodes m_0 and then adds new nodes one at a time. Each new node gets to connect to $m \leq m_0$ other nodes, and each connection to existing node v_i depends on the degree of v_i (i.e., $P(v_i) = \frac{d_i}{\sum_j d_j}$). Intrinsically, higher degree nodes get more attention from newly added nodes. Note that the initial m_0 nodes must have at least degree 1 for probability $P(v_i) = \frac{d_i}{\sum_j d_j}$ to be nonzero.

The model incorporates two ingredients – (1) the *growth* element and (2) the *preferential attachment* element – to achieve a scale-free network. The growth is realized by adding nodes as time goes by. The preferential attachment is realized by connecting to node v_i based on its degree probability, $P(v_i) = \frac{d_i}{\sum_j d_j}$. Removing any one of these ingredients generates networks that are not scale-free (see Exercises). Next, we show that preferential attachment models are capable of generating networks with a power-law degree distribution. They are also capable of generating small average path length, but unfortunately fail to generate the high clustering coefficients observed in real-world networks.

4.4.1 *Properties of the Preferential Attachment Model*

Degree Distribution

We first demonstrate that the preferential attachment model generates scale-free networks and can therefore model real-world networks. Empirical evidence found by simulating the preferential attachment model suggests that this model generates a scale-free network with exponent $b = 2.9 \pm 0.1$ [Barabási and Albert, 1999]. Theoretically, a *mean-field* [Newman, Barabasi, and Watts, 2006] proof can be provided as follows.

Let d_i denote the degree for node v_i. The probability of an edge connecting from a new node to v_i is

$$P(v_i) = \frac{d_i}{\sum_j d_j}. \tag{4.24}$$

The expected increase to the degree of v_i is proportional to d_i (this is true on average). Assuming a mean-field setting, the expected temporal change in d_i is

$$\frac{\mathrm{d}d_i}{\mathrm{d}t} = mP(v_i) = \frac{md_i}{\sum_j d_j} = \frac{md_i}{2mt} = \frac{d_i}{2t}. \tag{4.25}$$

Note that at each time step, m edges are added; therefore, mt edges are added over time, and the degree sum $\sum_j d_j$ is $2mt$. Rearranging and solving this differential equation, we get

$$d_i(t) = m \left(\frac{t}{t_i} \right)^{0.5}. \tag{4.26}$$

Here, t_i represents the time that v_i was added to the network, and because we set the expected degree to m in preferential attachment, then $d_i(t_i) = m$. The probability that d_i is less than d is

$$P(d_i(t) < d) = P(t_i > m^2 t/d^2). \tag{4.27}$$

Assuming uniform intervals of adding nodes,

$$P(t_i > m^2 t/d^2) = 1 - P(t_i \le m^2 t/d^2) = 1 - \frac{m^2 t}{d^2} \frac{1}{(t + m_0)}. \tag{4.28}$$

The factor $\frac{1}{(t+m_0)}$ shows the probability that one time step has passed because, at the end of the simulation, $t + m_0$ nodes are in the network. The probability density for $P(d)$

$$P(d) = \frac{\partial P(d_i(t) < d)}{\partial d}, \tag{4.29}$$

is what we are interested in, which, when solved, gives

$$P(d) = \frac{2m^2 t}{d^3(t + m_0)}$$

and the stationary solution ($t \to \infty$),

$$P(d) = \frac{2m^2}{d^3},\tag{4.30}$$

which is a power-law degree distribution with exponent $b = 3$. Note that in real-world networks, the exponent varies in a range (e.g., [2, 3]); however, there is no variance in the exponent of the introduced model. To overcome this issue, several other models are proposed. Interested readers can refer to the bibliographical notes for further references.

Clustering Coefficient

In general, not many triangles are formed by the Barábasi-Albert model, because edges are created independently and one at a time. Again, using a mean-field analysis, the expected clustering coefficient can be calculated as

$$C = \frac{m_0 - 1}{8} \frac{(\ln t)^2}{t},\tag{4.31}$$

where t is the time passed in the system during the simulation. We avoid the details of this calculation due to techniques beyond the scope of this book. Unfortunately, as time passes, the clustering coefficient gets smaller and fails to model the high clustering coefficient observed in real-world networks.

Average Path Length

The average path length of the preferential attachment model increases logarithmically with the number of nodes present in the network:

$$l \sim \frac{\ln |V|}{\ln(\ln |V|)}.\tag{4.32}$$

This indicates that, on average, preferential attachment models generate shorter path lengths than random graphs. Random graphs are considered accurate in approximating the average path lengths. The same holds for preferential attachment models.

Table 4.6. *A Comparison between Real-World Networks and Simulated Graphs using Preferential Attachment. C denotes the average clustering coefficient. The last two columns show the average path length and the clustering coefficient for the preferential-attachment graph simulated for the real-world network. Note that average path lengths are modeled properly, whereas the clustering coefficient is underestimated*

| Network | Size | Original Network | | | Simulated Graph | |
		Average Degree	Average Path Length	C	Average Path Length	C
Film Actors	225,226	61	3.65	0.79	4.90	≈0.005
Medline Coauthorship	1,520,251	18.1	4.6	0.56	5.36	≈0.0002
E. Coli	282	7.35	2.9	0.32	2.37	0.03
C. Elegans	282	14	2.65	0.28	1.99	0.05

4.4.2 Modeling Real-World Networks with the Preferential Attachment Model

As with random graphs, we can simulate real-world networks by generating a preferential attachment model by setting the expected degree m (see Algorithm 4.2). Table 4.6 demonstrates the simulation results for various real-world networks. The preferential attachment model generates a realistic degree distribution and, as observed in the table, small average path lengths; however, the generated networks fail to exhibit the high clustering coefficient observed in real-world networks.

4.5 Summary

In this chapter, we discussed three well-established models that generate networks with commonly observed characteristics of real-world networks: random graphs, the small-world model, and preferential attachment. Random graphs assume that connections are completely random. We discussed two variants of random graphs: $G(n, p)$ and $G(n, m)$. Random graphs exhibit a Poisson degree distribution, a small clustering coefficient p, and a realistic average path length $\frac{\ln |V|}{\ln c}$.

The small-world model assumes that individuals have a fixed number of connections in addition to random connections. This model generates networks with high transitivity and short path lengths, both commonly observed in real-world networks. Small-world models are created through a process where a parameter β controls how edges are randomly rewired from an initial regular ring lattice. The clustering coefficient of the model is approximately $(1 - p)^3$ times the clustering coefficient of a regular lattice.

No analytical solution to approximate the average path length with respect to a regular ring lattice has been found. Empirically, when between 1% to 10% of edges are rewired ($0.01 \leq \beta \leq 0.1$), the model resembles many real-world networks. Unfortunately, the small-world model generates a degree distribution similar to the Poisson degree distribution observed in random graphs.

Finally, the preferential attachment model assumes that friendship formation likelihood depends on the number of friends individuals have. The model generates a scale-free network; that is, a network with a power-law degree distribution. When k denotes the degree of a node, and p_k the fraction of nodes having degree k, then in a power-law degree distribution,

$$p_k = ak^{-b}. \tag{4.33}$$

Networks created using a preferential attachment model have a power-law degree distribution with exponent $b = 2.9 \pm 0.1$. Using a mean-field approach, we proved that this model has a power-law degree distribution. The preferential attachment model also exhibits realistic average path lengths that are smaller than the average path lengths in random graphs. The basic caveat of the model is that it generates a small clustering coefficient, which contradicts high clustering coefficients observed in real-world networks.

4.6 Bibliographic Notes

General reviews of the topics in this chapter can be found in [Newman, Barabasi, and Watts, 2006; Newman, 2010; Barrat, Barthelemy, and Vespignani, 2008; Jackson, 2010].

Initial random graph papers can be found in the works of Paul Erdős and Alfred Rényi [1959, 1960, 1961] as well as Edgar Gilbert [1959] and Solomonoff and Rapoport [1951]. As a general reference, readers can refer to [Bollobás, 2001; Newman, Watts, and Strogatz, 2002; Newman, 2002b]. Random graphs described in this chapter did not have any specific degree distribution; however, random graphs can be generated with a specific degree distribution. For more on this refer to [Newman, 2010; Newman, Strogatz, and Watts, 2000].

Small-worlds were first noticed in a short story by Hungarian writer F. Karinthy in 1929. Works of Milgram in 1969 and Kochen and Pool in 1978 treated the subject more systematically. Milgram designed an experiment in which he asked random participants in Omaha, Nebraska, or Wichita, Kansas, to help send letters to a target person in Boston. Individuals were only allowed to send the letter directly to the target person if they knew the person on a first-name basis. Otherwise, they had to forward it to someone who was more likely to know the target. The results showed that the letters were on average forwarded 5.5 to 6 times until they reached the target in Boston. Other recent research on small-world model dynamics can be found in [Watts, 1999, 2002].

Price [1965, 1976] was among the first who described power laws observed in citation networks and models capable of generating them. Power-law distributions are commonly found in social networks and the web [Faloutsos et al., 1999; Mislove et al., 2007]. The first developers of preferential attachment models were Yule [1925], who described these models for generating power-law distributions in plants, and Herbert A. Simon [1955], who developed these models for describing power laws observed in various phenomena: distribution of words in prose, scientists by citations, and cities by population, among others. Simon used what is known as the *master equation* to prove that preferential attachment models generate power-law degree distributions. A more rigorous proof for estimating the power-law exponent of the preferential attachment model using the master equation method can be found in [Newman, 2010]. The preferential attachment model introduced in this chapter has a fixed exponent $b = 3$, but, as mentioned, real-world networks have exponents in the range [2, 3]. To solve this issue, extensions have been proposed in [Krapivsky, Redner, and Leyvraz, 2000; Albert and Barabási, 2000].

4.7 Exercises

Properties of Real-World Networks

1. A *scale invariant* function $f(.)$ is one such that, for a scalar α,

$$f(\alpha x) = \alpha^c f(x), \tag{4.34}$$

for some constant c. Prove that the power-law degree distribution is scale invariant.

Random Graphs

2. Assuming that we are interested in a sparse random graph, what should we choose as our p value?

3. Construct a random graph as follows. Start with n nodes and a given k. Generate all the possible combinations of k nodes. For each combination, create a k-cycle with probability $\frac{\alpha}{\binom{n-1}{2}}$, where α is a constant.
   • Calculate the node mean degree and the clustering coefficient.

- What is the node mean degree if you create a complete graph instead of the k-cycle?

4. When does phase transition happen in the evolution of random graphs? What happens in terms of changes in network properties at that time?

Small-World Model

5. Show that in a regular lattice the number of connections between neighbors is given by $\frac{3}{8}c(c-2)$, where c is the average degree.

6. Show how the clustering coefficient can be computed in a regular lattice of degree k.

7. Why are random graphs incapable of modeling real-world graphs? What are the differences between random graphs, regular lattices, and small-world models?

8. Compute the average path length in a regular lattice.

Preferential Attachment Model

9. As a function of k, what fraction of pages on the web have k in-links, assuming that a normal distribution governs the probability of web-pages choosing their links? What if we have a power-law distribution instead?

10. In the Barábasi-Albert model (**BA**) two elements are considered: growth and preferential attachment. The growth (**G**) is added to the model by allowing new nodes to connect via m edges. The preferential attachment (**A**) is added by weighting the probability of connection by the degree. For the sake of brevity, we will consider the model as **BA** = **A** + **G**. Now, consider models that only have one element: **G**, or **A**, and not both. In the **G** model, the probability of connection is uniform ($P = \frac{1}{m_0+t-1}$), and in **A**, the number of nodes remain the same throughout the simulation and no new node is added. In **A**, at each time step, a node within the network is randomly selected based on degree probability and then connected to another one within the network.
    - Compute the degree distribution for these two models.
    - Determine if these two models generate scale-free networks. What does this prove?

5

Data Mining Essentials

Mountains of raw data are generated daily by individuals on social media. Around 6 billion photos are uploaded monthly to Facebook, the blogosphere doubles every five months, 72 hours of video are uploaded every minute to YouTube, and there are more than 400 million daily tweets on Twitter. With this unprecedented rate of content generation, individuals are easily overwhelmed with data and find it difficult to discover content that is relevant to their interests. To overcome these challenges, we need tools that can analyze these massive unprocessed sources of data (i.e., *raw data*) and extract useful patterns from them. Examples of useful patterns in social media are those that describe online purchasing habits or individuals' website visit duration. *Data mining* provides the necessary tools for discovering patterns in data. This chapter outlines the general process for analyzing social media data and ways to use data mining algorithms in this process to extract actionable patterns from raw data.

The process of extracting useful patterns from raw data is known as *Knowledge discovery in databases (KDD)*. It is illustrated in Figure 5.1. The KDD process takes raw data as input and provides statistically significant patterns found in the data (i.e., *knowledge*) as output. From the raw data, a subset is selected for processing and is denoted as *target data*. Target data is *preprocessed* to make it ready for analysis using data mining algorithm. Data mining is then performed on the preprocessed (and transformed) data to extract interesting patterns. The patterns are *evaluated* to ensure their validity and soundness and *interpreted* to provide insights into the data.

KNOWLEDGE DISCOVERY IN DATABASES (KDD)

In social media mining, the raw data is the content generated by individuals, and the knowledge encompasses the interesting patterns observed in this data. For example, for an online book seller, the raw data is the list of books individuals buy, and an interesting pattern could describe books that individuals often buy.

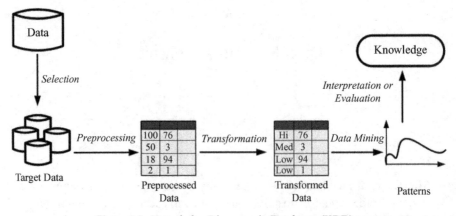

Figure 5.1. Knowledge Discovery in Databases (KDD) process.

To analyze social media, we can either collect this raw data or use available repositories that host collected data from social media sites.[1] When collecting data, we can either use APIs provided by social media sites for data collection or scrape the information from those sites. In either case, these sites are often networks of individuals where one can perform graph traversal algorithms to collect information from them. In other words, we can start collecting information from a subset of nodes on a social network, subsequently collect information from their neighbors, and so on. The data collected this way needs to be represented in a unified format for analysis. For instance, consider a set of tweets in which we are looking for common patterns. To find patterns in these tweets, they need to be first represented using a consistent data format. In the next section, we discuss data, its representation, and its types.

5.1 Data

In the KDD process, data is represented in a *tabular* format. Consider the example of predicting whether an individual who visits an online book seller is going to buy a specific book. This prediction can be performed by analyzing the individual's interests and previous purchase history. For instance, when John has spent a lot of money on the site, has bought similar books, and visits the site frequently, it is likely for John to buy that specific book. John is an example of an *instance*. Instances are also called *points*, *data points*, or *observations*. A *dataset* consists of one or more instances:

INSTANCE,
POINT,
DATA POINT,
OR
OBSERVATION

Attributes				Class
Name	Money Spent	Bought Similar	Visits	Will Buy
John	High	Yes	Frequently	?
Mary	High	Yes	Rarely	Yes

A dataset is represented using a set of *features*, and an instance is represented using values assigned to these features. Features are also known
as *measurements* or *attributes*. In this example, the features are Name,
Money Spent, Bought Similar, and Visits; feature values for the
first instance are John, High, Yes, and Frequently. Given the feature
values for one instance, one tries to predict its *class* (or *class attribute*)
value. In our example, the class attribute is Will Buy, and our class value
prediction for first instance is Yes. An instance such as John in which the
class attribute value is unknown is called an *unlabeled* instance. Similarly, a
labeled instance is an instance in which the class attribute value in known.
Mary in this dataset represents a labeled instance. The class attribute is
optional in a dataset and is only necessary for prediction or classification
purposes. One can have a dataset in which no class attribute is present, such
as a list of customers and their characteristics.

There are different types of features based on the characteristics of the
feature and the values they can take. For instance, Money Spent can be
represented using numeric values, such as $25. In that case, we have a
continuous feature, whereas in our example it is a *discrete* feature, which
can take a number of ordered values: {High, Normal, Low}.

Different types of features were first introduced by psychologist Stanley
Smith Stevens [1996] as "levels of measurement" in the theory of scales.
He claimed that there are four types of features. For each feature type, there
exists a set of permissible operations (statistics) using the feature values
and transformations that are allowed.

- **Nominal (categorical)**. These features take values that are often represented as strings. For instance, a customer's name is a nominal
  feature. In general, a few statistics can be computed on nominal features. Examples are the chi-square statistic (χ^2) and the *mode* (most
  common feature value). For example, one can find the most common first name among customers. The only possible transformation
  on the data is comparison. For example, we can check whether our
  customer's name is John or not. Nominal feature values are often
  presented in a set format.

FEATURES,
MEASUREMENTS,
OR
ATTRIBUTES

LABELED
AND
UNLABELED

LEVELS OF
MEASUREMENT

- **Ordinal**. Ordinal features lay data on an ordinal scale. In other words, the feature values have an intrinsic order to them. In our example, Money Spent is an ordinal feature because a High value for Money Spent is more than a Low one.
- **Interval**. In interval features, in addition to their intrinsic ordering, differences are meaningful whereas ratios are meaningless. For interval features, addition and subtraction are allowed, whereas multiplications and division are not. Consider two time readings: 6:16 PM and 3:08 PM. The difference between these two time readings is meaningful (3 hours and 8 minutes); however, there is no meaning to $\frac{6:16 \ PM}{3:08 \ PM} \neq 2$.
- **Ratio**. Ratio features, as the name suggests, add the additional properties of multiplication and division. An individual's income is an example of a ratio feature where not only differences and additions are meaningful but ratios also have meaning (e.g., an individual's income can be twice as much as John's income).

In social media, individuals generate many types of nontabular data, such as text, voice, or video. These types of data are first converted to tabular data and then processed using data mining algorithms. For instance, voice can be converted to feature values using approximation techniques such as the fast Fourier transform (FFT) and then processed using data mining algorithms. To convert text into the tabular format, we can use a process VECTORIZATION denoted as *vectorization*. A variety of vectorization methods exist. A well-known method for vectorization is the *vector-space model* introduced by Salton, Wong, and Yang [1975].

Vector Space Model

In the vector space model, we are given a set of documents D. Each document is a set of words. The goal is to convert these textual documents to [feature] vectors. We can represent document i with vector d_i,

$$d_i = (w_{1,i}, w_{2,i}, \ldots, w_{N,i}), \tag{5.1}$$

where $w_{j,i}$ represents the weight for word j that occurs in document i and N is the number of words used for vectorization.[2] To compute $w_{j,i}$, we can set it to 1 when the word j exists in document i and 0 when it does not. We can also set it to the number of times the word j is observed in document i. A more generalized approach is to use the *term frequency-inverse document frequency (TF-IDF)* weighting scheme. In the TF-IDF scheme, $w_{j,i}$ is calculated as

$$w_{j,i} = tf_{j,i} \times idf_j, \tag{5.2}$$

where $tf_{j,i}$ is the frequency of word j in document i. idf_j is the inverse frequency of word j across all documents,

$$idf_j = \log_2 \frac{|D|}{|\{\text{document} \in D \mid j \in \text{document}\}|}, \tag{5.3}$$

which is the logarithm of the total number of documents divided by the number of documents that contain word j. TF-IDF assigns higher weights to words that are less frequent across documents and, at the same time, have higher frequencies within the document they are used. This guarantees that words with high TF-IDF values can be used as representative examples of the documents they belong to and also, that stop words, such as "the," which are common in all documents, are assigned smaller weights.

Example 5.1. *Consider the words "apple" and "orange" that appear 10 and 20 times in document d_1. Let $|D| = 20$ and assume the word "apple" only appears in document d_1 and the word "orange" appears in all 20 documents. Then, TF-IDF values for "apple" and "orange" in document d_1 are*

$$tf - idf(\text{"apple"}, d_1) = 10 \times \log_2 \frac{20}{1} = 43.22, \tag{5.4}$$

$$tf - idf(\text{"orange"}, d_1) = 20 \times \log_2 \frac{20}{20} = 0. \tag{5.5}$$

Example 5.2. *Consider the following three documents:*

$$d_1 = \text{"social media mining"} \tag{5.6}$$

$$d_2 = \text{"social media data"} \tag{5.7}$$

$$d_3 = \text{"financial market data"} \tag{5.8}$$

The tf values are as follows:

	social	media	mining	data	financial	market
d_1	1	1	1	0	0	0
d_2	1	1	0	1	0	0
d_3	0	0	0	1	1	1

The idf values are

$$idf_{\text{social}} = \log_2(3/2) = 0.584 \qquad (5.9)$$

$$idf_{\text{media}} = \log_2(3/2) = 0.584 \qquad (5.10)$$

$$idf_{\text{mining}} = \log_2(3/1) = 1.584 \qquad (5.11)$$

$$idf_{\text{data}} = \log_2(3/2) = 0.584 \qquad (5.12)$$

$$idf_{\text{financial}} = \log_2(3/1) = 1.584 \qquad (5.13)$$

$$idf_{\text{market}} = \log_2(3/1) = 1.584. \qquad (5.14)$$

The TF-IDF values can be computed by multiplying tf values with the idf values:

	social	media	mining	data	financial	market
d_1	0.584	0.584	1.584	0	0	0
d_2	0.584	0.584	0	0.584	0	0
d_3	0	0	0	0.584	1.584	1.584

After vectorization, documents are converted to vectors, and common data mining algorithms can be applied. However, before that can occur, the quality of data needs to be verified.

5.1.1 Data Quality

When preparing data for use in data mining algorithms, the following four data quality aspects need to be verified:

1. **Noise** is the distortion of the data. This distortion needs to be removed or its adverse effect alleviated before running data mining algorithms because it may adversely affect the performance of the algorithms. Many filtering algorithms are effective in combating noise effects.
2. **Outliers** are instances that are considerably different from other instances in the dataset. Consider an experiment that measures the average number of followers of users on Twitter. A celebrity with many followers can easily distort the average number of followers per

individuals. Since the celebrities are outliers, they need to be removed from the set of individuals to accurately measure the average number of followers. Note that in special cases, outliers represent useful patterns, and the decision to removing them depends on the context of the data mining problem.

3. **Missing Values** are feature values that are missing in instances. For example, individuals may avoid reporting profile information on social media sites, such as their age, location, or hobbies. To solve this problem, we can (1) remove instances that have missing values, (2) estimate missing values (e.g., replacing them with the most common value), or (3) ignore missing values when running data mining algorithms.

4. **Duplicate data** occurs when there are multiple instances with the exact same feature values. Duplicate blog posts, duplicate tweets, or profiles on social media sites with duplicate information are all instances of this phenomenon. Depending on the context, these instances can either be removed or kept. For example, when instances need to be unique, duplicate instances should be removed.

After these quality checks are performed, the next step is preprocessing or transformation to prepare the data for mining.

5.2 Data Preprocessing

Often, the data provided for data mining is not immediately ready. Data preprocessing (and transformation in Figure 5.1) prepares the data for mining. Typical data preprocessing tasks are as follows:

- **Aggregation**. This task is performed when multiple features need to be combined into a single one or when the scale of the features change. For instance, when storing image dimensions for a social media website, one can store by image width and height or equivalently store by image area (width × height). Storing image area saves storage space and tends to reduce data variance; hence, the data has higher resistance to distortion and noise.

- **Discretization.** Consider a continuous feature such as money spent in our previous example. This feature can be converted into discrete values – High, Normal, and Low – by mapping different ranges to different discrete values. The process of converting continuous features to discrete ones and deciding the continuous range that is being assigned to a discrete value is called *discretization*.

- **Feature Selection**. Often, not all features gathered are useful. Some may be irrelevant, or there may be a lack of computational power to make use of all the features, among many other reasons. In these cases, a subset of features are selected that could ideally enhance the performance of the selected data mining algorithm. In our example, customer's name is an irrelevant feature to the value of the class attribute and the task of predicting whether the individual will buy the given book or not.

- **Feature Extraction**. In contrast to feature selection, *feature extraction* converts the current set of features to a new set of features that can perform the data mining task better. A transformation is performed on the data, and a new set of features is extracted. The example we provided for aggregation is also an example of feature extraction where a new feature (area) is constructed from two other features (width and height).

- **Sampling**. Often, processing the whole dataset is expensive. With the massive growth of social media, processing large streams of data is nearly impossible. This motivates the need for *sampling*. In sampling, a small random subset of instances are selected and processed instead of the whole data. The selection process should guarantee that the sample is representative of the distribution that governs the data, thereby ensuring that results obtained on the sample are close to ones obtained on the whole dataset. The following are three major sampling techniques:

  1. **Random sampling**. In random sampling, instances are selected uniformly from the dataset. In other words, in a dataset of size n, all instances have equal probability $\frac{1}{n}$ of being selected. Note that other probability distributions can also be used to sample the dataset, and the distribution can be different from uniform.

  2. **Sampling with or without replacement**. In sampling with replacement, an instance can be selected multiple times in the sample. In sampling without replacement, instances are removed from the selection pool once selected.

  3. **Stratified sampling**. In stratified sampling, the dataset is first partitioned into multiple bins; then a fixed number of instances are selected from each bin using random sampling. This technique is particularly useful when the dataset does not have a uniform distribution for class attribute values (i.e., *class imbalance*). For instance, consider a set of 10 females and 5 males. A sample of

5 females and 5 males can be selected using stratified sampling from this set.

In social media, a large amount of information is represented in network form. These networks can be sampled by selecting a subset of their nodes and edges. These nodes and edges can be selected using the aforementioned sampling methods. We can also sample these networks by starting with a small set of nodes (*seed nodes*) and sample

(a) the connected components they belong to;

(b) the set of nodes (and edges) connected to them directly; or

(c) the set of nodes and edges that are within n-hop distance from them.

After preprocessing is performed, the data is ready to be mined. Next, we discuss two general categories of data mining algorithms and how each can be evaluated.

5.3 Data Mining Algorithms

Data mining algorithms can be divided into several categories. Here, we discuss two well-established categories: *supervised learning* and *unsupervised learning*. In supervised learning, the class attribute exists, and the task is to predict the class attribute value. Our previous example of predicting the class attribute "will buy" is an example of supervised learning. In unsupervised learning, the dataset has no class attribute, and our task is to find similar instances in the dataset and group them. By grouping these similar instances, one can find significant patterns in a dataset. For example, unsupervised learning can be used to identify events on Twitter, because the frequency of tweeting is different for various events. By using unsupervised learning, tweets can be grouped based on the times at which they appear and hence, identify the tweets' corresponding real-world events. Other categories of data mining algorithms exist; interested readers can refer to the bibliographic notes for pointers to these categories.

5.4 Supervised Learning

The first category of algorithms, supervised learning algorithms, are those for which the class attribute values for the dataset are known before running the algorithm. This data is called *labeled* data or *training* data. Instances in

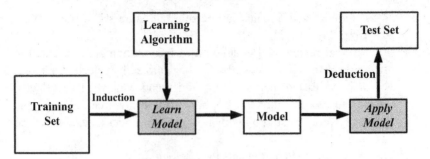

Figure 5.2. Supervised Learning.

this set are tuples in the format $(\mathbf{x}, y)$, where $\mathbf{x}$ is a vector and y is the class attribute, commonly a scalar. Supervised learning builds a model that maps $\mathbf{x}$ to y. Roughly, our task is to find a mapping $m(.)$ such that $m(\mathbf{x}) = y$. We are also given an unlabeled dataset or *test* dataset, in which instances are in the form $(\mathbf{x}, ?)$ and y values are unknown. Given $m(.)$ learned from training data and $\mathbf{x}$ of an unlabeled instance, we can compute $m(\mathbf{x})$, the result of which is prediction of the label for the unlabeled instance.

Consider the task of detecting spam emails. A set of emails is given where users have manually identified spam versus non-spam (training data). Our task is to use a set of features such as words in the email $(\mathbf{x})$ to identify the spam/non-spam status (y) of unlabeled emails (test data). In this case, $y = \{spam, non\text{-}spam\}$.

Supervised learning can be divided into *classification* and *regression*. When the class attribute is discrete, it is called classification; when the class attribute is continuous, it is regression. We introduce classification methods such as *decision tree learning, naive Bayes classifier, k-nearest neighbor classifier*, and *classification with network information* and regression methods such as *linear regression* and *logistic regression*. We also introduce how supervised learning algorithms are evaluated. Before we delve into supervised learning techniques, we briefly discuss the systematic process of a supervised learning algorithm.

This process is depicted in Figure 5.2. It starts with a training set (i.e., labeled data) where both features and labels (class attribute values) are known. A supervised learning algorithm is run on the training set in a process known as *induction*. In the induction process, the *model* is generated. The model maps the feature values to the class attribute values. The model is used on a *test set* in which the class attribute value is unknown to predict these unknown class attribute values (*deduction* process).

Table 5.1. *A Sample Dataset. In this dataset, features are characteristics of individuals on Twitter, and the class attribute denotes whether they are influential or not*

ID	Celebrity	Verified Account	# Followers	Influential?
1	Yes	No	1.25 M	No
2	No	Yes	1 M	No
3	No	Yes	600 K	No
4	Yes	Unknown	2.2 M	No
5	No	No	850 K	Yes
6	No	Yes	750 K	No
7	No	No	900 K	Yes
8	No	No	700 K	No
9	Yes	Yes	1.2 M	No
10	No	Unknown	950 K	Yes

5.4.1 Decision Tree Learning

Consider the dataset shown in Table 5.1. The last attribute represents the class attribute, and the other attributes represent the features. In decision tree classification, a decision tree is learned from the training dataset, and that tree is later used to predict the class attribute value for instances in the test dataset. As an example, two learned decision trees from the dataset shown in Table 5.1 are provided in Figure 5.3. As shown in this figure, multiple decision trees can be learned from the same dataset, and these decision trees can both correctly predict the class attribute values for all instances in the dataset. Construction of decision trees is based on heuristics, as different heuristics generate different decision trees from the same dataset.

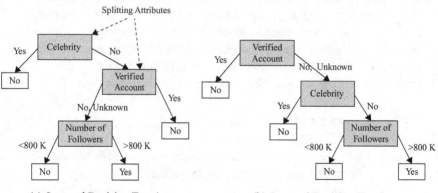

(a) Learned Decision Tree 1   (b) Learned Decision Tree 2

Figure 5.3. Decision Trees Learned from Data Provided in Table 5.1.

Decision trees classify examples based on their feature values. Each non-leaf node in a decision tree represents a feature, and each branch represents a value that the feature can take. Instances are classified by following a path that starts at the root node and ends at a leaf by following branches based on instance feature values. The value of the leaf determines the class attribute value predicted for the instance (see Figure 5.3).

Decision trees are constructed recursively from training data using a top-down greedy approach in which features are sequentially selected. In Figure 5.3(a), the feature selected for the root node is `Celebrity`. After selecting a feature for each node, based on its values, different branches are created: For Figure 5.3(a), since the `Celebrity` feature can only take either `Yes` or `No`, two branches are created: one labeled `Yes` and one labeled `No`. The training set is then partitioned into subsets based on the feature values, each of which fall under the respective feature value branch; the process is continued for these subsets and other nodes. In Figure 5.3(a), instances 1, 4, and 9 from Table 5.1 represent the subset that falls under the `Celebrity=Yes` branch, and the other instances represent the subset that falls under the `Celebrity=No` branch.

When selecting features, we prefer features that partition the set of instances into subsets that are more *pure*. A pure subset has instances that all have the same class attribute value. In Figure 5.3(a), the instances that fall under the left branch of the root node (`Celebrity=Yes`) form a pure subset in which all instances have the same class attribute value `Influential?=No`. When reaching pure subsets under a branch, the decision tree construction process no longer partitions the subset, creates a leaf under the branch, and assigns the class attribute value for subset instances as the leaf's predicted class attribute value. In Figure 5.3(a), the instances that fall under the right branch of the root node form an impure dataset; therefore, further branching is required to reach pure subsets. Purity of subsets can be determined with different measures. A common measure of purity is *entropy*. Over a subset of training instances, T, with a binary class attribute (values $\in \{+, -\}$), the entropy of T is defined as

$$entropy(T) = -p_+ \log p_+ - p_- \log p_-, \qquad (5.15)$$

where p_+ is the proportion of instances with $+$ class attribute value in T and p_- is the proportion of instances with $-$ class attribute value.

Example 5.3. *Assume that there is a subset T, containing 10 instances. Seven instances have a positive class attribute value, and three instances* *have a negative class attribute value* $[7+, 3-]$. *The entropy for subset T is*

$$entropy(T) = -\frac{7}{10} \log \frac{7}{10} - \frac{3}{10} \log \frac{3}{10} = 0.881. \tag{5.16}$$

Note that if the number of positive and negative instances in the set are equal ($p_+ = p_- = 0.5$), then the entropy is 1.

In a pure subset, all instances have the same class attribute value and the entropy is 0. If the subset being measured contains an unequal number of positive and negative instances, the entropy is between 0 and 1.

5.4.2 Naive Bayes Classifier

Among many methods that use the Bayes theorem, the naive Bayes classifier (NBC) is the simplest. Given two random variables X and Y, Bayes theorem states that

$$P(Y|X) = \frac{P(X|Y)P(Y)}{P(X)}. \tag{5.17}$$

In NBC, Y represents the class variable and X represents the instance features. Let X be $(x_1, x_2, x_3, \ldots, x_m)$, where x_i represents the value of feature i. Let $\{y_1, y_2, \ldots, y_n\}$ represent the values the class attribute Y can take. Then, the class attribute value of instance X can be calculated by measuring

$$\arg\max_{y_i} P(y_i|X). \tag{5.18}$$

Based on the Bayes theorem,

$$P(y_i|X) = \frac{P(X|y_i)P(y_i)}{P(X)}. \tag{5.19}$$

Note that $P(X)$ is constant and independent of y_i, so we can ignore the denominator of Equation 5.19 when maximizing Equation 5.18. The NBC also assumes conditional independence to make the calculations easier; that is, given the class attribute value, other feature attributes become conditionally independent. This condition, though unrealistic, performs well in practice and greatly simplifies calculation.

$$P(X|y_i) = \Pi_{j=1}^{m} P(x_j|y_i). \tag{5.20}$$

Substituting $P(X|y_i)$ from Equation 5.20 in Equation 5.19, we get

$$P(y_i|X) = \frac{\left(\Pi_{j=1}^{m} P(x_j|y_i)\right) P(y_i)}{P(X)}. \tag{5.21}$$

We clarify how the naive Bayes classifier works with an example.

Table 5.2. *Naive Bayes Classifier (NBC) Toy Dataset*

No.	Outlook (O)	Temperature (T)	Humidity (H)	Play Golf (PG)
1	sunny	hot	high	N
2	sunny	mild	high	N
3	overcast	hot	high	Y
4	rain	mild	high	Y
5	sunny	cool	normal	Y
6	rain	cool	normal	N
7	overcast	cool	normal	Y
8	sunny	mild	high	?

Example 5.4. *Consider the dataset in Table 5.2.*

We predict the label for instance 8 (i_8) using the naive Bayes classifer and the given dataset. We have

$$P(PG = Y|i_8) = \frac{P(i_8|PG = Y)P(PG = Y)}{P(i_8)}$$

$$= P(O = Sunny, T = mild, H = high|PG = Y)$$
$$\times \frac{P(PG = Y)}{P(i_8)}$$

$$= P(O = Sunny|PG = Y) \times P(T = mild|PG = Y)$$
$$\times P(H = high|PG = Y) \times \frac{P(PG = Y)}{P(i_8)}$$

$$= \frac{1}{4} \times \frac{1}{4} \times \frac{2}{4} \times \frac{\frac{4}{7}}{P(i_8)} = \frac{1}{28P(i_8)}. \tag{5.22}$$

Similarly,

$$P(PG = N|i_8) = \frac{P(i_8|PG = N)P(PG = N)}{P(i_8)}$$

$$= P(O = Sunny, T = mild, H = high|PG = N)$$
$$\times \frac{P(PG = N)}{P(i_8)}$$

$$= P(O = Sunny|PG = N) \times P(T = mild|PG = N)$$
$$\times P(H = high|PG = N) \times \frac{P(PG = N)}{P(i_8)}$$

$$= \frac{2}{3} \times \frac{1}{3} \times \frac{2}{3} \times \frac{\frac{3}{7}}{P(i_8)} = \frac{4}{63P(i_8)}. \tag{5.23}$$

Algorithm 5.1 k-Nearest Neighbor Classifier

Require: Instance i, A Dataset of Real-Value Attributes, k (number of neighbors), distance measure d

1: **return** Class label for instance i

2: Compute k nearest neighbors of instance i based on distance measure d.

3: $l =$ the majority class label among neighbors of instance i. If more than one majority label, select one randomly.

4: Classify instance i as class l

Since $\frac{4}{63 P(i_8)} > \frac{1}{28 P(i_8)}$, for instance i_8, and based on NBC calculations, we have Play Golf = N.

5.4.3 Nearest Neighbor Classifier

As the name suggests, k-nearest neighbor or kNN uses the k nearest instances, called neighbors, to perform classification. The instance being classified is assigned the label (class attribute value) that the majority of its k neighbors are assigned. The algorithm is outlined in Algorithm 5.1. When $k = 1$, the closest neighbor's label is used as the predicted label for the instance being classified. To determine the neighbors of an instance, we need to measure its distance to all other instances based on some distance metric. Commonly, Euclidean distance is employed; however, for higher dimensional spaces, Euclidean distance becomes less meaningful and other distance measures can be used.

Example 5.5. *Consider the example depicted in Figure 5.4. As shown, depending on the value of k, different labels can be predicted for the circle. In our example, $k = 5$ and $k = 9$ generate different labels for the instance (triangle and square, respectively).*

As shown in our example, an important issue with the k-nearest neighbor algorithm is the choice of k. The choice of k can easily change the label of the instance being predicted. In general, we are interested in a value of k that maximizes the performance of the learning algorithm.

5.4.4 Classification with Network Information

Consider a friendship network on social media and a product being marketed to this network. The product seller wants to know who the potential buyers

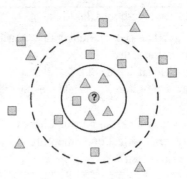

Figure 5.4. *k*-Nearest Neighbor Example. In this figure, our goal is to predict the label for the instance shown using a circle. When $k = 5$, the predicted label is ▲ and when $k = 9$ the predicted label is ■.

are for this product. Assume we are given the network with the list of individuals who decided to buy or not buy the product. Our goal is to predict the decision for the undecided individuals. This problem can be formulated as a classification problem based on features gathered from individuals. However, in this case, we have additional friendship information that may be helpful in building more accurate classification models. This is an example of *classification with network information*.

Assume we are not given any profile information, but only connections and class labels (i.e., the individual bought/will not buy). By using the rows of the adjacency matrix of the friendship network for each node as features and the decision (e.g., buy/not buy) as a class label, we can predict the label for any unlabeled node using its connections; that is, its row in the adjacency matrix. Let $P(y_i = 1|N(v_i))$ denote the probability of node v_i having class attribute value 1 given its neighbors. Individuals' decisions are often highly influenced by their immediate neighbors. Thus, we can approximate $P(y_i = 1)$ using the neighbors of the individual by assuming that

$$P(y_i = 1) \approx P(y_i = 1|N(v_i)). \tag{5.24}$$

We can estimate $P(y_i = 1|N(v_i))$ via different approaches. The weighted-vote relational-neighbor (wvRN) classifier is one such approach. It estimates $P(y_i = 1|N(v_i))$ as

WEIGHTED-
VOTE
RELATIONAL-
NEIGHBOR
CLASSIFIER

$$P(y_i = 1|N(v_i)) = \frac{1}{|N(v_i)|} \sum_{v_j \in N(v_i)} P(y_j = 1|N(v_j)). \tag{5.25}$$

In other words, the probability of node v_i having class attribute value 1 is the average probability of its neighbors having this class attribute

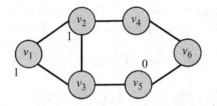

Figure 5.5. Weighted-Vote Relational-Neighbor (wvRN) Example. Labeled nodes have their class attribute values next to them. The goal is to predict labels for other nodes in the network.

value. Note that $P(y_i = 1|N(v_i))$ is *only* calculated for v_i's that are unlabeled. For node v_k, which is labeled 1, $p(y_k = 1|N(v_k)) = 1$ and the probability is never estimated. Similarly, if v_k will not buy the product, $p(y_k = 0|N(v_k)) = 1$. Since the probability of a node having class attribute value 1 depends on the probability of its neighbors having the same value, the probability of the node is affected if the probabilities of its neighbors change. Thus, the order of updating nodes can affect the estimated probabilities. In practice, one follows an order sequence for estimating node probabilities. Starting with an initial probability estimate for all unlabeled nodes and following this order, we estimate probabilities until probabilities no longer change (i.e., converge). We can assume the initial probability estimate to be $P(y_i = 1|N(v_i)) = 0.5$ for all unlabeled nodes.[3] We show how the wvRN classifier learns probabilities using the following example.

Example 5.6. *Consider the network given in Figure 5.5. Labeled nodes have their class attribute values next to them. Therefore,*

$$P(y_1 = 1|N(v_1)) = 1, \tag{5.26}$$

$$P(y_2 = 1|N(v_2)) = 1, \tag{5.27}$$

$$P(y_5 = 1|N(v_5)) = 0. \tag{5.28}$$

We have three unlabeled nodes $\{v_3, v_4, v_6\}$. We choose their natural order to update their probabilities. Thus, we start with v_3:

$$P(y_3|N(v_3))$$

$$= \frac{1}{|N(v_3)|} \sum_{v_j \in N(v_3)} P(y_j = 1|N(v_j))$$

$$= \frac{1}{3}(P(y_1 = 1|N(v_1)) + P(y_2 = 1|N(v_2)) + P(y_5 = 1|N(v_5)))$$

$$= \frac{1}{3}(1 + 1 + 0) = 0.67. \tag{5.29}$$

$P(y_3|N(v_3))$ *does not need to be computed again because its neighbors are all labeled (thus, this probability estimation has converged). Similarly,*

$$P(y_4|N(v_4)) = \frac{1}{2}(1 + 0.5) = 0.75, \tag{5.30}$$

$$P(y_6|N(v_6)) = \frac{1}{2}(0.75 + 0) = 0.38. \tag{5.31}$$

We need to recompute both $P(y_4|N(v_4))$ and $P(y_6|N(v_6))$ until convergence. Let $P_{(t)}(y_i|N(v_i))$ denote the estimated probability after t computations. Then,

$$P_{(1)}(y_4|N(v_4)) = \frac{1}{2}(1 + 0.38) = 0.69, \tag{5.32}$$

$$P_{(1)}(y_6|N(v_6)) = \frac{1}{2}(0.69 + 0) = 0.35, \tag{5.33}$$

$$P_{(2)}(y_4|N(v_4)) = \frac{1}{2}(1 + 0.35) = 0.68, \tag{5.34}$$

$$P_{(2)}(y_6|N(v_6)) = \frac{1}{2}(0.68 + 0) = 0.34, \tag{5.35}$$

$$P_{(3)}(y_4|N(v_4)) = \frac{1}{2}(1 + 0.34) = 0.67, \tag{5.36}$$

$$P_{(3)}(y_6|N(v_6)) = \frac{1}{2}(0.67 + 0) = 0.34, \tag{5.37}$$

$$P_{(4)}(y_4|N(v_4)) = \frac{1}{2}(1 + 0.34) = 0.67, \tag{5.38}$$

$$P_{(4)}(y_6|N(v_6)) = \frac{1}{2}(0.67 + 0) = 0.34. \tag{5.39}$$

After four iterations, both probabilities converge. So, from these probabilities (Equations 5.29, 5.38, and 5.39), we can tell that nodes v_3 and v_4 will likely have class attribute value 1 and node v_6 will likely have class attribute value 0.

5.4.5 Regression

In classification, class attribute values are discrete. In regression, class attribute values are real numbers. For instance, we wish to predict the stock market value (class attribute) of a company given information about the company (features). The stock market value is continuous; therefore, regression must be used to predict it. The input to the regression method is a dataset where attributes are represented using $x_1, x_2, \ldots, x_m$ (also known as *regressors*) and class attribute is represented using Y (also known as the *dependent variable*), where the class attribute is a real number. We want to find the relation between Y and the vector $X = (x_1, x_2, \ldots, x_m)$. We discuss two basic regression techniques: linear regression and logistic regression.

Linear Regression

In linear regression, we assume that the class attribute Y has a linear relation with the regressors (feature set) X by considering a linear error ϵ. In other words,

$$Y = XW + \epsilon, \tag{5.40}$$

where W represents the vector of regression coefficients. The problem of regression can be solved by estimating W using the training dataset and its labels Y such that fitting error ϵ is minimized. A variety of methods have been introduced to solve the linear regression problem, most of which use least squares or maximum-likelihood estimation. We employ the least squares technique here. Interested readers can refer to the bibliographic notes for more detailed analyses. In the least square method, we find W using regressors X and labels Y such that the square of fitting error *epsilon* is minimized.

$$\epsilon^2 = ||\epsilon^2|| = ||Y - XW||^2. \tag{5.41}$$

To minimize ϵ, we compute the gradient and set it to zero to find the optimal W:

$$\frac{\partial ||Y - XW||^2}{\partial W} = 0. \tag{5.42}$$

We know that for any X, $||X||^2 = (X^T X)$; therefore,

$$
\begin{aligned}
\frac{\partial ||Y - XW||^2}{\partial W} &= \frac{\partial (Y - XW)^T (Y - XW)}{\partial W} \\
&= \frac{\partial (Y^T - W^T X^T)(Y - XW)}{\partial W} \\
&= \frac{\partial (Y^T Y - Y^T XW - W^T X^T Y + W^T X^T XW)}{\partial W} \\
&= -2X^T Y + 2X^T XW = 0. \tag{5.43}
\end{aligned}
$$

Therefore,

$$X^T Y = X^T X W. \tag{5.44}$$

Since $X^T X$ is invertible for any X, by multiplying both sides by $(X^T X)^{-1}$, we get

$$W = (X^T X)^{-1} X^T Y. \tag{5.45}$$

Alternatively, one can compute the singular value decomposition (SVD) of $X = U \Sigma V^T$:

$$
\begin{aligned}
W &= (X^T X)^{-1} X^T Y \\
  &= (V \Sigma U^T U \Sigma V^T)^{-1} V \Sigma U^T Y \\
  &= (V \Sigma^2 V^T)^{-1} V \Sigma U^T Y \\
  &= V \Sigma^{-2} V^T V \Sigma U^T Y \\
  &= V \Sigma^{-1} U^T Y,
\end{aligned} \tag{5.46}
$$

and since we can have zero singular values,

$$W = V \Sigma^+ U^T Y, \tag{5.47}$$

where Σ^+ is the submatrix of Σ with nonzero singular values.

Logistic Regression

Logistic regression provides a probabilistic view of regression. For simplicity, let us assume that the class attribute can only take values of 0 and 1. Formally, logistic regression finds probability p such that

$$P(Y = 1|X) = p, \tag{5.48}$$

where X is the vector of features and Y is the class attribute. We can use linear regression to approximate p. In other words, we can assume that probability p depends on X; that is,

$$p = \beta X, \tag{5.49}$$

where β is a vector of coefficients. Unfortunately, βX can take unbounded values because X can take on any value and there are no constraints on how β's are chosen. However, probability p must be in range [0, 1]. Since βX is unbounded, we can perform a transformation $g(.)$ on p such that it also

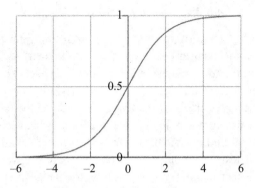

Figure 5.6. Logistic Function.

becomes unbounded. Then, we can fit $g(p)$ to βX. One such transformation $g(.)$ for p is

$$g(p) = \ln \frac{p}{1-p}, \tag{5.50}$$

which for any p between $[0, 1]$ generates a value in range $[-\infty, +\infty]$. The function $g(.)$ is known as the *logit* function. The transformed p can be approximated using a linear function of feature vector X,

$$g(p) = \beta X. \tag{5.51}$$

Combining Equations 5.50 and 5.51 and solving for p, we get

$$p = \frac{e^{\beta X}}{e^{\beta X} + 1} = \frac{1}{e^{-\beta X} + 1}. \tag{5.52}$$

This function is known as the logistic function and is plotted in Figure 5.6. An interesting property of this function is that, for any real value (negative to positive infinity), it will generate values between 0 and 1. In other words, it acts as a probability function.

Our task is to find β's such that $P(Y|X)$ is maximized. Unlike linear regression models, there is no closed form solution to this problem, and it is usually solved using iterative maximum likelihood methods (See Bibliographic Notes).

After β's are found, similar to the Naive Bayes Classifier (NBC), we compute the probability $P(Y|X)$ using Equation 5.52. In a situation where the class attribute takes two values, when this probability is larger than 0.5, the class attribute is predicted 1; otherwise, 0 is predicted.

5.4.6 Supervised Learning Evaluation

Supervised learning algorithms often employ a *training-testing* framework in which a training dataset (i.e., the labels are known) is used to train a model and then the model is evaluated on a test dataset. The performance of the supervised learning algorithm is measured by how accurate it is in predicting the correct labels of the test dataset. Since the correct labels of the test dataset are unknown, in practice, the training set is divided into two parts, one used for training and the other used for testing. Unlike the original test set, for this test set the labels are known. Therefore, when testing, the labels from this test set are removed. After these labels are predicted using the model, the predicted labels are compared with the masked labels (*ground truth*). This measures how well the trained model is generalized to predict class attributes. One way of dividing the training set into train/test sets is to divide the training set into *k* equally sized partitions, or *folds*, and then using all folds but one to train, with the one left out for testing. This technique is LEAVE-ONE- called *leave-one-out* training. Another way is to divide the training set into OUT *k* equally sized sets and then run the algorithm *k* times. In round *i*, we use all folds but fold *i* for training and fold *i* for testing. The average performance of the algorithm over *k* rounds measures the *generalization accuracy* of the *k*-FOLD algorithm. This robust technique is known as *k-fold cross validation*. CROSS VALIDATION To compare the masked labels with the predicted labels, depending on the type of supervised learning algorithm, different evaluation techniques can be used. In classification, the class attribute is discrete so the values it can take are limited. This allows us to use *accuracy* to evaluate the classifier. The accuracy is the fraction of labels that are predicted correctly. Let *n* be the size of the test dataset and let *c* be the number of instances from the test dataset for which the labels were predicted correctly using the trained model. Then the accuracy of this model is

$$accuracy = \frac{c}{n}. \tag{5.53}$$

In the case of regression, however, it is unreasonable to assume that the label can be predicted precisely because the labels are real values. A small variation in the prediction would result in extremely low accuracy. For instance, if we train a model to predict the temperature of a city in a given day and the model predicts the temperature to be 71.1 degrees Fahrenheit and the actual observed temperature is 71, then the model is highly accurate; however, using the accuracy measure, the model is 0% accurate. In general, for regression, we check if the predictions are highly correlated with the ground truth using correlation analysis, or we can fit lines to both ground

Table 5.3. *Distance Measures*

Measure Name	Formula	Description
Mahalanobis	$d(X, Y) = \sqrt{(X - Y)^T \Sigma^{-1}(X - Y)}$	X, Y are features vectors and Σ is the covariance matrix of the dataset
Manhattan (L_1 norm)	$d(X, Y) = \sum_i |x_i - y_i|$	X, Y are features vectors
L_p-norm	$d(X, Y) = (\sum_i |x_i - y_i|^n)^{\frac{1}{n}}$	X, Y are features vectors

truth and prediction results and check if these lines are close. The smaller the distance between these lines, the more accurate the models learned from the data.

5.5 Unsupervised Learning

Unsupervised learning is the unsupervised division of instances into groups of similar objects. In this topic, we focus on *clustering*. In clustering, the   CLUSTERING data is often unlabeled. Thus, the label for each instance is not known to the clustering algorithm. This is the main difference between supervised and unsupervised learning.

Any clustering algorithm requires a distance measure. Instances are put into different clusters based on their distance to other instances. The most popular distance measure for continuous features is the *Euclidean distance*:

$$d(X, Y) = \sqrt{(x_1 - y_1)^2 + (x_2 - y_2)^2 + \cdots + (x_n - y_n)^2}$$

$$= \sqrt{\sum_{i=1}^{n}(x_i - y_i)^2}, \tag{5.54}$$

where $X = (x_1, x_2, \ldots, x_n)$ and $Y = (y_1, y_2, \ldots, y_n)$ are n-dimensional feature vectors in $\mathbb{R}^n$. A list of some commonly used distance measures is provided in Table 5.3.

Once a distance measure is selected, instances are grouped using it. Clusters are usually represented by compact and abstract notations. "Cluster centroids" are one common example of this abstract notation. Finally, clusters are evaluated. There is still a large debate on the issue of evaluating clustering because of the lack of cluster labels in unsupervised learning.

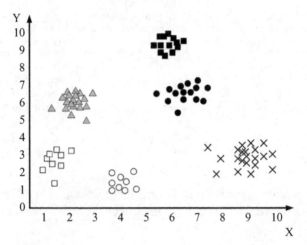

Figure 5.7. *k*-Means Output on a Sample Dataset. Instances are two-dimensional vectors shown in the 2-D space. *k*-means is run with $k = 6$, and the clusters found are visualized using different symbols.

Clustering validity and the definition of valid clusters are two of the challenges in the ongoing research.

5.5.1 Clustering Algorithms

There are many clustering algorithm types. In this section, we discuss *partitional* clustering algorithms, which are the most frequently used clustering algorithms. In Chapter 6, we discuss two other types of clustering algorithms: spectral clustering and hierarchical clustering.

Partitional Algorithms

Partitional clustering algorithms partition the dataset into a set of clusters. In other words, each instance is assigned to a cluster exactly once, and no instance remains unassigned to clusters. *k*-means [Jain and Dubes, 1999] is a well-known example of a partitional algorithm. The output of the *k*-means algorithm ($k = 6$) on a sample dataset is shown in Figure 5.7. In this figure, the dataset has two features, and instances can be visualized in a two-dimensional space. The instances are shown using symbols that represent the cluster to which they belong. The pseudocode for *k*-means algorithm is provided in Algorithm 5.2.

Algorithm 5.2 k-Means Algorithm

Require: A Dataset of Real-Value Attributes, k (number of Clusters)
 1: **return** A Clustering of Data into k Clusters
 2: Consider k random instances in the data space as the initial cluster centroids.
 3: **while** centroids have not converged **do**
 4:   Assign each instance to the cluster that has the closest cluster centroid.
 5:   If all instances have been assigned then recalculate the cluster centroids by averaging instances inside each cluster
 6: **end while**

The algorithm starts with k initial centroids. In practice, these centroids are randomly chosen instances from the dataset. These initial instances form the initial set of k clusters. Then, we assign each instance to one of these clusters based on its distance to the centroid of each cluster. The calculation of distances from instances to centroids depends on the choice of distance measure. Euclidean distance is the most widely used distance measure. After assigning all instances to a cluster, the centroids, are recomputed by taking the average (mean) of all instances inside the clusters (hence, the name k-means). This procedure is repeated using the newly computed centroids. Note that this procedure is repeated until convergence. The most common criterion to determine convergence is to check whether centroids are no longer changing. This is equivalent to clustering assignments of the data instances stabilizing. In practice, the algorithm execution can be stopped when the Euclidean distance between the centroids in two consecutive steps is bounded above by some small positive ϵ. As an alternative, k-means implementations try to minimize an *objective function*. A well-known objective function in these implementations is the squared distance error:

$$\sum_{i=1}^{k}\sum_{j=1}^{n(i)} ||x_j^i - c_i||^2, \qquad (5.55)$$

where x_j^i is the jth instance of cluster i, $n(i)$ is the number of instances in cluster i, and c_i is the centroid of cluster i. The process stops when the difference between the objective function values of two consecutive iterations of the k-means algorithm is bounded by some small value ϵ.

Note that k-means is highly sensitive to the initial k centroids, and different clustering results can be obtained on a single dataset depending on the initial k centroids. This problem can be mitigated by running k-means multiple times and selecting the clustering assignment that is observed most often or is more desirable based on an objective function, such as the squared error. Since k-means assumes that instances that belong to the same cluster are the ones that found the cluster's centroid closer than other centroids in the dataset, one can safely assume that all the instances inside a cluster fall into a hyper-sphere, with the centroid being its center. The radius for this hyper-sphere is defined based on the farthest instance inside this cluster. If clusters that need to be extracted are nonspherical (globular), k-means has problems detecting them. This problem can be addressed by a preprocessing step in which a transformation is performed on the dataset to solve this issue.

5.5.2 Unsupervised Learning Evaluation

When clusters are found, there is a need to evaluate how accurately the task has been performed. When ground truth is available, we have prior knowledge of which instances should belong to which cluster, as discussed in Chapter 6 in detail. However, evaluating clustering is a challenge because ground truth is often not available. When ground truth is unavailable, we incorporate techniques that analyze the clusters found and describe the quality of clusters found. In particular, we can use techniques that measure *cohesiveness* or *separateness* of clusters.

Cohesiveness

In evaluating clustering, we are interested in clusters that exhibit *cohesiveness*. In cohesive clusters, instances inside the clusters are close to each other. In statistical terms, this is equivalent to having a small standard deviation (i.e., being close to the mean value). In clustering, this translates to being close to the centroid of the cluster. So cohesiveness is defined as the distance from instances to the centroid of their respective clusters,

$$cohesiveness = \sum_{i=1}^{k} \sum_{j=1}^{n(i)} ||x_j^i - c_i||^2, \qquad (5.56)$$

which is the squared distance error (also known as SSE) discussed previously. Small values of cohesiveness denote highly cohesive clusters in which all instances are close to the centroid of the cluster.

Example 5.7. *Figure 5.8 shows a dataset of four one-dimensional instances. The instances are clustered into two clusters. Instances in cluster*

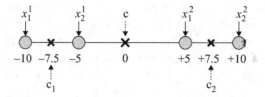

Figure 5.8. Unsupervised Learning Evaluation.

1 are x_1^1 and x_2^1, and instances in cluster 2 are x_1^2 and x_2^2. The centroids of these two clusters are denoted as c_1 and c_2. For these two clusters, the cohesiveness is

$$cohesiveness = |-10 - (-7.5)|^2 + |-5 - (-7.5)|^2 + |5 - 7.5|^2$$
$$+ |10 - 7.5|^2 = 25. \tag{5.57}$$

Separateness

We are also interested in clustering of the data that generates clusters that are well separated from one another. To measure this distance between clusters, we can use the *separateness* measure. In statistics, separateness can be measured by standard deviation. Standard deviation is maximized when instances are far from the mean. In clustering terms, this is equivalent to cluster centroids being far from the mean of the entire dataset:

$$separateness = \sum_{i=1}^{k} ||c - c_i||^2, \tag{5.58}$$

where $c = \frac{1}{n} \sum_{i=1}^{n} x_i$ is the centroid of all instances and c_i is the centroid of cluster i. Large values of separateness denote clusters that are far apart.

Example 5.8. *For the dataset shown in Figure 5.8, the centroid for all instances is denoted as c. For this dataset, the separateness is*

$$separateness = |-7.5 - 0|^2 + |7.5 - 0|^2 = 112.5. \tag{5.59}$$

In general, we are interested in clusters that are both cohesive and separate. The silhouette index combines both these measures.

Silhouette Index

The *silhouette index* combines both cohesiveness and separateness. It compares the average distance value between instances in the same cluster and the average distance value between instances in different clusters. In a well-clustered dataset, the average distance between instances in the same cluster is small (cohesiveness), and the average distance between instances in different clusters is large (separateness). Let $a(x)$ denote the average distance between instance x of cluster C and all other members of C:

$$a(x) = \frac{1}{|C| - 1} \sum_{y \in C, y \neq x} ||x - y||^2. \tag{5.60}$$

Let $G \neq C$ denote the cluster that is closest to x in terms of the average distance between x and members of G. Let $b(x)$ denote the average distance between instance x and instances in cluster G:

$$b(x) = \min_{G \neq C} \frac{1}{|G|} \sum_{y \in G} ||x - y||^2. \tag{5.61}$$

Since we want distance between instances in the same cluster to be smaller than distance between instances in different clusters, we are interested in $a(x) < b(x)$. The silhouette clustering index is formulated as

$$s(x) = \frac{b(x) - a(x)}{\max(b(x), a(x))}, \tag{5.62}$$

$$silhouette = \frac{1}{n} \sum_x s(x). \tag{5.63}$$

The silhouette index takes values between $[-1, 1]$. The best clustering happens when $\forall x \; a(x) \ll b(x)$. In this case, $silhouette \approx 1$. Similarly when $silhouette < 0$, that indicates that many instances are closer to other clusters than their assigned cluster, which shows low-quality clustering.

Example 5.9. *In Figure 5.8, the $a(.)$, $b(.)$, and $s(.)$ values are*

$$a(x_1^1) = |-10 - (-5)|^2 = 25 \tag{5.64}$$

$$b(x_1^1) = \frac{1}{2}(|-10 - 5|^2 + |-10 - 10|^2) = 312.5 \tag{5.65}$$

$$s(x_1^1) = \frac{312.5 - 25}{312.5} = 0.92 \tag{5.66}$$

$$a(x_2^1) = |-5 - (-10)|^2 = 25 \tag{5.67}$$

$$b(x_2^1) = \frac{1}{2}(|-5 - 5|^2 + |-5 - 10|^2) = 162.5 \tag{5.68}$$

$$s(x_2^1) = \frac{162.5 - 25}{162.5} = 0.84 \tag{5.69}$$

$$a(x_1^2) = |5 - 10|^2 = 25 \tag{5.70}$$

$$b(x_1^2) = \frac{1}{2}(|5 - (-10)|^2 + |5 - (-5)|^2) = 162.5 \tag{5.71}$$

$$s(x_1^2) = \frac{162.5 - 25}{162.5} = 0.84 \tag{5.72}$$

$$a(x_2^2) = |10 - 5|^2 = 25 \tag{5.73}$$

$$b(x_2^2) = \frac{1}{2}(|10 - (-5)|^2 + |10 - (-10)|^2) = 312.5 \tag{5.74}$$

$$s(x_2^2) = \frac{312.5 - 25}{312.5} = 0.92. \tag{5.75}$$

Given the $s(.)$ values, the silhouette index is

$$silhouette = \frac{1}{4}(0.92 + 0.84 + 0.84 + 0.92) = 0.88. \tag{5.76}$$

5.6 Summary

This chapter covered data mining essentials. The general process for analyzing data is known as knowledge discovery in databases (KDD). The first step in the KDD process is data representation. Data instances are represented in tabular format using features. These instances can be labeled or unlabeled. There exist different feature types: nominal, ordinal, interval, and ratio. Data representation for text data can be performed using the vector space model. After having a representation, quality measures need to be addressed and preprocessing steps completed before processing the data. Quality measures include noise removal, outlier detection, missing values handling, and duplicate data removal. Preprocessing techniques commonly performed are aggregation, discretization, feature selection, feature extraction, and sampling.

We covered two categories of data mining algorithms: supervised and unsupervised learning. Supervised learning deals with mapping feature values to class labels, and unsupervised learning is the unsupervised division of instances into groups of similar objects.

When labels are discrete, the supervised learning is called classification, and when labels are real numbers, it is called regression. We covered these classification methods: decision tree learning, naive Bayes classifier (NBC), nearest neighbor classifier, and classifiers that use network information. We also discussed linear and logistic regression.

To evaluate supervised learning, a training-testing framework is used in which the labeled dataset is partitioned into two parts, one for training and the other for testing. Different approaches for evaluating supervised learning such as leave-one-out or k-fold cross validation were discussed.

Any clustering algorithm requires the selection of a distance measure. We discussed partitional clustering algorithms and k-means from these algorithms, as well as methods of evaluating clustering algorithms. To evaluate clustering algorithms, one can use clustering quality measures such as cohesiveness, which measures how close instances are inside clusters, or separateness, which measures how separate different clusters are from one another. Silhouette index combines the cohesiveness and separateness into one measure.

5.7 Bibliographic Notes

A general review of data mining algorithms can be found in the machine learning and pattern recognition [Bishop, 2006; Duda, Hart, and Stork, 2012; Mitchell, 1997; Quinlan, 1986, 1993; Langley, 1995], data mining [Friedman et al., 2009; Han et al., 2006; Witten et al., 2011; Tan et al., 2005; Han et al., 2006], and pattern recognition [Bishop, 1995; Duda, Hart, and Stork, 2012] literature.

Among preprocessing techniques, feature selection and feature extraction have gained much attention due to their importance. General references for feature selection and extraction can be found in [Liu and Motoda, 1998; Dash and Liu, 1997, 2000; Guyon, 2006; Zhao and Liu, 2011; Liu and Motoda, 1998; Liu and Yu, 2005]. Feature selection has also been discussed in social media data in [Tang and Liu, 2012a,b, 2013]. Although not much research is dedicated to sampling in social media, it plays an important role in the experimental outcomes of social media research. Most experiments are performed using sampled social media data, and it is important for these samples to be representative samples of the site that is under study. For instance, Morstatter et al. [2013] studied whether Twitter's heavily sampled Streaming API, a free service for social media data, accurately portrays the true activity on Twitter. They show that the bias introduced by the Streaming API is significant.

In addition to the data mining categories covered in this chapter, there are other important categories in the area of data mining and machine learning. In particular, an interesting category is *semi-supervised* learning. In semi-supervised learning, the label is available for some instances, but not all. The model uses the labeled information and the feature distribution of the unlabeled data to learn a model. *Expectation maximization* (EM) is a well-established technique from this area. In short, EM learns a model from the data that is partially labeled (expectation step). Then, it uses this model to predict labels for the unlabeled instances (maximization step). The predicted labels for instances are used once again to refine the learned model and revise predictions for unlabeled instances in an iterative fashion until convergence in reached. In addition to supervised methods covered, neural networks deserve mention [Haykin, 1994]. More on regression techniques in available in [Neter et al., 1996; Bishop, 2006].

Clustering is one of the most popular areas in the field of machine learning research. A taxonomy of clustering algorithms can be found in [Berkhin, 2006; Jain et al., 1999; Xu and Wunsch, 2005; Mirkin, 2005]. Among clustering algorithms, some of which use data density of cluster data, DBSCAN [Ester et al., 1996], GDBSCAN [Sander et al., 1998], CLARANS [Ng and Han, 1994], and OPTICS [Ankerst et al., 1999] are some of the most well known and practiced algorithms. Most of the previous contributions in the area of clustering consider the number of clusters as an input parameter. Early literature in clustering had attempted to solve this by running algorithms for several Ks (number of clusters) and selecting the best K that optimizes some coefficients [Milligan and Cooper, 1985; Berkhin, 2006]. For example, the distance between two cluster centroids normalized by a cluster's standard deviation could be used as a coefficient. After the coefficient is selected, the coefficient values are plotted as a function of K (number of clusters) and the best K is selected.

An interesting application of data mining is *sentiment analysis* in which the level of subjective content in information is quantified; for example, identifying the polarity (i.e., being positive/negative) of a digital camera review. General references for sentiment analysis can be found in [Pang and Lee, 2008; Liu, 2007], and examples of recent developments in social media are available in [Hu et al., 2013a,b].

5.8 Exercises

1. Describe how methods from this chapter can be applied in social media.

2. Outline a framework for using the supervised learning algorithm for unsupervised learning.

Data

3. Describe methods that can be used to deal with missing data.

4. Given a continuous attribute, how can we convert it to a discrete attribute? How can we convert discrete attributes to continuous ones?

5. If you had the chance of choosing either instance selection or feature selection, which one would you choose? Please justify.

6. Given two text documents that are vectorized, how can we measure document similarity?

7. In the example provided for TF-IDF (Example 5.1), the word "orange" received zero score. Is this desirable? What does a high TF-IDF value show?

Supervised Learning

8. Provide a pseudocode for decision tree induction.

9. How many decision trees containing n attributes and a binary class can be generated?

10. What does zero entropy mean?

11. • What is the time complexity for learning a naive Bayes classifer?
    • What is the time complexity for classifying using the naive Bayes classifier?
    • **Linear separability**: Two sets of two-dimensional instances are linearly separable if they can be completely separated using one line. In n-dimensional space, two set of instances are linearly separable if one can separate them by a hyper-plane. A classical example of nonlinearity is the XOR function. In this function, the two instance sets are the black-and-white instances (see Figure 5.9), which cannot be separated using a single line. This is an example of a nonlinear binary function. Can a naive Bayes classifier learn nonlinear binary functions? Provide details.
    • What about linear separability and K-NN? Are K-NNs capable of solving such problems?

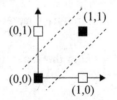

Figure 5.9. Nonlinearity of XOR Function.

12. Describe how the least square solution can be determined for regression.

Unsupervised Learning

13. (a) Given k clusters and their respective cluster sizes $s_1, s_2, \ldots, s_k$, what is the probability that two random (with replacement) data vectors (from the clustered dataset) belong to the same cluster?
    (b) Now, assume you are given this probability (you do not have s_i's and k), and the fact that clusters are equally sized, can you find k? This gives you an idea how to predict the number of clusters in a dataset.

14. Give an example of a dataset consisting of four data vectors where there exist two different optimal (minimum SSE) 2-means (k-means, $k = 2$) clusterings of the dataset.
    - Calculate the optimal SSE value for your example.
    - In general, how should datasets look like geometrically so that we have more than one optimal solution?
    - What defines the number of optimal solutions?

    Perform two iterations of the k-means algorithm in order to obtain two clusters for the input instances given in Table 5.4. Assume that the first centroids are instances 1 and 3. Explain if more iterations are needed to get the final clusters.

Table 5.4. *Dataset*

Instance	X	Y
1	12.0	15.0
2	12.0	33.0
3	18.0	15.0
4	18.0	27.0
5	24.0	21.0
6	36.0	42.0

16. What is the usual shape of clusters generated by k-means? Give an example of cases where k-means has limitations in detecting the patterns formed by the instances.

17. Describe a preprocessing strategy that can help detect nonspherical clusters using k-means.

Part II
Communities and Interactions

6

Community Analysis

In November 2010, a team of Dutch law enforcement agents dismantled a community of 30 million infected computers across the globe that were sending more than 3.6 billion daily spam mails. These distributed networks of infected computers are called *botnets*. The community of computers in a botnet transmit spam or viruses across the web without their owner's permission. The members of a botnet are rarely known; however, it is vital to identify these botnet communities and analyze their behavior to enhance internet security. This is an example of *community analysis*. In this chapter, we discuss community analysis in social media.

Also known as *groups*, *clusters*, or *cohesive subgroups*, communities have been studied extensively in many fields and, in particular, the social sciences. In social media mining, analyzing communities is essential. Studying communities in social media is important for many reasons. First, individuals often form groups based on their interests, and when studying individuals, we are interested in identifying these groups. Consider the importance of finding groups with similar reading tastes by an online book seller for recommendation purposes. Second, groups provide a clear global view of user interactions, whereas a local-view of individual behavior is often noisy and ad hoc. Finally, some behaviors are *only* observable in a group setting and not on an individual level. This is because the individual's behavior can fluctuate, but group collective behavior is more robust to change. Consider the interactions between two opposing political groups on social media. Two individuals, one from each group, can hold similar opinions on a subject, but what is important is that their communities can exhibit opposing views on the same subject.

In this chapter, we discuss communities and answer the following three questions in detail:

1. *How can we detect communities?* This question is discussed in different disciplines, and in diverse forms. In particular, quantization in

electrical engineering, discretization in statistics, and clustering in machine learning tackle a similar challenge. As discussed in Chapter 5, in clustering, data points are grouped together based on a similarity measure. In community detection, data points represent actors in social media, and similarity between these actors is often defined based on the interests these users share. The major difference between clustering and community detection is that in community detection, individuals are connected to others via a network of links, whereas in clustering, data points are not embedded in a network.

2. *How do communities evolve and how can we study evolving communities?* Social media forms a dynamic and evolving environment. Similar to real-world friendships, social media interactions evolve over time. People join or leave groups; groups expand, shrink, dissolve, or split over time. Studying the temporal behavior of communities is necessary for a deep understanding of communities in social media.

3. *How can we evaluate detected communities?* As emphasized in our botnet example, the list of community members (i.e., ground truth) is rarely known. Hence, community evaluation is a challenging task and often means to evaluating detected communities in the absence of ground truth.

Social Communities

Broadly speaking, a real-world community is a body of individuals with common economic, social, or political interests/characteristics, often living in relatively close proximity. A virtual community comes into existence when like-minded users on social media form a link and start interacting with each other. In other words, formation of any community requires (1) a set of at least two nodes sharing some interest and (2) interactions with respect to that interest.

As a real-world community example, consider the interactions of a college karate club collected by Wayne Zachary in 1977. The example is often ZACHARY'S referred to as *Zachary's Karate Club* [Zachary, 1977] in the literature. Fig-KARATE CLUB ure 6.1 depicts the interactions in a college karate club over two years. The links show friendships between members. During the observation period, individuals split into two communities due to a disagreement between the club administrator and the karate instructor, and members of one community left to start their own club. In this figure, node colors demonstrate the communities to which individuals belong. As observed in this figure, using

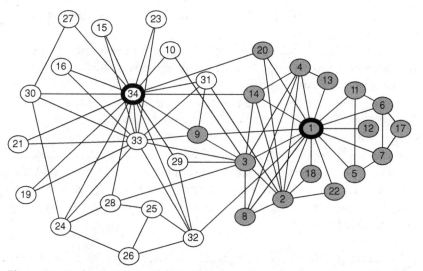

Figure 6.1. Zachary's Karate Club. Nodes represent karate club members and edges represent friendships. A conflict in the club divided the members into two groups. The color of the nodes denotes which one of the two groups the nodes belong to.

graphs is a convenient way to depict communities because color-coded nodes can denote memberships and edges can be used to denote relations. Furthermore, we can observe that individuals are more likely to be friends with members of their own group, hence, creating tightly knit components in the graph.

Zachary's Karate Club is an example of two *explicit communities*. An explicit community, also known as an *emic* community, satisfies the following three criteria:

    EXPLICIT
    (EMIC)
    COMMUNITIES

1. Community members understand that they are its members.
2. Nonmembers understand who the community members are.
3. Community members often have more interactions with each other than with nonmembers.

In contrast to explicit communities, in implicit communities, also known as *etic* communities, individuals tacitly interact with others in the form of an unacknowledged community. For instance, individuals calling Canada from the United States on a daily basis need not be friends and do not consider each other as members of the same explicit community. However, from the phone operator's point of view, they form an implicit community that needs to be marketed the same promotions. Finding implicit communities is of

    IMPLICIT
    (ETIC)
    COMMUNITIES

major interest, and this chapter focuses on finding these communities in social media.

Communities in social media are more or less representatives of communities in the real world. As mentioned, in the real world, members of communities are often geographically close to each other. The geographical location becomes less important in social media, and many communities on social media consist of highly diverse people from all around the planet. In general, people in real-world communities tend to be more similar than those of social media. People do not need to share language, location, and the like to be members of social media communities. Similar to real-world communities, communities in social media can be labeled as explicit or implicit. Examples of explicit communities in well-known social media sites include the following:

- **Facebook.** In Facebook, there exist a variety of explicit communities, such as *groups* and *communities*. In these communities, users can post messages and images, comment on other messages, like posts, and view activities of others.
- **Yahoo! Groups**. In Yahoo! groups, individuals join a group mailing list where they can receive emails from all or a selection of group members (administrators) directly.
- **LinkedIn.** LinkedIn provides its users with a feature called *Groups and Associations*. Users can join professional groups where they can post and share information related to the group.

Because these sites represent explicit communities, individuals have an understanding of when they are joining them. However, there exist implicit communities in social media as well. For instance, consider individuals with the same taste for certain movies on a movie rental site. These individuals are rarely all members of the same explicit community. However, the movie rental site is particularly interested in finding these implicit communities so it can better market to them by recommending movies similar to their tastes. We discuss techniques to find these implicit communities next.

6.1 Community Detection

As mentioned earlier, communities can be explicit (e.g., Yahoo! groups), or implicit (e.g., individuals who write blogs on the same or similar topics). In contrast to explicit communities, in many social media sites, implicit communities and their members are obscure to many people. Community detection finds these implicit communities.

In the simplest form, similar to the graph shown in Figure 6.1, community detection algorithms are often provided with a graph where nodes represent individuals and edges represent friendships between individual. This definition can be generalized. Edges can also be used to represent contents or attributes shared by individuals. For instance, we can connect individuals at the same location, with the same gender, or who bought the same product using edges. Similarly, nodes can also represent products, sites, and webpages, among others. Formally, for a graph $G(V, E)$, the task of community detection is to find a set of communities $\{C_i\}_{i=1}^{n}$ in a G such that $\cup_{i=1}^{n} C_i \subseteq V$.

6.1.1 Community Detection Algorithms

There are a variety of community detection algorithms. When detecting communities, we are interested in detecting communities with either (1) *specific members* or (2) *specific forms* of communities. We denote the former as *member-based community detection* and the latter as *group-based community detection*. Consider the network of 10 individuals shown in Figure 6.2 where 7 are wearing black t-shirts and 3 are wearing white ones. If we group individuals based on their t-shirt color, we end up having a community of three and a community of seven. This is an example of member-based community detection, where we are interested in *specific members* characterized by their t-shirts' color. If we group the same set based on the density of interactions (i.e., internal edges), we get two other communities. This is an instance of group-based community detection, where we are interested in *specific communities* characterized by their interactions' density.

Member-based community detection uses community detection algorithms that group members based on attributes or measures such as similarity, degree, or reachability. In group-based community detection, we are interested in finding communities that are modular, balanced, dense, robust, or hierarchical.

6.1.2 Member-Based Community Detection

The intuition behind member-based community detection is that members with the same (or similar) characteristics are more often in the same community. Therefore, a community detection algorithm following this approach should assign members with similar characteristics to the same community.

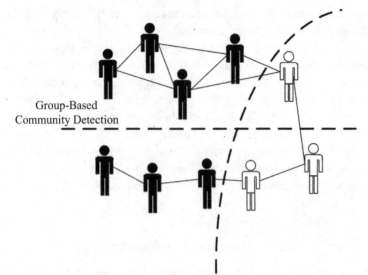

Group-Based
Community Detection

Member-Based
Community Detection

Figure 6.2. Community Detection Algorithms Example. Member-based community detection groups members based on their characteristics. Here, we divide the network based on color. In group-based community detection, we find communities based on group properties. Here, groups are formed based on the density of interactions among their members.

Let us consider a simple example. We can assume that nodes that belong to a cycle form a community. This is because they share the same characteristic: being in the cycle. Figure 6.3 depicts a 4-cycle. For instance, we can search for all n-cycles in the graph and assume that they represent a community. The choice for n can be based on empirical evidence or heuristics, or n can be in a range $[\alpha_1, \alpha_2]$ for which all cycles are found. A well-known example is the search for 3-cycles (triads) in graphs.

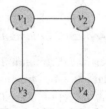

Figure 6.3. A 4-Cycle.

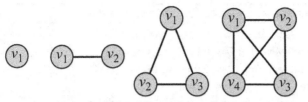

Figure 6.4. First Four Complete Graphs.

In theory, any subgraph can be searched for and assumed to be a community. In practice, only subgraphs that have nodes with specific characteristics are considered as communities. Three general node characteristics that are frequently used are *node similarity, node degree (familiarity),* and *node reachibility.*

When employing node degrees, we seek subgraphs, which are often connected, such that each node (or a subset of nodes) has a certain node degree (number of incoming or outgoing edges). Our 4-cycle example follows this property, the degree of each node being two. In reachability, we seek subgraphs with specific properties related to paths existing between nodes. For instance, our 4-cycle instance also follows the reachability characteristic where all pairs of nodes can be reached via two independent paths. In node similarity, we assume nodes that are highly similar belong to the same community.

Node Degree

The most common subgraph searched for in networks based on node degrees is a *clique.* A clique is a maximum complete subgraph in which all pairs of nodes inside the subgraph are connected. In terms of the node degree characteristic, a clique of size k is a subgraph of k nodes where all node degrees in the induced subgraph are $k - 1$. The only difference between cliques and complete graphs is that cliques are subgraphs, whereas complete graphs contain the whole node set V. The simplest four complete graphs (or cliques, when these are subgraphs) are represented in Figure 6.4.

To find communities, we can search for the maximum clique (the one with the largest number of vertices) or for all maximal cliques (cliques that are not subgraphs of a larger clique; i.e., cannot be expanded further). However, both problems are NP-hard, as is verifying whether a graph contains a clique larger than size k. To overcome these theoretical barriers, for sufficiently small networks or subgraphs, we can (1) use brute force, (2) add some constraints such that the problem is relaxed and polynomially solvable, or (3) use cliques as the seed or core of a larger community.

Algorithm 6.1 Brute-Force Clique Identification

Require: Adjacency Matrix A, Vertex v_x
  1: **return** Maximal Clique C containing v_x
  2: CliqueStack $= \{\{v_x\}\}$, Processed $= \{\}$;
  3: **while** CliqueStack not empty **do**
  4:     C=pop(CliqueStack); push(Processed,C);
  5:     $v_{last} = $ Last node added to C;
  6:     $N(v_{last}) = \{v_i \mid A_{v_{last},v_i} = 1\}$.
  7:     **for all** $v_{temp} \in N(v_{last})$ **do**
  8:         **if** $C \bigcup \{v_{temp}\}$ is a clique **then**
  9:             push(CliqueStack, $C \bigcup \{v_{temp}\}$);
  10:         **end if**
  11:     **end for**
  12: **end while**
  13: Return the largest clique from Processed

Brute-force clique identification. The brute force method can find all maximal cliques in a graph. For each vertex v_x, we try to find the maximal clique that contains node v_x. The brute-force algorithm is detailed in Algorithm 6.1.

The algorithm starts with an empty stack of cliques. This stack is initialized with the node v_x that is being analyzed (a clique of size 1). Then, from the stack, a clique is popped (C). The last node added to clique C is selected (v_{last}). All the neighbors of v_{last} are added to the popped clique C sequentially, and if the new set of nodes creates a larger clique (i.e., the newly added node is connected to all of the other members), then the new clique is pushed back into the stack. This procedure is followed until nodes can no longer be added.

The brute-force algorithm becomes impractical for large networks. For instance, for a complete graph of only 100 nodes, the algorithm will generate at least $2^{99} - 1$ different cliques starting from any node in the graph (why?).

The performance of the brute-force algorithm can be enhanced by pruning specific nodes and edges. If the cliques being searched for are of size k or larger, we can simply assume that the clique, if found, should contain nodes that have degrees equal to or more than $k - 1$. We can first prune all nodes (and edges connected to them) with degrees less than $k - 1$. Due to the power-law distribution of node degrees, many nodes exist with small degrees (1, 2, etc.). Hence, for a large enough k many nodes and edges

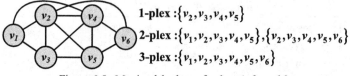

$$\text{1-plex}:\{v_2,v_3,v_4,v_5\}$$
$$\text{2-plex}:\{v_1,v_2,v_3,v_4,v_5\},\{v_2,v_3,v_4,v_5,v_6\}$$
$$\text{3-plex}:\{v_1,v_2,v_3,v_4,v_5,v_6\}$$

Figure 6.5. Maximal k-plexes for $k = 1, 2,$ and 3.

will be pruned, which will reduce the computation drastically. This pruning works for both directed and undirected graphs.

Even with pruning, there are intrinsic properties with cliques that make them a less desirable means for finding communities. Cliques are rarely observed in the real world. For instance, consider a clique of 1,000 nodes. This subgraph has $\frac{999 \times 1000}{2} = 499,500$ edges. A single edge removal from this many edges results in a subgraph that is no longer a clique. That represents less than 0.0002% of the edges, which makes finding cliques a challenging task.

In practice, to overcome this challenge, we can either relax the clique structure or use cliques as a seed or core of a community.

Relaxing cliques. A well-known clique relaxation that comes from sociology is the k-plex concept. In a clique of size k, all nodes have the degree of $k - 1$; however, in a k-plex, all nodes have a minimum degree that is not necessarily $k - 1$ (as opposed to cliques of size k). For a set of vertices V, the structure is called a k-plex if we have $\quad$ k-PLEX

$$d_v \geq |V| - k, \forall v \in V, \tag{6.1}$$

where d_v is the degree of v in the induced subgraph (i.e., the number of nodes from the set V that are connected to v).

Clearly, a clique of size k is a 1-plex. As k gets larger in a k-plex, the structure gets increasingly relaxed, because we can remove more edges from the clique structure. Finding the maximum k-plex in a graph still tends to be NP-hard, but in practice, finding it is relatively easier due to smaller search space. Figure 6.5 shows maximal k-plexes for $k = 1, 2,$ and 3. A k-plex is maximal if it is not contained in a larger k-plex (i.e., with more nodes).

Using cliques as a seed of a community. When using cliques as a seed or core of a community, we assume communities are formed from a set of $\quad$ CLIQUE cliques (small or large) in addition to edges that connect these cliques. A $\quad$ PERCOLATION well-known algorithm in this area is the clique percolation method (CPM) $\quad$ METHOD (CPM)

Algorithm 6.2 Clique Percolation Method (CPM)

Require: parameter k
  1: **return** Overlapping Communities
  2: $Cliques_k$ = find all cliques of size k
  3: Construct clique graph $G(V, E)$, where $|V| = |Cliques_k|$
  4: $E = \{e_{ij} \mid$ clique i and clique j share $k - 1$ nodes$\}$
  5: Return all connected components of G

Palla et al. [2005]. The algorithm is provided in Algorithm 6.2. Given parameter k, the method starts by finding all cliques of size k. Then a graph is generated (clique graph) where all cliques are represented as nodes, and cliques that share $k - 1$ vertices are connected via edges. Communities are then found by reporting the connected components of this graph. The algorithm searches for all cliques of size k and is therefore computationally intensive. In practice, when using the CPM algorithm, we often solve CPM for a small k. Relaxations discussed for cliques are desirable to enable the algorithm to perform faster. Lastly, CPM can return overlapping communities.

Example 6.1. *Consider the network depicted in Figure 6.6(a). The corresponding clique graph generated by the CPM algorithm for $k = 3$ is provided in Figure 6.6(b). All cliques of size $k = 3$ have been identified and cliques that share $k - 1 = 2$ nodes are connected. Connected components are returned as communities ($\{v_1, v_2, v_3\}$, $\{v_8, v_9, v_{10}\}$, and $\{v_3, v_4, v_5, v_6, v_7, v_8\}$). Nodes v_3 and v_8 belong to two communities, and these communities are overlapping.*

Node Reachability

When dealing with reachability, we are seeking subgraphs where nodes are reachable from other nodes via a path. The two extremes of reachability are achieved when nodes are assumed to be in the same community if (1) there is a path between them (regardless of the distance) or (2) they are so close as to be immediate neighbors. In the first case, any graph traversal algorithm such as BFS or DFS can be used to identify connected components (communities). However, finding connected components is not very useful in large social media networks. These networks tend to have a large-scale connected component that contains most nodes, which are connected to each other via short paths. Therefore, finding connected

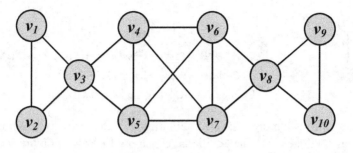

(a) Graph

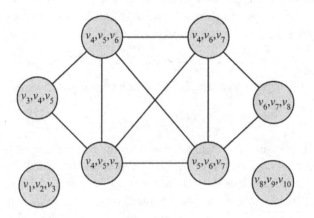

(b) CPM Clique Graph

Figure 6.6. Clique Percolation Method (CPM) Example for $k = 3$.

components is less powerful for detecting communities in them. In the second case, when nodes are immediate neighbors of all other nodes, cliques are formed, and as discussed previously, finding cliques is considered a very challenging process.

To overcome these issues, we can find communities that are in between cliques and connected components in terms of connectivity and have small shortest paths between their nodes. There are predefined subgraphs, with roots in social sciences, with these characteristics. Well-known ones include the following:

- k-**Clique** is a maximal subgraph where the shortest path between any two nodes is always less than or equal to k. Note that in k-cliques, nodes on the shortest path should not necessarily be part of the subgraph.

k-CLIQUE, k-CLUB, AND k-CLAN

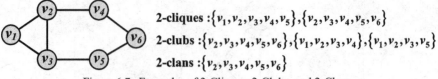

2-cliques : $\{v_1, v_2, v_3, v_4, v_5\}, \{v_2, v_3, v_4, v_5, v_6\}$

2-clubs : $\{v_2, v_3, v_4, v_5, v_6\}, \{v_1, v_2, v_3, v_4\}, \{v_1, v_2, v_3, v_5\}$

2-clans : $\{v_2, v_3, v_4, v_5, v_6\}$

Figure 6.7. Examples of 2-Cliques, 2-Clubs, and 2-Clans.

- k-**Club** is a more restricted definition; it follows the same definition as k-cliques with the additional constraint that nodes on the shortest paths should be part of the subgraph.
- k-**Clan** is a k-clique where, for all shortest paths within the subgraph, the distance is less than or equal to k. All k-clans are k-cliques and k-clubs, but not vice versa. In other words,

$$k\text{-Clans} = k\text{-Cliques} \cap k\text{-Clubs}.$$

Figure 6.7 depicts an example of the three discussed models.

Node Similarity

Node similarity attempts to determine the similarity between two nodes v_i and v_j. Similar nodes (or most similar nodes) are assumed to be in the same community. Often, once the similarities between nodes are determined, a classical clustering algorithm (see Chapter 5) is applied to find communities. Determining similarity between two nodes has been addressed in different STRUCTURAL fields; in particular, the problem of *structural equivalence* in the field of EQUIVALENCE sociology considers the same problem. In structural equivalence, similarity is based on the overlap between the neighborhood of the vertices. Let $N(v_i)$ and $N(v_j)$ be the neighbors of vertices v_i and v_j, respectively. In this case, a measure of vertex similarity can be defined as follows:

$$\sigma(v_i, v_j) = |N(v_i) \cap N(v_j)|. \tag{6.2}$$

For large networks, this value can increase rapidly, because nodes may share many neighbors. Generally, similarity is attributed to a value that is bounded and usually in the range $[0, 1]$. For that to happen, various normalization procedures such as the Jaccard similarity or the cosine similarity can be done:

$$\sigma_{\text{Jaccard}}(v_i, v_j) = \frac{|N(v_i) \cap N(v_j)|}{|N(v_i) \cup N(v_j)|}, \tag{6.3}$$

$$\sigma_{\text{Cosine}}(v_i, v_j) = \frac{|N(v_i) \cap N(v_j)|}{\sqrt{|N(v_i)||N(v_j)|}}. \tag{6.4}$$

Example 6.2. *Consider the graph in Figure 6.7. The similarity values between nodes v_2 and v_5 are*

$$\sigma_{\text{Jaccard}}(v_2, v_5) = \frac{|\{v_1, v_3, v_4\} \cap \{v_3, v_6\}|}{|\{v_1, v_3, v_4, v_6\}|} = 0.25, \quad (6.5)$$

$$\sigma_{\text{Cosine}}(v_2, v_5) = \frac{|\{v_1, v_3, v_4\} \cap \{v_3, v_6\}|}{\sqrt{|\{v_1, v_3, v_4\}||\{v_3, v_6\}|}} = 0.40. \quad (6.6)$$

In general, the definition of neighborhood $N(v_i)$ excludes the node itself (v_i). This, however, leads to problems with the aforementioned similarity values because nodes that are connected and do not share a neighbor will be assigned zero similarity. This can be rectified by assuming that nodes are included in their own neighborhood.

A generalization of structural equivalence is known as *regular equivalence*. Consider the situation of two basketball players in two different countries. Though sharing no neighborhood overlap, the social circles of these players (coach, players, fans, etc.) might look quite similar due to their social status. In other words, nodes are regularly equivalent when they are connected to nodes that are themselves similar (a self-referential definition). For more details on regular equivalence, refer to Chapter 3.

6.1.3 Group-Based Community Detection

When considering community characteristics for community detection, we are interested in communities that have certain group properties. In this section, we discuss communities that are balanced, robust, modular, dense, or hierarchical.

Balanced Communities

As mentioned before, community detection can be thought of as the problem of clustering in data mining and machine learning. Graph-based clustering techniques have proven to be useful in identifying communities in social networks. In graph-based clustering, we cut the graph into several partitions and assume these partitions represent communities.

Formally, a *cut* in a graph is a partitioning (cut) of the graph into two (or more) sets (*cutsets*). The size of the cut is the number of edges that are being cut and the summation of weights of edges that are being cut in a weighted graph. A *minimum cut* (min-cut) is a cut such that the size of the

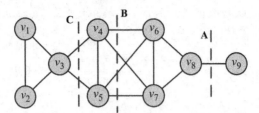

Figure 6.8. Minimum Cut (A) and Two More Balanced Cuts (B and C) in a Graph.

MINIMUM
CUT

cut is minimized. Figure 6.8 depicts several cuts in a graph. For example, cut B has size 4, and A is the minimum cut.

Based on the well-known *max-flow min-cut* theorem, the minimum cut of a graph can be computed efficiently. However, minimum cuts are not always preferred for community detection. Often, they result in cuts where a partition is only one node (singleton), and the rest of the graph is in the other. Typically, communities with balanced sizes are preferred. Figure 6.8 depicts an example where the minimum cut (A) creates unbalanced partitions, whereas, cut C is a more balanced cut.

RATIO CUT
AND
NORMALIZED
CUT

To solve this problem, variants of minimum cut define an objective function, minimizing (or maximizing) that during the cut-finding procedure, results in a more balanced and natural partitioning of the data. Consider a graph $G(V, E)$. A partitioning of G into k partitions is a tuple $P = (P_1, P_2, P_3, \ldots, P_k)$, such that $P_i \subseteq V$, $P_i \cap P_j = \emptyset$ and $\bigcup_{i=1}^{k} P_i = V$. Then, the objective function for the ratio cut and normalized cut are defined as follows:

$$\text{Ratio Cut}(P) = \frac{1}{k} \sum_{i=1}^{k} \frac{\text{cut}(P_i, \bar{P}_i)}{|P_i|}, \tag{6.7}$$

$$\text{Normalized Cut}(P) = \frac{1}{k} \sum_{i=1}^{k} \frac{\text{cut}(P_i, \bar{P}_i)}{\text{vol}(P_i)}, \tag{6.8}$$

where $\bar{P}_i = V - P_i$ is the complement cut set, $cut(P_i, \bar{P}_i)$ is the size of the cut, and volume $vol(P_i) = \sum_{v \in P_i} d_v$. Both objective functions provide a more balanced community size by normalizing the cut size either by the number of vertices in the outset or the volume (total degree).

Both the ratio cut and normalized cut can be formulated in a matrix format. Let matrix $X \in \{0, 1\}^{|V| \times k}$ denote the *community membership* matrix, where $X_{i,j} = 1$ if node i is in community j; otherwise, $X_{i,j} = 0$. Let $D = \text{diag}(d_1, d_2, \ldots, d_n)$ represent the diagonal degree matrix. Then the

i^{th} entry on the diagonal of $X^T A X$ represents the number of edges that are inside community i. Similarly, the ith element on the diagonal of $X^T D X$ represents the number of edges that are connected to members of community i. Hence, the ith element on the diagonal of $X^T(D - A)X$ represents the number of edges that are in the cut that separates community i from all other nodes. In fact, the ith diagonal element of $X^T(D - A)X$ is equivalent to the summation term $cut(P_i, \bar{P}_i)$ in both the ratio and normalized cut. Thus, for ratio cut, we have

$$\text{Ratio Cut}(P) = \frac{1}{k} \sum_{i=1}^{k} \frac{cut(P_i, \bar{P}_i)}{|P_i|} \tag{6.9}$$

$$= \frac{1}{k} \sum_{i=1}^{k} \frac{X_i^T(D - A)X_i}{X_i^T X_i} \tag{6.10}$$

$$= \frac{1}{k} \sum_{i=1}^{k} \hat{X}_i^T(D - A)\hat{X}_i, \tag{6.11}$$

where $\hat{X}_i = X_i/(X_i^T X_i)^{1/2}$. A similar approach can be followed to formulate the normalized cut and to obtain a different $\hat{X}_i$. To formulate the summation in both the ratio and normalized cut, we can use the trace of matrix $(tr(\hat{X}) = \sum_{i=1}^{n} \hat{X}_{ii})$. Using the trace, the objectives for both the ratio and normalized cut can be formulated as trace-minimization problems,

$$\min_{\hat{X}} \text{Tr}(\hat{X}^T L \hat{X}), \tag{6.12}$$

where L is the *(normalized) graph Laplacian*, defined as follows:

$$L = \begin{cases} D - A & \text{Ratio Cut Laplacian (\textit{Unnormalized Laplacian})}; \\ I - D^{-1/2} A D^{-1/2} & \text{Normalized Cut Laplacian (\textit{Normalized Laplacian})}. \end{cases}$$

$$\tag{6.13}$$

It has been shown that both ratio cut and normalized cut minimization are NP-hard; therefore, approximation algorithms using relaxations are desired. Spectral clustering is one such relaxation:

$$\min_{\hat{X}} \text{Tr}(\hat{X}^T L \hat{X}), \tag{6.14}$$

$$s.t. \ \hat{X}^T \hat{X} = I_k. \tag{6.15}$$

NORMALIZED AND UNNORMALIZED GRAPH LAPLACIAN

The solution to this problem is the top eigenvectors of L.[1] Given L, the top k eigenvectors corresponding to the smallest eigen values are computed and used as $\hat{X}$, and then k-means is run on $\hat{X}$ to extract communities memberships (X). The first eigenvector is meaningless (why?); hence, the rest of the eigenvectors $(k-1)$ are used as k-means input.

Example 6.3. *Consider the graph in Figure 6.8. We find two communities in this graph using spectral clustering (i.e., $k = 2$). Then, we have*

$$D = diag(2, 2, 4, 4, 4, 4, 4, 3, 1). \tag{6.16}$$

The adjacency matrix A and the unnormalized laplacian L are

$$A = \begin{bmatrix} 0 & 1 & 1 & 0 & 0 & 0 & 0 & 0 & 0 \\ 1 & 0 & 1 & 0 & 0 & 0 & 0 & 0 & 0 \\ 1 & 1 & 0 & 1 & 1 & 0 & 0 & 0 & 0 \\ 0 & 0 & 1 & 0 & 1 & 1 & 1 & 0 & 0 \\ 0 & 0 & 1 & 1 & 0 & 1 & 1 & 0 & 0 \\ 0 & 0 & 0 & 1 & 1 & 0 & 1 & 1 & 0 \\ 0 & 0 & 0 & 1 & 1 & 1 & 0 & 1 & 0 \\ 0 & 0 & 0 & 0 & 0 & 1 & 1 & 0 & 1 \\ 0 & 0 & 0 & 0 & 0 & 0 & 0 & 1 & 0 \end{bmatrix}, \tag{6.17}$$

$$L = D - A = \begin{bmatrix} 2 & -1 & -1 & 0 & 0 & 0 & 0 & 0 & 0 \\ -1 & 2 & -1 & 0 & 0 & 0 & 0 & 0 & 0 \\ -1 & -1 & 4 & -1 & -1 & 0 & 0 & 0 & 0 \\ 0 & 0 & -1 & 4 & -1 & -1 & -1 & 0 & 0 \\ 0 & 0 & -1 & -1 & 4 & -1 & -1 & 0 & 0 \\ 0 & 0 & 0 & -1 & -1 & 4 & -1 & -1 & 0 \\ 0 & 0 & 0 & -1 & -1 & -1 & 4 & -1 & 0 \\ 0 & 0 & 0 & 0 & 0 & -1 & -1 & 3 & -1 \\ 0 & 0 & 0 & 0 & 0 & 0 & 0 & -1 & 1 \end{bmatrix}. \tag{6.18}$$

We aim to find two communities; therefore, we get two eigenvectors corresponding to the two smallest eigenvalues from L:

$$\hat{X} = \begin{matrix} 1 \\ 2 \\ 3 \\ 4 \\ 5 \\ 6 \\ 7 \\ 8 \\ 9 \end{matrix} \begin{bmatrix} 0.33 & -0.46 \\ 0.33 & -0.46 \\ 0.33 & -0.26 \\ 0.33 & \approx 0.01 \\ 0.33 & \approx 0.01 \\ 0.33 & 0.13 \\ 0.33 & 0.13 \\ 0.33 & 0.33 \\ 0.33 & 0.59 \end{bmatrix}. \tag{6.19}$$

As mentioned, the first eigenvector is meaningless, because it assigns all nodes to the same community. The second is used with k-means; based on the vector signs, we get communities {1, 2, 3} and {4, 5, 6, 7, 8, 9}.

Robust Communities

When seeking robust communities, our goal is to find subgraphs robust enough such that removing some edges or nodes does not disconnect the subgraph. A k-vertex connected graph (or k-connected) is an example of such a graph. In this graph, k is the minimum number of nodes that must be removed to disconnect the graph (i.e., there exist at least k independent paths between any pair of nodes). A similar subgraph is the k-edge graph, where at least k edges must be removed to disconnect the graph. An upper-bound analysis on *k-edge connectivity* shows that the minimum degree for any node in the graph should not be less than k (why?). For example, a complete graph of size n is a unique n-connected graph, and a cycle is a 2-connected graph. k-CONNECTED

Modular Communities

Modularity is a measure that defines how likely the community structure found is created at random. Clearly, community structures should be far from random. Consider an undirected graph $G(V, E)$, $|E| = m$ where the degrees are known beforehand, but edges are not. Consider two nodes v_i and v_j, with degrees d_i and d_j, respectively. What is the expected number of edges between these two nodes? Consider node v_i. For any edge going out of v_i randomly, the probability of this edge getting connected to node v_j is $\frac{d_j}{\sum_i d_i} = \frac{d_j}{2m}$. Because the degree for v_i is d_i, we have d_i number of such edges; hence, the expected number of edges between v_i and v_j is $\frac{d_i d_j}{2m}$. So, given a degree distribution, the expected number of edges between any pair of vertices can be computed. Real-world communities are far from random; therefore, the more distant they are from randomly generated communities, the more structure they exhibit. Modularity defines this distance, and modularity maximization tries to maximize this distance. Consider a partitioning of the graph G into k partitions, $P = (P_1, P_2, P_3, \ldots, P_k)$. For partition P_x, this distance can be defined as

MODULARITY

$$\sum_{v_i, v_j \in P_x} A_{ij} - \frac{d_i d_j}{2m}. \qquad (6.20)$$

This distance can be generalized for partitioning P with k partitions,

$$\sum_{x=1}^{k} \sum_{v_i, v_j \in P_x} A_{ij} - \frac{d_i d_j}{2m}. \qquad (6.21)$$

The summation is over all edges (m), and because all edges are counted twice $(A_{ij} = A_{ji})$, the normalized version of this distance is defined as *modularity* [Newman, 2006]:

$$Q = \frac{1}{2m} \left(\sum_{x=1}^{k} \sum_{v_i, v_j \in P_x} A_{ij} - \frac{d_i d_j}{2m} \right). \qquad (6.22)$$

We define the modularity matrix as $B = A - \mathbf{d}\mathbf{d}^T/2m$, where $\mathbf{d} \in \mathbb{R}^{n \times 1}$ is the degree vector for all nodes. Similar to spectral clustering matrix formulation, modularity can be reformulated as

$$Q = \frac{1}{2m} \text{Tr}(X^T B X), \qquad (6.23)$$

where $X \in \mathbb{R}^{n \times k}$ is the indicator (partition membership) function; that is, $X_{ij} = 1$ iff. $v_i \in P_j$. This objective can be maximized such that the best membership function is extracted with respect to modularity. The problem is NP-hard; therefore, we relax X to $\hat{X}$ that has an orthogonal structure $(\hat{X}^T \hat{X} = I_k)$. The optimal $\hat{X}$ can be computed using the top k eigenvectors of B corresponding to the largest positive eigenvalues. Similar to spectral clustering, to find X, we can run k-means on $\hat{X}$. Note that this requires that B has at least k positive eigenvalues.

Dense Communities

Often, we are interested in dense communities, which have sufficiently frequent interactions. These communities are of particular interest in social media where we would like to have enough interactions for analysis to make statistical sense. When we are measuring density in communities, the community may or may not be connected as long as it satisfies the properties required, assuming connectivity is not one such property. Cliques, clubs, and clans are examples of connected dense communities. Here, we focus on subgraphs that have the possibility of being disconnected. Density-based community detection has been extensively discussed in the field of clustering (see Chapter 5, Bibliographic Notes).

The density γ of a graph defines how close a graph is to a clique. In other words, the density γ is the ratio of the number of edges $|E|$ that graph G has over the maximum it can have $\binom{|V|}{2}$: GRAPH DENSITY

$$\gamma = \frac{|E|}{\binom{|V|}{2}}. \tag{6.24}$$

A graph $G = (V, E)$ is γ-dense if $|E| \geq \gamma \binom{|V|}{2}$. Note that a 1-dense graph is a clique. Here, we discuss the interesting scenario of connected dense graphs (i.e., quasi-cliques). A quasi-clique (or γ-clique) is a connected γ-dense graph. Quasi-cliques can be searched for using approaches previously discussed for finding cliques. We can utilize the brute-force clique identification algorithm (Algorithm 6.1) for finding quasi-cliques as well. The only part of the algorithm that needs to be changed is the part where the clique condition is checked (Line 8). This can be replaced with a quasi-clique checking condition. In general, because there is less regularity in quasi-cliques, searching for them becomes harder. Interested readers can refer to the bibliographic notes for faster algorithms. QUASI-CLIQUE

Hierarchical Communities

All previously discussed methods have considered communities at a single level. In reality, it is common to have hierarchies of communities, in which each community can have sub/super communities. Hierarchical clustering deals with this scenario and generates community hierarchies. Initially, n

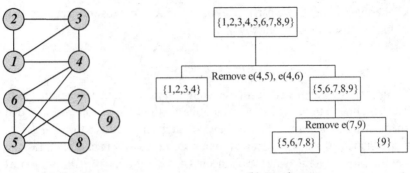

(a) Graph   (b) Dendrogram

Figure 6.9. An Example of Girvan-Newman Algorithm Example: (a) graph and (b) its hierarchical clustering dendrogram based on edge betweenness.

nodes are considered as either 1 or n communities in hierarchical clustering. These communities are gradually merged or split (*agglomerative* or *divisive* hierarchical clustering algorithms), depending on the type of algorithm, until the desired number of communities are reached. A dendrogram is a visual demonstration of how communities are merged or split using hierarchical clustering. The Girvan-Newman [2002] algorithm is specifically designed for finding communities using divisive hierarchical clustering.

The assumption underlying this algorithm is that, if a network has a set of communities and these communities are connected to one another with a few edges, then all shortest paths between members of different communities should pass through these edges. By removing these edges (at times referred to as *weak ties*), we can recover (i.e., disconnect) communities in a network. To find these edges, the Girvan-Newman algorithm uses a measure called *edge betweenness* and removes edges with higher edge betweenness. For an edge e, edge betweenness is defined as the number of shortest paths between node pairs (v_i, v_j) such that the shortest path between v_i and v_j passes through e. For instance, in Figure 6.9(a), edge betweenness for edge $e(1, 2)$ is $6/2 + 1 = 4$, because all the shortest paths from 2 to $\{4, 5, 6, 7, 8, 9\}$ have to either pass $e(1, 2)$ or $e(2, 3)$, and $e(1, 2)$ is the shortest path between 1 and 2. Formally, the Girvan-Newman algorithm is as follows:

EDGE
BETWEENNESS

GIRVAN-
NEWMAN
ALGORITHM

1. Calculate edge betweeness for all edges in the graph.
2. Remove the edge with the highest betweenness.

3. Recalculate betweenness for all edges affected by the edge removal.
4. Repeat until all edges are removed.

Example 6.4. *Consider the graph depicted in Figure 6.9(a). For this graph, the edge-betweenness values are as follows:*

$$
\begin{bmatrix}
 & 1 & 2 & 3 & 4 & 5 & 6 & 7 & 8 & 9 \\
\hline
1 & 0 & 4 & 1 & 9 & 0 & 0 & 0 & 0 & 0 \\
2 & 4 & 0 & 4 & 0 & 0 & 0 & 0 & 0 & 0 \\
3 & 1 & 4 & 0 & 9 & 0 & 0 & 0 & 0 & 0 \\
4 & 9 & 0 & 9 & 0 & 10 & 10 & 0 & 0 & 0 \\
5 & 0 & 0 & 0 & 10 & 0 & 1 & 6 & 3 & 0 \\
6 & 0 & 0 & 0 & 10 & 1 & 0 & 6 & 3 & 0 \\
7 & 0 & 0 & 0 & 0 & 6 & 6 & 0 & 2 & 8 \\
8 & 0 & 0 & 0 & 0 & 3 & 3 & 2 & 0 & 0 \\
9 & 0 & 0 & 0 & 0 & 0 & 0 & 8 & 0 & 0
\end{bmatrix}.
\tag{6.25}
$$

Therefore, by following the algorithm, the first edge that needs to be removed is $e(4, 5)$ (or $e(4, 6)$). By removing $e(4, 5)$, we compute the edge betweenness once again; this time, $e(4, 6)$ has the highest betweenness value: 20. This is because all shortest paths between nodes $\{1,2,3,4\}$ to nodes $\{5,6,7,8,9\}$ must pass $e(4, 6)$; therefore, it has betweenness $4 \times 5 = 20$. By following the first few steps of the algorithm, the dendrogram shown in Figure 6.9(b) and three disconnected communities ($\{1, 2, 3, 4\}$, $\{5, 6, 7, 8\}$, $\{9\}$) can be obtained.

We discussed various community detection algorithms in this section. Figure 6.10 summarizes the two categories of community detection algorithms.

6.2 Community Evolution

Community detection algorithms discussed so far assume that networks are static; that is, their nodes and edges are fixed and do not change over time. In reality, with the rapid growth of social media, networks and their internal communities change over time. Earlier community detection algorithms have to be extended to deal with evolving networks. Before analyzing evolving networks, we need to answer the question, *How do networks evolve?* In this section, we discuss how networks evolve in general and then how

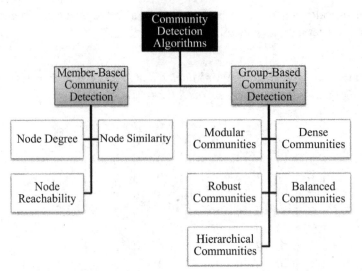

Figure 6.10. Community Detection Algorithms.

communities evolve over time. We also demonstrate how communities can be found in these evolving networks.

6.2.1 How Networks Evolve

Large social networks are highly dynamic, where nodes and links appear or disappear over time. In these evolving networks, many interesting patterns are observed; for instance, when distances (in terms of shortest path distance) between two nodes increase, their probability of getting connected decreases.[2] We discuss three common patterns that are observed in evolving networks: segmentation, densification, and diameter shrinkage.

Network Segmentation

Often, in evolving networks, segmentation takes place, where the large network is decomposed over time into three parts:

1. **Giant Component**: As network connections stabilize, a giant component of nodes is formed, with a large proportion of network nodes and edges falling into this component.
2. **Stars**: These are isolated parts of the network that form star structures. A star is a tree with one internal node and n leaves.

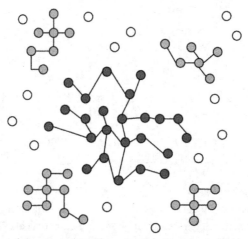

Figure 6.11. Network Segmentation. The network is decomposed into a giant component (dark gray), star components (medium gray), and singletons (light gray).

3. **Singletons**: These are orphan nodes disconnected from all nodes in the network.

Figure 6.11 depicts a segmented network and these three components.

Graph Densification

It is observed in evolving graphs that the density of the graph increases as the network grows. In other words, the number of edges increases faster than the number of nodes. This phenomenon is called *densification*. Let $V(t)$ denote nodes at time t and let $E(t)$ denote edges at time t,

$$|E(t)| \propto |V(t)|^{\alpha}. \tag{6.26}$$

If densification happens, then we have $1 \le \alpha \le 2$. There is linear growth when $\alpha = 1$, and we get clique structures when $\alpha = 2$ (why?). Networks exhibit α values between 1 and 2 when evolving. Figure 6.12 depicts a log-log graph for densification for a physics citation network and a patent citation network. During the evolution process in both networks, the number of edges is recorded as the number of nodes grows. These recordings show that both networks have $\alpha \approx 1.6$ (i.e., the log-log graph of $|E|$ with respect to $|V|$ is a straight line with slope 1.6). This value also implies that when V is given, to realistically model a social network, we should generate $O(|V|^{1.6})$ edges.

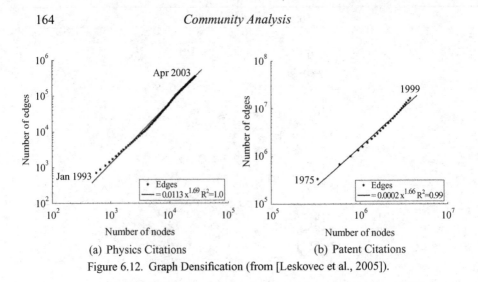

(a) Physics Citations   (b) Patent Citations

Figure 6.12. Graph Densification (from [Leskovec et al., 2005]).

Diameter Shrinkage

Another property observed in large networks is that the network diameter shrinks in time. This property has been observed in random graphs as well (see Chapter 4). Figure 6.13 depicts the diameter shrinkage for the same patent network discussed in Figure 6.12.

In this section we discussed three phenomena that are observed in evolving networks. Communities in evolving networks also evolve. They appear,

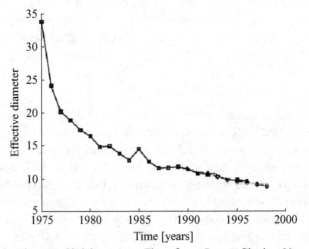

Figure 6.13. Diameter Shrinkage over Time for a Patent Citation Network (from [Leskovec et al., 2005]).

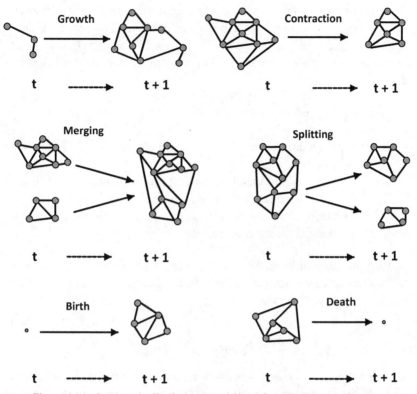

Figure 6.14. Community Evolution (reproduced from [Palla et al., 2007]).

grow, shrink, split, merge, or even dissolve over time. Figure 6.14 depicts different situations that can happen during community evolution.

Both networks and their internal communities evolve over time. Given evolution information (e.g., when edges or nodes are added), how can we study evolving communities? And can we adapt static (nontemporal) methods to use this temporal information? We discuss these questions next.

6.2.2 Community Detection in Evolving Networks

Consider an instant messaging (IM) application in social media. In these IM systems, members become "available" or "offline" frequently. Consider individuals as nodes and messages between them as edges. In this example, we are interested in finding a community of individuals who send messages to one another frequently. Clearly, community detection at any time stamp is not a valid solution because interactions are limited at any point in time.

A valid solution to this problem needs to use temporal information and interactions between users over time. In this section, we present community detection algorithms that incorporate temporal information. To incorporate temporal information, we can extend previously discussed static methods as follows:

1. Take t snapshots of the network, $G_1, G_2, \ldots, G_t$, where G_i is a snapshot at time i.
2. Perform a static community detection algorithm on all snapshots independently.
3. Assign community members based on communities found in all t different time stamps. For instance, we can assign nodes to communities based on voting. In voting, we assign nodes to communities they belong to the most over time.

Unfortunately, this method is unstable in highly dynamic networks because community memberships are always changing. An alternative is to use evolutionary clustering.

Evolutionary Clustering

In evolutionary clustering, it is assumed that communities do not change most of the time; hence, it tries to minimize an objective function that considers both communities at different time stamps (snapshot cost or SC) and how they evolve throughout time (temporal cost or TC). Then, the objective function for evolutionary clustering is defined as a linear combination of the snapshot cost and temporal cost (SC and TC),

$$Cost = \alpha \, SC + (1 - \alpha) \, TC, \tag{6.27}$$

where $0 \leq \alpha \leq 1$. Let us assume that spectral clustering (discussed in Section 6.1.3) is used to find communities at each time stamp. We know that the objective for spectral clustering is $Tr(X^T L X)$ s.t. $X^T X = I_m$, so we will have the objective function at time t as

$$Cost_t = \alpha \, SC + (1 - \alpha) \, TC, \tag{6.28}$$

$$= \alpha \, Tr(X_t^T L X_t) + (1 - \alpha) \, TC, \tag{6.29}$$

where X_t is the community membership matrix at time t. To define TC, we can compute the distance between the community assignments of two snapshots:

$$TC = ||X_t - X_{t-1}||^2. \tag{6.30}$$

Unfortunately, this requires both X_t and X_{t-1} to have the same number of columns (number of communities). Moreover, X_t is not unique and can change by orthogonal transformations;[3] therefore, the distance value $||X_t - X_{t-1}||^2$ can change arbitrarily. To remove the effect of orthogonal transformations and allow different numbers of columns, TC is defined as

$$
\begin{aligned}
TC &= \frac{1}{2}||X_t X_t^T - X_{t-1} X_{t-1}^T||^2, \\
&= \frac{1}{2} Tr\left((X_t X_t^T - X_{t-1} X_{t-1}^T)^T (X_t X_t^T - X_{t-1} X_{t-1}^T)\right), \\
&= \frac{1}{2} Tr\left(X_t X_t^T X_t X_t^T - 2 X_t X_t^T X_{t-1} X_{t-1}^T + X_{t-1} X_{t-1}^T X_{t-1} X_{t-1}^T\right), \\
&= Tr\left(I - X_t X_t^T X_{t-1} X_{t-1}^T\right), \\
&= Tr\left(I - X_t^T X_{t-1} X_{t-1}^T X_t\right), \tag{6.31}
\end{aligned}
$$

where $\frac{1}{2}$ is for mathematical convenience, and $Tr(AB) = Tr(BA)$ is used. Therefore, evolutionary clustering objective can be stated as

$$
\begin{aligned}
Cost_t &= \alpha\, Tr\left(X_t^T L X_t\right) + (1-\alpha)\frac{1}{2}||X_t X_t^T - X_{t-1} X_{t-1}^T||^2, \\
&= \alpha\, Tr\left(X_t^T L X_t\right) + (1-\alpha)\, Tr\left(I - X_t^T X_{t-1} X_{t-1}^T X_t\right), \\
&= \alpha\, Tr\left(X_t^T L X_t\right) + (1-\alpha)\, Tr\left(X_t^T I X_t - X_t^T X_{t-1} X_{t-1}^T X_t\right), \\
&= Tr\left(X_t^T \alpha L X_t\right) + Tr\left(X_t^T (1-\alpha) I X_t - X_t^T (1-\alpha) X_{t-1} X_{t-1}^T X_t\right).
\end{aligned}
\tag{6.32}
$$

Assuming the normalized Laplacian is used in spectral clustering, $L = I - D_t^{-1/2} A_t D_t^{-1/2}$,

$$
\begin{aligned}
Cost_t &= Tr\left(X_t^T \alpha \left(I - D_t^{-1/2} A_t D_t^{-1/2}\right) X_t\right) \\
&\quad + Tr\left(X_t^T (1-\alpha) I X_t - X_t^T (1-\alpha) X_{t-1} X_{t-1}^T X_t\right), \\
&= Tr\left(X_t^T \left(I - \alpha D_t^{-1/2} A_t D_t^{-1/2} - (1-\alpha) X_{t-1} X_{t-1}^T\right) X_t\right), \\
&= Tr(X_t \hat{L} X_t), \tag{6.33}
\end{aligned}
$$

where $\hat{L} = I - \alpha D_t^{-1/2} A_t D_t^{-1/2} - (1-\alpha) X_{t-1} X_{t-1}^T$. Similar to spectral clustering, X_t can be obtained by taking the top eigenvectors of $\hat{L}$.

Community 1   *Community* 2   *Community* 3

Figure 6.15. Commmunity Evaluation Example. Circles represent communities, and items inside the circles represent members. Each item is represented using a symbol, +, ×, or △, that denotes the item's true label.

Note that at time t, we can obtain X_t directly by solving spectral clustering for the laplacian of the graph at time t, but then we are not employing any temporal information. Using evolutionary clustering and the new laplacian $\hat{L}$, we incorporate temporal information into our community detection algorithm and disallow user memberships in communities at time t: X_t to change dramatically from X_{t-1}.

6.3 Community Evaluation

When communities are found, one must evaluate how accurately the detection task has been performed. In terms of evaluating communities, the task is similar to evaluating clustering methods in data mining. Evaluating clustering is a challenge because ground truth may not be available. We consider two scenarios: when ground truth is available and when it is not.

6.3.1 Evaluation with Ground Truth

When ground truth is available, we have at least partial knowledge of what communities should look like. Here, we assume that we are given the correct community (clustering) assignments. We discuss four measures: precision and recall, F-measure, purity, and normalized mutual information (NMI). Consider Figure 6.15, where three communities are found and the points are shown using their true labels.

Precision and Recall

Community detection can be considered a problem of assigning all similar nodes to the same community. In the simplest case, any two similar nodes should be considered members of the same community. Based on our assignments, four cases can occur:

1. True Positive (**TP**) Assignment: when similar members are assigned to the same community. This is a *correct* decision.
2. True Negative (**TN**) Assignment: when dissimilar members are assigned to different communities. This is a *correct* decision.
3. False Negative (**FN**) Assignment: when similar members are assigned to different communities. This is an *incorrect* decision.
4. False Positive (**FP**) Assignment: when dissimilar members are assigned to the same community. This is an *incorrect* decision.

Precision (P) and Recall (R) are defined as follows,

$$P = \frac{TP}{TP + FP},\qquad(6.34)$$

$$R = \frac{TP}{TP + FN}.\qquad(6.35)$$

Precision defines the fraction of pairs that have been correctly assigned to the same community. Recall defines the fraction of pairs that the community detection algorithm assigned to the same community of all the pairs that should have been in the same community.

Example 6.5. *We compute these values for Figure 6.15. For TP, we need to compute the number of pairs with the same label that are in the same community. For instance, for label × and community 1, we have $\binom{5}{2}$ such pairs. Therefore,*

$$TP = \underbrace{\binom{5}{2}}_{\text{Community 1}} + \underbrace{\binom{6}{2}}_{\text{Community 2}} + \underbrace{(\binom{4}{2} + \binom{2}{2})}_{\text{Community 3}} = 32.\qquad(6.36)$$

For FP, we need to compute dissimilar pairs that are in the same community. For instance, for community 1, this is $(5 \times 1 + 5 \times 1 + 1 \times 1)$. Therefore,

$$FP = \underbrace{(5 \times 1 + 5 \times 1 + 1 \times 1)}_{\text{Community 1}} + \underbrace{(6 \times 1)}_{\text{Community 2}} + \underbrace{(4 \times 2)}_{\text{Community 3}} = 25.$$

$$(6.37)$$

FN computes similar members that are in different communities. For instance, for label +, this is $(6 \times 1 + 6 \times 2 + 2 \times 1)$. Similarly,

$$FN = \underbrace{(5 \times 1)}_{\times} + \underbrace{(6 \times 1 + 6 \times 2 + 2 \times 1)}_{+} + \underbrace{(4 \times 1)}_{\triangle} = 29. \qquad (6.38)$$

Finally, TN computes the number of dissimilar pairs in dissimilar communities:

$$TN = \underbrace{(\overbrace{5 \times 6}^{\times,+} + \overbrace{1 \times 1}^{+,\times} + \overbrace{1 \times 6}^{\triangle,+} + \overbrace{1 \times 1}^{\triangle,\times})}_{\text{Communities 1 and 2}}$$

$$+ \underbrace{(\overbrace{5 \times 4}^{\times,\triangle} + \overbrace{5 \times 2}^{\times,+} + \overbrace{1 \times 4}^{+,\triangle} + \overbrace{1 \times 2}^{\triangle,+})}_{\text{Communities 1 and 3}}$$

$$+ \underbrace{(\overbrace{6 \times 4}^{+,\triangle} + \overbrace{1 \times 2}^{\times,+} + \overbrace{1 \times 4}^{\times,\triangle}}_{\text{Communities 2 and 3}} = 104. \qquad (6.39)$$

Hence,

$$P = \frac{32}{32 + 25} = 0.56 \qquad (6.40)$$

$$R = \frac{32}{32 + 29} = 0.52. \qquad (6.41)$$

F-Measure

To consolidate precision and recall into one measure, we can use the harmonic mean of precision and recall:

$$F = 2 \cdot \frac{P \cdot R}{P + R}. \qquad (6.42)$$

Computed for the same example, we get $F = 0.54$.

Purity

In purity, we assume that the majority of a community represents the community. Hence, we use the label of the majority of the community against the label of each member of the community to evaluate the algorithm. For instance, in Figure 6.15, the majority in Community 1 is ×; therefore, we assume majority label × for that community. The purity is then defined as the fraction of instances that have labels equal to their community's majority label. Formally,

$$Purity = \frac{1}{N} \sum_{i=1}^{k} \max_j |C_i \cap L_j|,$$

(6.43)

where k is the number of communities, N is the total number of nodes, L_j is the set of instances with label j in all communities, and C_i is the set of members in community i. In the case of our example, purity is $\frac{5+6+4}{20} = 0.75$.

Normalized Mutual Information

Purity can be easily manipulated to generate high values; consider when nodes represent singleton communities (of size 1) or when we have very large pure communities (ground truth = majority label). In both cases, purity does not make sense because it generates high values.

A more precise measure to solve problems associated with purity is the normalized mutual information (NMI) measure, which originates in information theory. Mutual information (MI) describes the amount of information that two random variables share. In other words, by knowing one of the variables, MI measures the amount of uncertainty reduced regarding the other variable. Consider the case of two independent variables; in this case, the mutual information is zero because knowing one does not help in knowing more information about the other. Mutual information of two variables X and Y is denoted as $I(X, Y)$. We can use mutual information to measure the information one clustering carries regarding the ground truth. It can be calculated using Equation 6.44, where L and H are labels and found communities; n_h and n_l are the number of data points in community h and with label l, respectively; $n_{h,l}$ is the number of nodes in community h and with label l; and n is the number of nodes.

$$MI = I(X, Y) = \sum_{h \in H} \sum_{l \in L} \frac{n_{h,l}}{n} \log \frac{n \cdot n_{h,l}}{n_h n_l}$$

(6.44)

Unfortunately, mutual information is unbounded; however, it is common for measures to have values in range [0,1]. To address this issue, we can normalize mutual information. We provide the following equation, without proof, which will help us normalize mutual information,

$$MI \leq min(H(L), H(H)), \tag{6.45}$$

where $H(\cdot)$ is the entropy function,

$$H(L) = -\sum_{l \in L} \frac{n_l}{n} \log \frac{n_l}{n} \tag{6.46}$$

$$H(H) = -\sum_{h \in H} \frac{n_h}{n} \log \frac{n_h}{n}. \tag{6.47}$$

From Equation 6.45, we have $MI \leq H(L)$ and $MI \leq H(H)$; therefore,

$$(MI)^2 \leq H(H)H(L). \tag{6.48}$$

Equivalently,

$$MI \leq \sqrt{H(H)}\sqrt{H(L)}. \tag{6.49}$$

Equation 6.49 can be used to normalize mutual information. Thus, we introduce the NMI as

$$NMI = \frac{MI}{\sqrt{H(L)}\sqrt{H(H)}}. \tag{6.50}$$

By plugging Equations 6.47, 6.46, and 6.44 into 6.50,

$$NMI = \frac{\sum_{h \in H} \sum_{l \in L} n_{h,l} \log \frac{n \cdot n_{h,l}}{n_h n_l}}{\sqrt{(\sum_{h \in H} n_h \log \frac{n_h}{n})(\sum_{l \in L} n_l \log \frac{n_l}{n})}}. \tag{6.51}$$

An NMI value close to one indicates high similarity between communities found and labels. A value close to zero indicates a long distance between them.

6.3.2 Evaluation without Ground Truth

When no ground truth is available, we can incorporate techniques based on semantics or clustering quality measures to evaluate community detection algorithms.

(a) U.S . Constitution   (b) Sports

Figure 6.16. Tag Clouds for Two Communities.

Evaluation with Semantics

A simple way of analyzing detected communities is to analyze other attributes (posts, profile information, content generated, etc.) of community members to see if there is a coherency among community members. The coherency is often checked via human subjects. For example, the Amazon Mechanical Turk platform[4] allows defining this task on its platform for human workers and hiring individuals from all around the globe to perform tasks such as community evaluation. To help analyze these communities, one can use word frequencies. By generating a list of frequent keywords for each community, human subjects determine whether these keywords represent a coherent topic. A more focused and single-topic set of keywords represents a coherent community. Tag clouds are one way of demonstrating these topics. Figure 6.16 depicts two coherent tag clouds for a community related to the U.S. Constitution and another for sports. Larger words in these tag clouds represent higher frequency of use.

Evaluation Using Clustering Quality Measures

When experts are not available, an alternative is to use clustering quality measures. This approach is commonly used when two or more community detection algorithms are available. Each algorithm is run on the target network, and the quality measure is computed for the identified communities. The algorithm that yields a more desirable quality measure value is considered a better algorithm. SSE (sum of squared errors) and inter-cluster distance are some of the quality measures. For other measures refer to Chapter 5.

We can also follow this approach for evaluating a single community detection algorithm; however, we must ensure that the clustering quality measure used to evaluate community detection is different from the measure used to find communities. For instance, when using node similarity to group individuals, a measure other than node similarity should be used to evaluate the effectiveness of community detection.

6.4 Summary

In this chapter, we discussed community analysis in social media, answering three general questions: (1) how can we detect communities, (2) how do communities evolve and how can we study evolving communities, and (3) how can we evaluate detected communities? We started with a description of communities and how they are formed. Communities in social media are either explicit (emic) or implicit (etic). Community detection finds implicit communities in social media.

We reviewed member-based and group-based community detection algorithms. In member-based community detection, members can be grouped based on their degree, reachability, and similarity. For example, when using degrees, cliques are often considered as communities. Brute-force clique identification is used to identify cliques. In practice, due to the computational complexity of clique identifications, cliques are either relaxed or used as seeds of communities. k-Plex is an example of relaxed cliques, and the clique percolation algorithm is an example of methods that use cliques as community seeds. When performing member-based community detection based on reachability, three frequently used subgraphs are the k-clique, k-club, and k-clan. Finally, in member-based community detection based on node similarity, methods such as Jaccard and Cosine similarity help compute node similarity. In group-based community detection, we described methods that find balanced, robust, modular, dense, or hierarchical communities. When finding balanced communities, one can employ spectral clustering. Spectral clustering provides a relaxed solution to the normalized cut and ratio cut in graphs. For finding robust communities, we search for subgraphs that are hard to disconnect. k-edge and k-vertex graphs are two examples of these robust subgraphs. To find modular communities, one can use modularity maximization and for dense communities, we discussed quasi-cliques. Finally, we provided hierarchical clustering as a solution to finding hierarchical communities, with the Girvan-Newman algorithm as an example.

In community evolution, we discussed when networks and, on a lower level, communities evolve. We also discussed how commmunities can be detected in evolving networks using evolutionary clustering. Finally, we presented how communities are evaluated when ground truth exists and when it does not.

6.5 Bibliographic Notes

A general survey of community detection in social media can be found in [Fortunato, 2009] and a review of heterogeneous community detection in [Tang and Liu, 2010]. In related fields, [Berkhin, 2006; Xu et al., 2005; Jain et al., 1999] provide surveys of clustering algorithms and [Wasserman and Faust, 1994] provides a sociological perspective. Comparative analysis of community detection algorithms can be found in [Lancichinetti and Fortunato, 2009] and [Leskovec et al., 2010]. The description of explicit communities in this chapter is due to Kadushin [2012].

For member-based algorithms based on node degree, refer to [Kumar et al., 1999], which provides a systematic approach to finding clique-based communities with pruning. In algorithms based on node reachability, one can find communities by finding connected components in the network. For more information on finding connected components of a graph refer to [Hopcroft and Tarjan, 1971]. In node similarity, we discussed structural equivalence, similarity measures, and regular equivalence. More information on structural equivalence can be found in [Lorrain and White, 1971; Leicht et al., 2005], on Jaccard similarity in [Jaccard, 1901], and on regular equivalence in [Stephen and Martin, 1993].

In group-based methods that find balanced communities, we are often interested in solving the max-flow min-cut theorem. Linear programming and Ford-Fulkerson [Cormen et al., 2009], Edmonds-Karp [Edmonds and Karp, 1972], and Push-Relabel [Goldberg and Tarjan, 1988] methods are some established techniques for solving the max-flow min-cut problem. We discussed quasi-cliques that help find dense communities. Finding the maximum quasi-clique is discussed in [Pattillo et al., 2012]. A well-known greedy algorithm for finding quasi-cliques is introduced by [Abello et al., 2002]. In their approach a local search with a pruning strategy is performed on the graph to enhance the speed of quasi-clique detection. They define a peel strategy, in which vertices that have some degree k along with their incident edges are recursively removed. There are a variety of algorithms to find dense subgraphs, such as the one discussed in [Gibson et al., 2005] where the authors propose an algorithm that recursively fingerprints the graph (shingling algorithm) and creates dense subgraphs. In group-based methods that find hierarchical communities, we described hierarchical clustering. Hierarchical clustering algorithms are usually variants of single link, average link, or complete link algorithms [Jain and Dubes, 1999]. In hierarchical clustering, COBWEB [Fisher, 1987] and CHAMELEON [Karypis et al., 1999] are two well-known algorithms.

In group-based community detection, latent space models [Handcock et al., 2007; Hoff et al., 2002] are also very popular, but are not discussed in this chapter. In addition to the topics discussed in this chapter, community detection can also be performed for networks with multiple types of interaction (edges) [Tang and Liu, 2009; Tang et al., 2012]. We also restricted our discussion to community detection algorithms that use graph information. One can also perform community detection based on the content that individuals share on social media. For instance, using tagging relations (i.e., individuals who shared the same tag) [Wang et al., 2010], instead of connections between users, one can discover overlapping communities, which provides a natural summarization of the interests of the identified communities.

In network evolution analysis, network segmentation is discussed in [Kumar et al., 2010]. Segment-based clustering [Sun et al., 2007] is another method not covered in this chapter.

NMI was first introduced in [Strehl et al., 2002] and in terms of clustering quality measures, the Davies-Bouldin [Davies and Bouldin, 1979] measure, Rand index [Rand, 1971], C-index [Dunn, 1974], Silhouette index [Rousseeuw, 1987], and Goodman-Kruskal index [Goodman and Kruskal, 1954] can be used.

6.6 Exercises

1. Provide an example to illustrate how community detection can be subjective.

Community Detection

2. Given a complete graph K_n, how many nodes will the clique percolation method generate for the clique graph for value k? How many edges will it generate?

3. Find all k-cliques, k-clubs, and k-clans in a complete graph of size 4.

4. For a complete graph of size n, is it m-connected? What possible values can m take?

5. Why is the smallest eigenvector meaningless when using an unnormalized laplacian matrix?

6. Modularity can be defined as

$$Q = \frac{1}{2m} \sum_{ij} \left[A_{ij} - \frac{d_i d_j}{2m} \right] \delta(c_i, c_j), \qquad (6.52)$$

where c_i and c_j are the communities for v_i and v_j, respectively.

$\delta(c_i, c_j)$ (Kronecker delta) is 1 when v_i and v_j both belong to the same community ($c_i = c_j$), and 0 otherwise.

• What is the range $[\alpha_1, \alpha_2]$ for Q values? Provide examples for both extreme values of the range and cases where modularity becomes zero.
• What are the limitations for modularity? Provide an example where modularity maximization does not seem reasonable.
• Find three communities in Figure 6.8 by performing modularity maximization.

7. For Figure 6.8:

• Compute Jaccard and Cosine similarity between nodes v_4 and v_8, assuming that the neighborhood of a node excludes the node itself.
• Compute Jaccard and Cosine similarity when the node is included in the neighborhood.

Community Evolution

8. What is the upper bound on densification factor α? Explain.

Community Evaluation

9. Normalized mutual information (NMI) is used to evaluate community detection results when the actual communities (labels) are known beforehand.

• What are the maximum and minimum values for the NMI? Provide details.
• Explain how NMI works (describe the intuition behind it).

10. Compute NMI for Figure 6.15.

11. Why is high precision not enough? Provide an example to show that both precision and recall are important.

12. Discuss situations where purity does not make sense.

13. Compute the following for Figure 6.17:

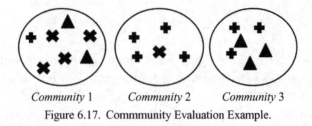

Community 1   Community 2   Community 3

Figure 6.17. Commmunity Evaluation Example.

- precision and recall
- F-measure
- NMI
- purity

7

Information Diffusion in Social Media

In February 2013, during the third quarter of Super Bowl XLVII, a power outage stopped the game for 34 minutes. Oreo, a sandwich cookie company, tweeted during the outage: "Power out? No Problem, You can still dunk it in the dark." The tweet caught on almost immediately, reaching nearly 15,000 retweets and 20,000 likes on Facebook in less than two days. A simple tweet diffused into a large population of individuals. It helped the company gain fame with minimum cost in an environment where companies spent as much as $4 million to run a 30-second ad. This is an example of *information diffusion*.

Information diffusion is a field encompassing techniques from a plethora of sciences. In this chapter, we discuss methods from fields such as sociology, epidemiology, and ethnography, which can help social media mining. Our focus is on techniques that can model information diffusion.

Societies provide means for individuals to exchange information through various channels. For instance, people share knowledge with their immediate network (friends) or broadcast it via public media (TV, newspapers, etc.) throughout the society. Given this flow of information, different research fields have disparate views of what is an information diffusion process. We define information diffusion as the *process by which a piece of information (knowledge) is spread and reaches individuals* through interactions. The diffusion process involves the following three elements:

1. **Sender(s).** A sender or a small set of senders initiate the information diffusion process.
2. **Receiver(s).** A receiver or a set of receivers receive diffused information. Commonly, the set of receivers is much larger than the set of senders and can overlap with the set of senders.
3. **Medium.** This is the medium through which the diffusion takes place. For example, when a rumor is spreading, the medium can be the personal communication between individuals.

179

This definition can be generalized to other domains. In a disease-spreading process, the disease is the analog to the information, and infection can be considered a diffusing process. The medium in this case is the air shared by the infecter and the infectee. An information diffusion can be interrupted. We define the process of interfering with information diffusion INTERVENTION by expediting, delaying, or even stopping diffusion as *intervention*.

Individuals in online social networks are situated in a network where they interact with others. Although this network is at times unavailable or unobservable, the information diffusion process takes place in it. Individuals facilitate information diffusion by making individual decisions that allow information to flow. For instance, when a rumor is spreading, individuals decide if they are interested in spreading it to their neighbors. They can make this decision either dependently (i.e., depending on the information they receive from others) or independently. When they make dependent decisions, it is important to gauge the level of dependence that individuals have on others. It could be *local dependence*, where an individual's LOCAL AND decision is dependent on all of his or her immediate neighbors (friends) GLOBAL or *global dependence*, where all individuals in the network are observed DEPENDENCE before making decisions.

In this chapter, we present in detail four general types of information diffusion: *herd behavior*, *information cascades*, *diffusion of innovation*, and *epidemics*.

Herd behavior takes place when individuals observe the actions of *all* others and act in an aligned form with them. An information cascade describes the process of diffusion when individuals merely observe their immediate neighbors. In information cascades and herd behavior, the network of individuals is observable; however, in herding, individuals decide based on global information (global dependence); whereas, in information cascades, decisions are made based on knowledge of immediate neighbors (local dependence).

Diffusion of innovations provides a bird's-eye view of how an innovation (e.g., a product, music video, or fad) spreads through a population. It assumes that interactions among individuals are unobservable and that the sole available information is the rate at which products are being adopted throughout a certain period of time. This information is particularly interesting for companies performing market research, where the sole available information is the rate at which their products are being bought. These companies have no access to interactions among individuals. Epidemic models are similar to diffusion of innovations models, with the difference that the innovation's analog is a pathogen and adoption is replaced by infection. Another difference is that in epidemic models, individuals do not decide

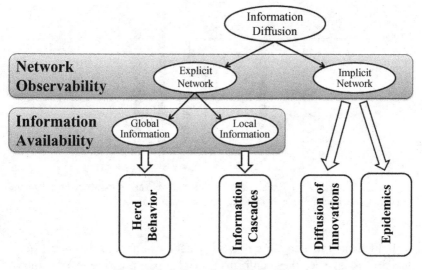

Figure 7.1. Information Diffusion Types.

whether to become infected or not and infection is considered a random natural process, as long as the individual is exposed to the pathogen. Figure 7.1 summarizes our discussion by providing a decision tree of the information diffusion types.

7.1 Herd Behavior

Consider people participating in an online auction. Individuals are connected via the auction's site where they cannot only observe the bidding behaviors of others but can also often view profiles of others to get a feel for their reputation and expertise. Individuals often participate actively in online auctions, even bidding on items that might otherwise be considered unpopular. This is because they trust others and assume that the high number of bids that the item has received is a strong signal of its value. In this case, *herd behavior* has taken place.

Herd behavior, a term first coined by British surgeon Wilfred Trotter [1916], describes when a group of individuals performs actions that are aligned without previous planning. It has been observed in flocks, herds of animals, and in humans during sporting events, demonstrations, and religious gatherings, to name a few examples. In general, any herd behavior requires two components:

1. connections between individuals
2. a method to transfer behavior among individuals or to observe their behavior

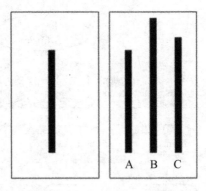

Figure 7.2. Solomon Asch Experiment. Participants were asked to match the line on the left card to the line on the right card that has the exact same length.

Individuals can also make decisions that are aligned with others (mindless decisions) when they conform to social or peer pressure. A well-known example is the set of experiments performed by Solomon Asch during the 1950s [Asch, 1956]. In one experiment, he asked groups of students to participate in a vision test where they were shown two cards (Figure 7.2), one with a single line segment and one with three lines, and told to match the line segments with the same length.

Each participant was put into a group where all the other group members were actually collaborators with Asch, although they were introduced as participants to the subject. Asch found that in control groups with no pressure to conform, in which the collaborators gave the correct answer, only 3% of the subjects provided an incorrect answer. However, when participants were surrounded by individuals providing an incorrect answer, up to 32% of the responses were incorrect.

In contrast to this experiment, we refer to the process in which individuals *consciously* make decisions aligned with others by observing the decisions of other individuals as *herding* or *herd behavior*. In theory, there is no need to have a network of people. In practice, there is a network, and this network is close to a complete graph, where nodes can observe at least most other nodes. Consider this example of herd behavior.

Example 7.1. *Diners Example [Banerjee, 1992]. Assume you are visiting a metropolitan area that you are not familiar with. Planning for dinner, you find restaurant A with excellent reviews online and decide to go there. When arriving at A, you see that A is almost empty and that restaurant B, which is next door and serves the same cuisine, is almost full. Deciding to* *go to* **B***, based on the belief that other diners have also had the chance of going to* **A***, is an example of herd behavior.*

In this example, when **B** is getting more and more crowded, herding is taking place. Herding happens because we consider *crowd intelligence* trustworthy. We assume that there must be private information not known to us, but known to the crowd, that resulted in the crowd preferring restaurant B over A. In other words, we assume that, given this private information, we would have also chosen B over A.

In general, when designing a herding experiment, the following four conditions need to be satisfied:

1. There needs to be a decision made. In this example, the decision involves going to a restaurant.
2. Decisions need to be in sequential order.
3. Decisions are not mindless, and people have private information that helps them decide.
4. No message passing is possible. Individuals do not know the private information of others, but can infer what others know from what they observe from their behavior.

Anderson and Holt [1996, 1997] designed an experiment satisfying these four conditions, in which students guess whether an urn containing red and blue marbles is majority red or majority blue. Each student had access to the guesses of students beforehand. Anderson and Holt observed a herd behavior where students reached a consensus regarding the majority color over time. It has been shown [Easley and Kleinberg, 2010] that Bayesian modeling is an effective technique for demonstrating why this herd behavior occurs. Simply put, computing conditional probabilities and selecting the most probable majority color result in herding over time. We detail this experiment and how conditional probabilities can explain why herding takes place next.

7.1.1 Bayesian Modeling of Herd Behavior

In this section, we show how Bayesian modeling can be used to explain herd behavior by describing in detail the urn experiment devised by Anderson and Holt [1996, 1997]. In front of a large class of students, there is an urn that has three marbles in it. These marbles are either blue (B) or red (R), and we are guaranteed to have at least one of each color. So, the urn is either majority blue (B,B,R) or majority red (R,R,B). We assume the probability of being either majority blue or majority red is 50%. During the experiment, each student comes to the urn, picks one marble, and checks its color in private. The student predicts majority blue or red, writes the prediction on the blackboard (which was blank initially), and puts the marble back in the urn. Other students cannot see the color of the marble taken out, but can see the predictions made by the students regarding the majority color and written on the blackboard. Let the BOARD variable denote the sequence of predictions written on the blackboard. So, before the first student, it is

BOARD: {}

We start with the first student. If the marble selected is red, the prediction will be majority red; if blue, it will be majority blue. Assuming it was blue, on the board we have

BOARD: {B}

The second student can pick a blue or a red marble. If blue, he also predicts majority blue because he knows that the previous student must have picked blue. If red, he knows that because he has picked red and the first student has picked blue, he can randomly assume majority red or blue. So, after the second student we either have

BOARD: {B,B} or BOARD: {B,R}

Assume we end up with BOARD: {B, B}. In this case, if the third student takes out a red ball, the conditional probability is higher for majority blue, although she observed a red marble. Hence, a herd behavior takes place, and on the board, we will have BOARD: {B,B,B}. From this student and onward, independent of what is being observed, everyone will predict majority blue. Let us demonstrate why this happens based on conditional probabilities and our problem setting. In our problem, we know that the first student predicts majority blue if $P(\text{majority blue}|student's\ obervation) > 1/2$ and majority red otherwise. We also know from the experiments setup that

$$P(\text{majority blue}) = P(\text{majority red}) = 1/2, \qquad (7.1)$$

$$P(\text{blue}|\text{majority blue}) = P(\text{red}|\text{majority red}) = 2/3. \qquad (7.2)$$

Let us assume that the first student observes blue; then,

$$P(\text{majority blue}|\text{blue}) = \frac{P(\text{blue}|\text{majority blue})P(\text{majority blue})}{P(\text{blue})} \quad (7.3)$$

$$P(\text{blue}) = P(\text{blue}|\text{majority blue})P(\text{majority blue})$$

$$+ P(\text{blue}|\text{majority red})P(\text{majority red}) \quad (7.4)$$

$$= 2/3 \times 1/2 + 1/3 \times 1/2 = 1/2. \quad (7.5)$$

Therefore, $P(\text{majority blue}|\text{blue}) = \frac{2/3 \times 1/2}{1/2} = 2/3$. So, if the first student picks blue, she will predict majority blue, and if she picks red, she will predict majority red. Assuming the first student picks blue, the same argument holds for the second student; if blue is picked, he will also predict majority blue. Now, in the case of the third student, assuming she has picked red, and having BOARD: {B,B} on the blackboard, then,

$$P(\text{majority blue}|\text{blue, blue, red}) = \frac{P(\text{blue,blue,red}|\text{majority blue})}{P(\text{blue,blue,red})}$$

$$\times P(\text{majority blue}) \quad (7.6)$$

$$P(\text{blue, blue, red}|\text{majority blue}) = 2/3 \times 2/3 \times 1/3 = 4/27 \quad (7.7)$$

$$P(\text{blue, blue, red}) = P(\text{blue, blue, red}|\text{majority blue})$$

$$\times P(\text{majority blue})$$

$$+ P(\text{blue, blue, red}|\text{majority red})$$

$$\times P(\text{majority red}) \quad (7.8)$$

$$= (2/3 \times 2/3 \times 1/3) \times 1/2$$

$$+ (1/3 \times 1/3 \times 2/3) \times 1/2 = 1/9.$$

Therefore, $P(\text{majority blue}|\textit{blue,blue,red}) = \frac{4/27 \times 1/2}{1/9} = 2/3$. So, the third student predicts majority blue even though she picks red. Any student after the third student also predicts majority blue regardless of what is being picked because the conditional remains above 1/2. Note that the urn can in fact be majority red. For instance, when *blue, blue, red* is picked, there is a $1 - ^2/_3 = ^1/_3$ chance that it is majority red; however, due to herding, the prediction could become incorrect. Figure 7.3 depicts the herding process. In the figure, rectangles represent the board status, and edge values represent the observations. Dashed arrows depict transitions between states that contain the same statistical information that is available to the students.

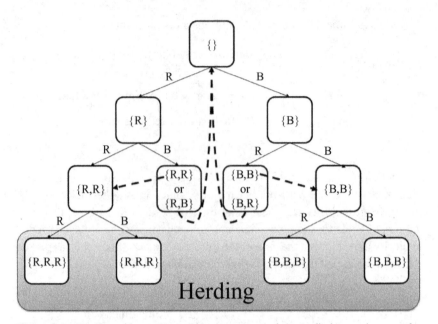

Figure 7.3. Urn Experiment. Rectangles represent student predictions written on the blackboard, and edge values represent what the students observe. Rectangles are filled with the most likely majority, computed from conditional probabilities.

7.1.2 Intervention

As herding converges to a consensus over time, it is interesting how one can intervene with this process. In general, intervention is possible by providing private information to individuals that was not previously available. Consider an urn experiment where individuals decide on majority red over time. Either (1) a private message to individuals informing them that the urn is majority blue or (2) writing the observations next to predictions on the board stops the herding and changes decisions.

7.2 Information Cascades

In social media, individuals commonly repost content posted by others in the network. This content is often received via immediate neighbors (friends). An *information cascade* occurs as information propagates through friends.

Formally, an information cascade is defined as a piece of information or decision being cascaded among a set of individuals, where (1) individuals are connected by a network and (2) individuals are only observing decisions of their immediate neighbors (friends). Therefore, cascade users have less information available to them compared to herding users, where almost all information about decisions are available.

There are many approaches to modeling information cascades. Next, we introduce a basic model that can help explain information cascades.

7.2.1 Independent Cascade Model (ICM)

In this section, we discuss the independent cascade model (ICM) [Kempe et al., 2003] that can be utilized to model information cascades. Variants of this model have been discussed in the literature. Here, we discuss the one detailed by Kempe et al. [2003]. Interested readers can refer to the bibliographic notes for further references. Underlying assumptions for this model include the following:

- The network is represented using a directed graph. Nodes are actors and edges depict the communication channels between them. A node can only influence nodes that it is connected to.
- Decisions are binary – nodes can be either *active* or *inactive*. An active nodes means that the node decided to adopt the behavior, innovation, or decision.
- A node, once activated, can activate its neighboring nodes.
- Activation is a *progressive* process, where nodes change from inactive to active, but not vice versa.[1]

Considering nodes that are active as senders and nodes that are being activated as receivers, in the independent cascade model (ICM) senders activate receivers. Therefore, ICM is denoted as a *sender-centric* model. In this model, the node that becomes active at time t has, in the next time step $t + 1$, one chance of activating each of its neighbors. Let v be an active node at time t. Then, for any neighbor w, there is a probability $p_{v,w}$ that node w gets activated at $t + 1$. A node v that has been activated at time t has a single chance of activating its neighbor w and that activation can only happen at $t + 1$. We start with a set of active nodes and we continue until no further activation is possible. Algorithm 7.1 details the process of the ICM model.

SENDER-CENTRIC MODEL

Example 7.2. *Consider the network in Figure 7.4 as an example. The network is undirected; therefore, we assume $p_{v,w} = p_{w,v}$. Since it is*

Algorithm 7.1 Independent Cascade Model (ICM)

Require: Diffusion graph $G(V, E)$, set of initial activated nodes A_0, activation probabilities $p_{v,w}$

1: **return** Final set of activated nodes A_∞
2: $i = 0$;
3: **while** $A_i \neq \{\}$ **do**
4:
5: $\quad i = i + 1$;
6: $\quad A_i = \{\}$;
7: $\quad$ **for all** $v \in A_{i-1}$ **do**
8: $\quad\quad$ **for all** w neighbor of v, $w \notin \cup_{j=0}^i A_j$ **do**
9: $\quad\quad\quad$ rand = generate a random number in $[0,1]$;
10: $\quad\quad\quad$ **if** rand $< p_{v,w}$ **then**
11: $\quad\quad\quad\quad$ activate w;
12: $\quad\quad\quad\quad$ $A_i = A_i \cup \{w\}$;
13: $\quad\quad\quad$ **end if**
14: $\quad\quad$ **end for**
15: $\quad$ **end for**
16: **end while**
17: $A_\infty = \cup_{j=0}^i A_j$;
18: Return A_∞;

---

undirected, for any two vertices connected via an edge, there is an equal chance of one activating the other. Consider the network in step 1. The values on the edges denote $p_{v,w}$'s. The ICM procedure starts with a set of nodes activated. In our case, it is node v_1. Each activated node gets one chance of activating its neighbors. The activated node generates a random number for each neighbor. If the random number is less than the respective $p_{v,w}$ of the neighbor (see Algorithm 7.1, lines 9–11), the neighbor gets activated. The random numbers generated are shown in Figure 7.4 in the form of inequalities, where the left-hand side is the random number generated and the right-hand side is the $p_{v,w}$. As depicted, by following the procedure after five steps, five nodes get activated and the ICM procedure converges.

Clearly, the ICM characterizes an information diffusion process.[2] It is sender-centered, and once a node is activated, it aims to activate all its neighboring nodes. Node activation in ICM is a probabilistic process. Thus, we might get different results for different runs.

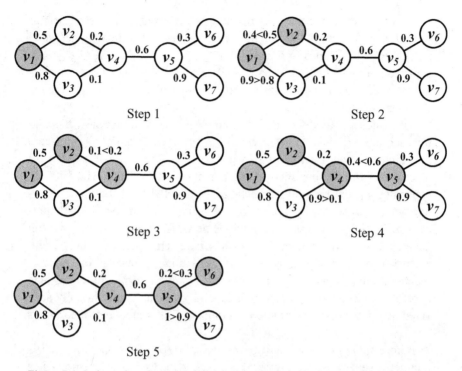

Figure 7.4. Independent Cascade Model (ICM) Simulation. The numbers on the edges represent the weights $p_{v,w}$. When there is an inequality, the activation condition is checked. The left number denotes the random number generated, and the right number denotes weight $p_{v,w}$.

One interesting question when dealing with the ICM model is that given a network, how to activate a small set of nodes initially such that the final number of activated nodes in the network is maximized. We discuss this next.

7.2.2 Maximizing the Spread of Cascades

Consider a network of users and a company that is marketing a product. The company is trying to advertise its product in the network. The company has a limited budget; therefore, not all users can be targeted. However, when users find the product interesting, they can talk with their friends (immediate neighbors) and market the product. Their neighbors, in turn, will talk about it with their neighbors, and as this process progresses, the news about the product is spread to a population of nodes in the network. The company plans on selecting a set of initial users such that the size of the final population talking about the product is *maximized*.

Formally, let S denote a set of initially activated nodes (seed set) in ICM. Let $f(S)$ denote the number of nodes that get ultimately activated in the network if nodes in S are initially activated. For our ICM example depicted in Figure 7.4, $|S| = 1$ and $f(S) = 5$. Given a budget k, our goal is to find a set S such that its size is equal to our budget $|S| = k$ and $f(S)$ is maximized.

Since the activations in ICM depend on the random number generated for each node (see line 9, Algorithm 7.1), it is challenging to determine the number of nodes that ultimately get activated $f(S)$ for a given set S. In other words, the number of ultimately activated individuals can be different depending on the random numbers generated. ICM can be made deterministic (nonrandom) by generating these random numbers in the beginning of the ICM process for the whole network. In other words, we can generate a random number $r_{u,w}$ for any connected pair of nodes. Then, whenever node v has a chance of activating u, instead of generating the random number, it can compare $r_{u,w}$ with $p_{v,w}$. Following this approach, ICM becomes deterministic, and given any set of initially activated nodes S, we can compute the number of ultimately activated nodes $f(S)$.

Before finding S, we detail properties of $f(S)$. The function $f(S)$ is non-negative because for any set of nodes S, in the worst case, no node gets activated. It is also monotone:

$$f(S \cup \{v\}) \geq f(S). \tag{7.9}$$

This is because when a node is added to the set of initially activated nodes, it either increases the number of ultimately activated nodes or keeps them the same. Finally, $f(S)$ is submodular. A set function f is submodular if for any finite set N, SUBMODULAR FUNCTION

$$\forall S \subset T \subset N, \forall v \in N \setminus T, f(S \cup \{v\}) - f(S) \geq f(T \cup \{v\}) - f(T). \tag{7.10}$$

The proof that function f is submodular is beyond the scope of this book, but interested readers are referred to [Kempe et al., 2003] for the proof. So, f is non-negative, monotone, and submodular. Unfortunately, for a submodular non-negative monotone function f, finding a k element set S such that $f(S)$ is maximized is an NP-hard problem [Kempe et al., 2003]. In other words, we know no efficient algorithm for finding this set.[3] Often, when a computationally challenging problem is at hand, approximation algorithms come in handy. In particular, the following theorem helps us approximate S.

Algorithm 7.2 Maximizing the spread of cascades – Greedy algorithm

Require: Diffusion graph $G(V, E)$, budget k
 1: **return** Seed set S (set of initially activated nodes)
 2: $i = 0$;
 3: $S = \{\}$;
 4: **while** $i \neq k$ **do**
 5:    $v = \arg\max_{v \in V \setminus S} f(S \cup \{v\})$;
       or equivalently $\arg\max_{v \in V \setminus S} f(S \cup \{v\}) - f(s)$
 6:    $S = S \cup \{v\}$;
 7:    $i = i + 1$;
 8: **end while**
 9: Return S;

Theorem 7.1. *[Kempe et al., 2003] Let f be a (1) non-negative, (2) mono-tone, and (3) submodular set function. Construct k-element set S, each time by adding node v, such that $f(S \cup \{v\})$ (or equivalently, $f(S \cup \{v\}) - f(s)$) is maximized. Let S^{Optimal} be the k-element set such that f is maximized. Then $f(S) \geq (1 - \frac{1}{e})f(S^{\text{Optimal}})$.*

This theorem states that by constructing the set S greedily one can get at least a $(1 - 1/e) \approx 63\%$ approximation of the optimal value. Algorithm 7.2 details this greedy approach. The algorithm starts with an empty set S and adds node v_1, which ultimately activates most other nodes if activated. For-mally, v_1 is selected such that $f(\{v_1\})$ is the maximum. The algorithm then selects the second node v_2 such that $f(\{v_1, v_2\})$ is maximized. The process is continued until the kth node v_k is selected. Following this algorithm, we find an approximately reasonable solution for the problem of cascade maximization.

Example 7.3. *For the following graph, assume that node i activates node j when $|i - j| \equiv 2$ (mod 3). Solve cascade maximization for $k = 2$.*

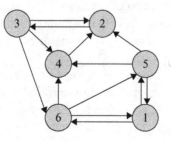

To find the first node v, we compute $f(\{v\})$ for all v. We start with node 1. At time 0, node 1 can only activate node 6, because

$$|1 - 6| \equiv 2 \ (mod \ 3), \tag{7.11}$$

$$|1 - 5| \not\equiv 2 \ (mod \ 3). \tag{7.12}$$

At time 1, node 1 can no longer activate others, but node 6 is active and can activate others. Node 6 has outgoing edges to nodes 4 and 5. From 4 and 5, node 6 can only activate 4:

$$|6 - 4| \equiv 2 \ (mod \ 3) \tag{7.13}$$

$$|6 - 5| \not\equiv 2 \ (mod \ 3). \tag{7.14}$$

At time 2, node 4 is activated. It has a single out-link to node 2 and since $|4 - 2| \equiv 2 \ (mod \ 3)$, 2 is activated. Node 2 cannot activate other nodes; therefore, $f(\{1\}) = 4$. Similarly, we find that $f(\{2\}) = 1$, $f(\{3\}) = 1$, $f(\{4\}) = 2$, $f(\{5\}) = 1$, and $f(\{6\}) = 4$. So, 1 or 6 can be chosen for our first node. Let us choose 6. If 6 is initially activated, nodes 1, 2, 4, and 6 will become activated at the end. Now, from the set $\{1, 2, 3, 4, 5, 6\} \setminus \{1, 2, 4, 6\} = \{3, 5\}$, we need to select one more node. This is because in the setting for this example, $f(\{6, 1\}) = f(\{6, 2\}) = f(\{6, 4\}) = f(\{6\}) = 4$. In general, one needs to compute $f(S \cup \{v\})$ for all $v \in V \setminus S$ (see Algorithm 7.2, line 5). We have $f(\{6, 3\}) = f(\{6, 5\}) = 5$, so we can select one node randomly. We choose 3. So, $S = \{6, 3\}$ and $f(S) = 5$.

7.2.3 Intervention

Consider a false rumor spreading in social media. This is an example where we are interested in stopping an information cascade in social media. Intervention in the independent cascade model can be achieved using three methods:

1. By limiting the number of out-links of the sender node and potentially reducing the chance of activating others. Note that when the sender node is not connected to others via directed edges, no one will get activated by the sender.
2. By limiting the number of in-links of receiver nodes and therefore reducing their chance of getting activated by others.
3. By decreasing the activation probability of a node ($p_{v,w}$) and therefore reducing the chance of activating others.

7.3 Diffusion of Innovations

Diffusion of innovations is a phenomenon observed regularly in social media. A music video going viral or a piece of news being retweeted many times are examples of innovations diffusing across social networks. As defined by Rogers [2003], an innovation is "an idea, practice, or object that is perceived as new by an individual or other unit of adoption." Innovations are created regularly; however, not all innovations spread through populations. The theory of diffusion of innovations aims to answer why and how these innovations spread. It also describes the reasons behind the diffusion process, the individuals involved, and the rate at which ideas spread. In this section, we review characteristics of innovations that are likely to be diffused through populations and detail well-known models in the diffusion of innovations. Finally, we provide mathematical models that can model the process of diffusion of innovations and describe how we can intervene with these models.

7.3.1 Innovation Characteristics

For an innovation to be adopted, the individual adopting it (adopter) and the innovation must have certain qualities.

Innovations must be highly *observable*, should have a *relative advantage* over current practices, should be *compatible* with the sociocultural paradigm to which it is being presented, should be observable under various trials (*trialability*), and should not be highly *complex*.

In terms of individual characteristics, many researchers [Rogers, 2003; Hirschman, 1980] claim that the adopter should adopt the innovation earlier than other members of his or her social circle (*innovativeness*).

7.3.2 Diffusion of Innovations Models

Some of the earliest models for diffusion of innovations were provided by Gabriel Tarde in the early 20th century Tarde [1907]. In this section, we review basic diffusion of innovations models. Interested readers may refer to the bibliographical notes for further study.

Ryan and Gross: Adopter Categories

Ryan and Gross [1943] studied the adoption of hybrid seed corn by farmers in Iowa [Strang and Soule, 1998]. The hybrid seed corn was highly resistant to diseases and other catastrophes such as droughts. However, farmers

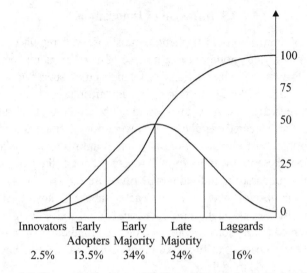

Figure 7.5. Types of Adopters and S-Shaped Cumulative Adoption Curve.

did not adopt it because of its high price and the seed's inability to reproduce. Their study showed that farmers received information through two main channels: mass communications from companies selling the seeds and interpersonal communications with other farmers. They found that although farmers received information from the mass channel, the influence on their behavior was coming from the interpersonal channel. They argued that adoption depended on a combination of information from both channels. They also observed that the adoption rate follows an *S*-shaped curve and that there are five different types of adopters based on the order in which they adopt the innovations: (1) *Innovators* (top 2.5%), (2) *Early Adopters* (13.5%), (3) *Early Majority* (34%), (4) *Late Majority* (34%), and (5) *Laggards* (16%). Figure 7.5 depicts the distribution of these adopters as well as the cumulative adoption S-shaped curve. As shown in the figure, the adoption rate is slow when innovators or early adopters adopt the product. Once early majority individuals start adopting, the adoption curve becomes linear, and the rate is constant until all late majority members adopt the product. After the late majority adopts the product, the adoption rate becomes slow once again as laggards start adopting, and the curve slowly approaches 100%.

Katz: Two-Step Flow Model

Elihu Katz, a professor of communication at the University of Pennsylvania, is a well-known figure in the study of the flow of information. In

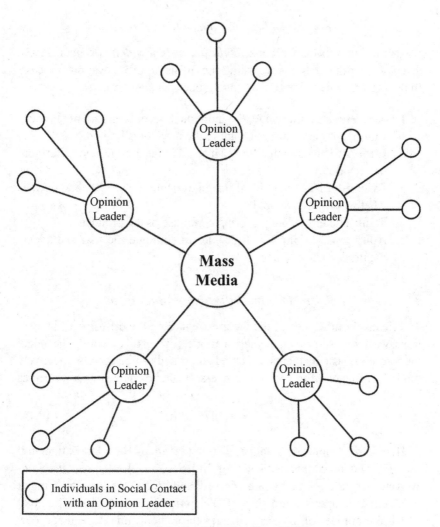

Figure 7.6. Katz Two-Step Flow Model.

addition to a study similar to the adoption of hybrid corn seed on how physicians adopted the new tetracycline drug [Coleman et al., 1966], Katz also developed a *two-step flow* model (also known as the *multistep flow model*) [Katz and Lazarsfeld, 2005] that describes how information is delivered through mass communication. The basic idea is depicted in Figure 7.6. Most information comes from mass media and is then directed toward influential figures called *opinion leaders*. These leaders then convey the information (or form opinions) and act as hubs for other members of the society.

Rogers in his well-known book, *Diffusion of Innovations* [Rogers, 2003], discusses various theories regarding the diffusion of innovations process. In particular, he describes a five stage process of adoption:

1. **Awareness**: In this stage, the individual becomes aware of the innovation, but her information about the product is limited.
2. **Interest**: The individual shows interest in the product and seeks more information.
3. **Evaluation**: The individual imagines using the product and decides whether or not to adopt it.
4. **Trial**: The individual performs a trial use of the product.
5. **Adoption**: The individual decides to continue the trial and adopts the product for full use.

7.3.3 Modeling Diffusion of Innovations

To effectively make use of the theories regarding the diffusion of innovations, we demonstrate a mathematical model for it in this section. The model incorporates basic elements discussed so far and can be used to effectively model a diffusion of innovations process. It can be concretely described as

$$\frac{dA(t)}{dt} = i(t)[P - A(t)]. \tag{7.15}$$

Here, $A(t)$ denotes the total population that adopted the innovation until time t. $i(t)$ denotes the coefficient of diffusion, which describes the innovativeness of the product being adopted, and P denotes the total number of potential adopters (until time t). This equation shows that the rate at which the number of adopters changes throughout time depends on how innovative is the product being adopted. The adoption rate only affects the potential adopters who have not yet adopted the product. Since $A(t)$ is the total population of adopters until time t, it is a cumulative sum and can be computed as follows:

$$A(t) = \int_{t_0}^{t} a(t)dt, \tag{7.16}$$

where $a(t)$ defines the adopters at time t. Let A_0 denote the number of adopters at time t_0. There are various methods of defining the diffusion coefficient [Mahajan, 1985]. One way is to define $i(t)$ as a linear combination of the cumulative number of adopters at different times $A(t)$,

$$i(t) = \alpha + \alpha_0 A_0 + \cdots + \alpha_t A(t) = \alpha + \sum_{i=t_0}^{t} \alpha_i A(i), \qquad (7.17)$$

where α_i's are the weights for each time step. Often a simplified version of this linear combination is used. In particular, the following three models for computing $i(t)$ are considered in the literature:

$$i(t) = \alpha, \qquad \text{External-Influence Model} \qquad (7.18)$$

$$i(t) = \beta A(t), \qquad \text{Internal-Influence Model} \qquad (7.19)$$

$$i(t) = \alpha + \beta A(t), \qquad \text{Mixed-Influence Model} \qquad (7.20)$$

where α is the *external-influence factor* and β is the *imitation factor*. EXTERNAL Equation 7.18 describes $i(t)$ in terms of α only and is independent of INFLUENCE the current number of adopters $A(t)$; therefore, in this model, the adoption FACTOR only depends on the external influence. In the second model, $i(t)$ depends on the number of adopters at any time and is therefore dependent on the internal factors of the diffusion process. β defines how much the current adopter population is going to affect the adoption and is therefore denoted as the *imitation* factor. The mixed-influence model is a model between the IMITATION two that uses a linear combination of both previous models. FACTOR

External-Influence Model

In the external-influence model, the adoption coefficient only depends on an external factor. One such example of external influence in social media is when important news goes viral. Often, people who post or read the news do not know each other; therefore, the importance of the news determines whether it goes viral. The external-influence model can be formulated as

$$\frac{dA(t)}{dt} = \alpha[P - A(t)]. \qquad (7.21)$$

By solving Equation 7.21,

$$A(t) = P(1 - e^{-\alpha t}), \qquad (7.22)$$

when $A(t = t_0 = 0) = 0$. The $A(t)$ function is shown in Figure 7.7. The number of adopters increases exponentially and then saturates near P.

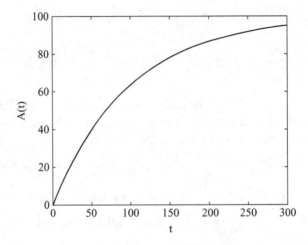

Figure 7.7. External-Influence Model for $P = 100$ and $\alpha = 0.01$.

Internal-Influence Model

In the internal-influence model, adoption depends on how many have adopted the innovation in the current time step.[4] In social media there is internal influence when a group of friends join a site due to peer pressure. Think of a group of individuals where the likelihood of joining a social networking site increases as more group members join the site. The internal influence model can be described as follows:

$$\frac{dA(t)}{dt} = \beta A(t)[P - A(t)].$$ (7.23)

PURE IMITATION MODEL Since the diffusion rate in this model depends on $\beta A(t)$, it is called the *pure imitation* model. The solution to this model is defined as

$$A(t) = \frac{P}{1 + \frac{P - A_0}{A_0} e^{-\beta P(t - t_0)}},$$ (7.24)

where $A(t = t_0) = A_0$. The $A(t)$ function is shown in Figure 7.8.

Mixed-Influence Model

As discussed, the mixed influence model is situated in between the internal- and external-influence models. The mixed-influence model is defined as

$$\frac{dA(t)}{dt} = (\alpha + \beta A(t))[P - A(t)].$$ (7.25)

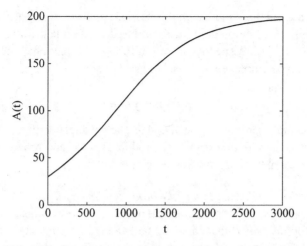

Figure 7.8. Internal-Influence Model for $A_0 = 30$, $\beta = 10^{-5}$, and $P = 200$.

By solving the differential equation, we arrive at

$$A(t) = \frac{P - \frac{\alpha(P-A_0)}{\alpha+\beta A_0} e^{-(\alpha+\beta P)(t-t_0)}}{1 + \frac{\beta(P-A_0)}{\alpha+\beta A_0} e^{-(\alpha+\beta P)(t-t_0)}}, \qquad (7.26)$$

where $A(t = t_0) = A_0$. The $A(t)$ function for the mixed-influence model is depicted in Figure 7.9.

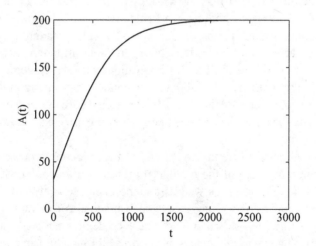

Figure 7.9. Mixed-Influence Model for $P = 200$, $\beta = 10^{-5}$, $A_0 = 30$, and $\alpha = 10^{-3}$.

We discussed three models in this section: internal, external, and mixed influence. Depending on the model used to describe the diffusion of innovations process, the respective equation for $A(t)$ (Equations 7.22, 7.24, or 7.26) should be employed to model the system.

7.3.4 Intervention

Consider a faulty product being adopted. The product company is planning to stop or delay adoptions until the product is fixed and re-released. This intervention can be performed by doing the following:

- *Limiting the distribution of the product or the audience that can adopt the product*. In our mathematical model, this is equivalent to reducing the population P that can potentially adopt the product.
- *Reducing interest in the product being sold*. For instance, the company can inform adopters of the faulty status of the product. In our models, this can be achieved by tampering α: setting α to a very small value in Equation 7.22 results in a slow adoption rate.
- *Reducing interactions within the population*. Reduced interactions result in less imitation of product adoptions and a general decrease in the trend of adoptions. In our models, this can be achieved by setting β to a small value.

7.4 Epidemics

In an epidemic, a disease spreads widely within a population. This process consists of a *pathogen* (the disease being spread), a population of *hosts* (humans, animals, and plants, among others), and a spreading mechanism (breathing, drinking, sexual activity, etc.). Unlike information cascades and herding, but similar to diffusion of innovations models, epidemic models assume an implicit network and unknown connections among individuals. This makes epidemic models more suitable when we are interested in global patterns, such as trends and ratios of people getting infected, and not in who infects whom.

In general, a complete understanding of the epidemic process requires substantial knowledge of the biological process within *each* host and the immune system process, as well as a comprehensive analysis of interactions among individuals. Other factors such as social and cultural attributes also play a role in how, when, and where epidemics happen. Large epidemics, also known as *pandemics*, have spread through human populations and include the Black Death in the 13th century (killing more than 50% of Europe's population), the Great Plague of London (100,000 deaths), the smallpox epidemic, in the 17th century (killing more than 90% of Massachusetts Bay Native Americans) and recent pandemics such as HIV/AIDS, SARS, H5N1 (Avian flu), and influenza. These pandemics motivated the introduction of epidemic models in the early 20th century and the establishment of the epidemiology field.

There are various ways of modeling epidemics. For instance, one can look at how hosts contact each other and devise methods that describe how epidemics happen in networks. These networks are called *contact networks*. CONTACT A contact network is a graph where nodes represent the hosts and edges NETWORKS represent the interactions between these hosts. For instance, in the case of the HIV/AIDS epidemic, edges represent sexual interactions, and in the case of influenza, nodes that are connected represent hosts that breathe the same air. Nodes that are close in a contact network are not necessarily close in terms of real-world proximity. Real-world proximity might be true for plants or animals, but diseases such as SARS or avian flu travel between continents because of the traveling patterns of hosts. This spreading pattern becomes clearer when the science of epidemics is employed to understand the propagation of computer viruses in cell phone networks or across the internet [Pastor-Satorras and Vespignani, 2001; Newman et al., 2002].

Another way of looking at epidemic models is to avoid considering network information and to analyze only the rates at which hosts get infected, recover, and the like. This analysis is known as the *fully mixed* FULLY MIXED technique, assuming that each host has an equal chance of meeting other TECHNIQUE hosts. Through these interactions, hosts have random probabilities of getting infected. Though simplistic, the technique reveals several useful methods of modeling epidemics that are often capable of describing various real-world outbreaks. In this section, we concentrate on the fully mixed models that avoid the use of contact networks.[5]

Note that the models of information diffusion that we have already discussed, such as the models in diffusion of innovations or information cascades, are more or less related to epidemic models. However, what makes epidemic models different is that, in the other models of information diffusion, actors decide whether to adopt the innovation or take the decision and the system is usually fully observable. In epidemics, however, the system has a high level of uncertainty, and individuals usually do not decide whether to get infected or not. The models discussed in this section assume that (1) no contact network information is available and (2) the process by which hosts get infected is unknown. These models can be applied to situations in social media where the decision process has a certain uncertainty to it or is ambiguous to the analyst.

7.4.1 Definitions

Since there is no network, we assume that we have a population where the disease is being spread. Let N define the size of this crowd. Any member of the crowd can be in either one of three states:

CLOSED-
WORLD
ASSUMPTION

1. **Susceptible**: When an individual is in the susceptible state, he or she can potentially get infected by the disease. In reality, infections can come from outside the population where the disease is being spread (e.g., by genetic mutation, contact with an animal, etc.); however, for simplicity, we make a *closed-world assumption*, where susceptible individuals can only get infected by infected people in the population. We denote the number of susceptibles at time t as $S(t)$ and the fraction of the population that is susceptible as $s(t) = S(t)/N$.
2. **Infected**: An infected individual has the chance of infecting susceptible parties. Let $I(t)$ denote the number of infected individuals at time t, and let $i(t)$ denote the fraction of individuals who are infected, $i(t) = I(t)/N$.
3. **Recovered (or Removed)**: These are individuals who have either recovered from the disease and hence have complete or partial immunity against the infection or were killed by the infection. Let $R(t)$ denote the size of this set at time t and $r(t)$ the fraction recovered, $r(t) = R(t)/N$.

Clearly, $N = S(t) + I(t) + R(t)$ for all t. Since we are assuming that there is some level of randomness associated with the values of $S(t)$, $I(t)$, and $R(t)$, we try to deal with expected values and assume S, I, and R represent these at time t.

7.4.2 SI Model

We start with the most basic model. In this model, the susceptible individuals get infected, and once infected, they will never get cured. Denote β as the contact probability. In other words, the probability of a pair of people meeting in any time step is β. So, if $\beta = 1$, everyone comes into contact with everyone else, and if $\beta = 0$, no one meets another individual. Assume

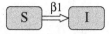

Figure 7.10. SI Model.

that when an infected individual meets a susceptible individual the disease is being spread with probability 1 (this can be generalized to other values). Figure 7.10 demonstrates the SI model and the transition between states that happens in this model for individuals. The value over the arrow shows that each susceptible individual meets at least βI infected individuals during the next time step.

Given this situation, infected individuals will meet βN people on average. We know from this set that only the fraction S/N will be susceptible and that the rest are infected already. So, each infected individual will infect $\beta N S/N = \beta S$ others. Since I individuals are infected, $\beta I S$ will be infected in the next time step. This means that the number of susceptible individuals will be reduced by this factor as well. So, to get different values of S and I at different times, we can solve the following differential equations:

$$\frac{dS}{dt} = -\beta I S, \tag{7.27}$$

$$\frac{dI}{dt} = \beta I S. \tag{7.28}$$

Since $S + I = N$ at all times, we can eliminate one equation by replacing S with $N - I$:

$$\frac{dI}{dt} = \beta I (N - I). \tag{7.29}$$

The solution to this differential equation is called the *logistic growth function*,

$$I(t) = \frac{N I_0 e^{\beta t}}{N + I_0 (e^{\beta t} - 1)}, \tag{7.30}$$

where I_0 is the number of individuals infected at time 0. In general, analyzing epidemics in terms of the number of infected individuals has nominal generalization power. To address this limitation, we can consider infected fractions. We therefore substitute $i_0 = \frac{I_0}{N}$ in the previous equation,

$$i(t) = \frac{i_0 e^{\beta t}}{1 + i_0 (e^{\beta t} - 1)}. \tag{7.31}$$

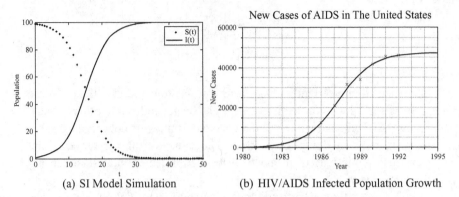

(a) SI Model Simulation (b) HIV/AIDS Infected Population Growth

Figure 7.11. SI model simulation compared to the HIV/AIDS growth in the United States.

Note that in the limit, the SI model infects all the susceptible population because there is no recovery in the model. Figure 7.11(a) depicts the logistic growth function (infected individuals) and susceptible individuals for $N = 100$, $I_0 = 1$, and $\beta = 0.003$. Figure 7.11(b) depicts the infected population for HIV/AIDS for the past 20 years. As observed, the infected population can be approximated well with the logistic growth function and follows the SI model. Note that in the HIV/AIDS graph, not everyone is getting infected. This is because not everyone in the United States is in the susceptible population, so not everyone will get infected in the end. Moreover, there are other factors that are far more complex than the details of the SI model that determine how people get infected with HIV/AIDS.

7.4.3 SIR Model

The SIR model, first introduced by Kermack and McKendrick [1932], adds more detail to the standard SI model. In the SIR model, in addition to the I and S states, a recovery state R is present. Figure 7.12 depicts the model. In the SIR model, hosts get infected, remain infected for a while, and then recover. Once hosts recover (or are removed), they can no longer get infected and are no longer susceptible. The process by which susceptible individuals get infected is similar to the SI model, where a parameter β defines the

Figure 7.12. SIR Model.

probability of contacting others. Similarly, a parameter γ in the SIR model defines how infected people recover, or the recovering probability of an infected individual in a time period Δt.

In terms of differential equations, the SIR model is

$$\frac{dS}{dt} = -\beta I S, \tag{7.32}$$

$$\frac{dI}{dt} = \beta I S - \gamma I, \tag{7.33}$$

$$\frac{dR}{dt} = \gamma I. \tag{7.34}$$

Equation 7.32 is identical to that of the SI model (Equation 7.27). Equation 7.33 is different from Equation 7.28 of the SI model by the addition of the term γI, which defines the number of infected individuals who recovered. These are removed from the infected set and are added to the recovered ones in Equation 7.34. Dividing Equation 7.32 by Equation 7.34, we get

$$\frac{dS}{dR} = -\frac{\beta}{\gamma} S, \tag{7.35}$$

and by assuming the number of recovered at time 0 is zero ($R_0 = 0$),

$$\log \frac{S_0}{S} = \frac{\beta}{\gamma} R. \tag{7.36}$$

$$S_0 = S e^{\frac{\beta}{\gamma} R} \tag{7.37}$$

$$S = S_0 e^{-\frac{\beta}{\gamma} R} \tag{7.38}$$

Since $I + S + R = N$, we replace I in Equation 7.34,

$$\frac{dR}{dt} = \gamma (N - S - R). \tag{7.39}$$

Now combining Equations 7.38 and 7.39,

$$\frac{dR}{dt} = \gamma (N - S_0 e^{-\frac{\beta}{\gamma} R} - R). \tag{7.40}$$

If we solve this equation for R, then we can determine S from 7.38 and I from $I = N - R - S$. The solution for R can be computed by solving the following integration:

$$t = \frac{1}{\gamma} \int_0^R \frac{dx}{N - S_0 e^{-\frac{\beta}{\gamma} x} - x}. \tag{7.41}$$

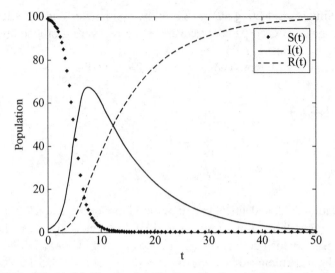

Figure 7.13. SIR Model Simulated with $S_0 = 99$, $I_0 = 1$, $R_0 = 0$, $\beta = 0.01$, and $\gamma = 0.1$.

However, there is no closed-form solution to this integration, and only numerical approximation is possible. Figure 7.13 depicts the behavior of the SIR model for a set of initial parameters.

The two models in the next two subsections are generalized versions of the two models discussed thus far: SI and SIR. These models allow individuals to have temporary immunity and to get reinfected.

7.4.4 SIS Model

The SIS model is the same as the SI model, with the addition of infected nodes recovering and becoming susceptible again (see Figure 7.14). The differential equations describing the model are

$$\frac{dS}{dt} = \gamma I - \beta IS, \tag{7.42}$$

$$\frac{dI}{dt} = \beta IS - \gamma I. \tag{7.43}$$

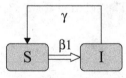

Figure 7.14. SIS Model.

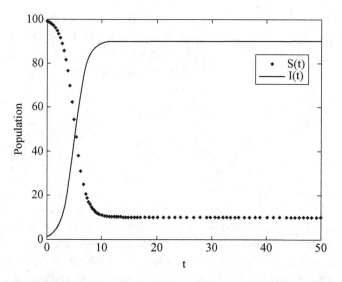

Figure 7.15. SIS Model Simulated with $S_0 = 99$, $I_0 = 1$, $\beta = 0.01$, and $\gamma = 0.1$.

By replacing S with $N - I$ in Equation 7.43, we arrive at

$$\frac{dI}{dt} = \beta I(N - I) - \gamma I = I(\beta N - \gamma) - \beta I^2. \qquad (7.44)$$

When $\beta N \leq \gamma$, the first term will be negative or zero at most; hence, the whole term becomes negative. Therefore, in the limit, the value $I(t)$ will decrease exponentially to zero. However, when $\beta N > \gamma$, we will have a logistic growth function as in the SI model. Having said this, as the simulation of the SIS model shows in Figure 7.15, the model will never infect everyone. It will reach a steady state, where both susceptibles and infecteds reach an equilibrium (see the epidemics exercises).

7.4.5 SIRS Model

The final model analyzed in this section is the SIRS model. Just as the SIS model extends the SI, the SIRS model extends the SIR, as shown in Figure 7.16. In this model, the assumption is that individuals who have

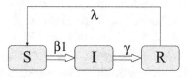

Figure 7.16. SIRS Model.

recovered will lose immunity after a certain period of time and will become susceptible again. A new parameter has been added to the model λ that defines the probability of losing immunity for a recovered individual. The set of differential equations that describe this model is

$$\frac{dS}{dt} = \lambda R - \beta I S, \tag{7.45}$$

$$\frac{dI}{dt} = \beta I S - \gamma I, \tag{7.46}$$

$$\frac{dR}{dt} = \gamma I - \lambda R. \tag{7.47}$$

Like the SIR model, this model has no closed-form solution, so numerical integration can be used. Figure 7.17 demonstrates a simulation of the SIRS model with given parameters of choice. As observed, the simulation outcome is similar to the SIR model simulation (see Figure 7.13). The major difference is that in the SIRS, the number of susceptible and recovered individuals changes non-monotonically over time. For example, in SIRS, the number of susceptible individuals decreases over time, but after reaching the minimum count, starts increasing again. On the contrary, in the SIR, both susceptible individuals and recovered individuals change monotonically, with the number of susceptible individuals decreasing over time and that of recovered individuals increasing over time. In both SIR and SIRS, the infected population changes non-monotonically.

7.4.6 Intervention

A pressing question in any pandemic or epidemic outbreak is how to stop the process. In this section, we discuss epidemic intervention based on a recent discovery [Christakis and Fowler, 2009]. In any epidemic outbreak, infected individuals infect susceptible individuals. Although in this chapter we discussed random infection in the real world, what actually takes place is quite different. Infected individuals have a limited number of contacts and can only infect them if said contacts are susceptible. A well-connected infected individual is more dangerous to the epidemic outbreak than someone who has no contacts. In other words, the epidemic takes place in a network. Unfortunately, it is often difficult to trace these contacts and outline the contact network. If this was possible, the best way to intervene with the epidemic outbreak would be to vaccinate the highly connected nodes and stop the epidemic. This would result in what is known as *herd immunity* and would stop the epidemic outbreak. Herd immunity

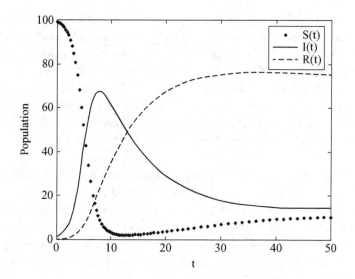

Figure 7.17. SIRS Model Simulated with $S_0 = 99$, $I_0 = 1$, $R_0 = 0$, $\gamma = 0.1$, $\beta = 0.01$, and $\lambda = 0.02$.

entails vaccinating a population inside a herd such that the pathogen cannot initiate an outbreak inside the herd. In general, creating herd immunity requires at least a **random** sample of 96% of the population to be vaccinated. Interestingly, we can achieve the same herd immunity by making use of friends in a network. In general, people know which of their friends have more friends. So, they know or have access to these higher-degree and more-connected nodes. Researchers found that if a random population of 30% of the herd is selected and then these 30% are asked for their highest degree friends, one can achieve herd immunity by vaccinating these friends. Of course, older intervention techniques such as separating those infected from those susceptible (quarantining them) or removing those infected (killing cows with mad cow disease) still work.

7.5 Summary

In this chapter, we discussed the concept of information diffusion in social networks. In the herd behavior, individuals observe the behaviors of others and act similarly to them based on their own benefit. We reviewed the well-known diners example and urn experiment and demonstrated how conditional probabilities can be used to determine why herding takes place. We discussed how herding experiments should be designed and ways to intervene with it.

Next, we discussed the information cascade problem with the constraint of sequential decision making. The independent cascade model (ICM) is a sender-centric model and has a level of stochasticity associated with it. The spread of cascades can be maximized in a network given a budget on how many initial nodes can be activated. Unfortunately, the problem is NP-hard; therefore, we introduced a greedy approximation algorithm that has guaranteed performance due to the submodularity of ICM's activation function. Finally, we discussed how to intervene with information cascades.

Our next topic was the diffusion of innovations. We discussed the characteristics of adoption both from the individual and innovation point of view. We reviewed well-known theories such as the models introduced by Ryan and Gross, Katz, and Rogers, in addition to experiments in the field, and different types of adopters. We also detailed mathematical models that account for internal, external, and mixed influences and their intervention procedures.

Finally, we moved on to epidemics, an area where decision making is usually performed unconsciously. We discussed four epidemic models: SI, SIR, SIS, and SIRS; the two last models allow for reinfected individuals. For each model we provided differential equations, numerical solutions, and closed-form solutions, when available. We concluded the chapter with intervention approaches to epidemic outbreaks and a review of herd immunity in epidemics. Although a 96% random vaccination is required for achieving herd immunity, it is also possible to achieve it by selecting a random population of 30% and then vaccinating their highest degree friends.

7.6 Bibliographic Notes

The concept of the herd has been well studied in psychology by Freud (crowd psychology), Carl Gustav Jung (the collective unconscious), and Gustave Le Bon (the popular mind). It has also been observed in economics by Veblen [1899] and in studies related to the *bandwagon effect* [Rohlfs and Varian, 2003; Simon, 1954; Leibenstein, 1950]. The behavior is also discussed in terms of *sociability* [Simmel and Hughes, 1949] in sociology.

Herding, first coined by Banerjee [1992], at times refers to a slightly different concept. In herd behaviour discussed in this chapter, the crowd does not necessarily start with the same decision, but will eventually reach one, whereas in herding the same behavior is usually observed. Moreover, in herd behavior, individuals decide whether the action they are taking has some benefits to themselves or is rational, and based on that, they will align with the population. In herding, some level of uncertainty is associated with the decision, and the individual does not know why he or she is following the crowd.

Another confusion is that the terms "herd behavior/herding" is often used interchangebly with "information cascades" [Bikhchandani et al., 1992; Welch, 1992]. To avoid this problem, we clearly define both in the chapter and assume that in herd behavior, decisions are taken based on global information, whereas in information cascades, local information is utilized.

Herd behavior has been studied in the context of financial markets [Cont and Bouchaud, 2000; Drehmann et al., 2005; Bikhchandani and Sharma, 2001; Devenow and Welch, 1996] and investment [Scharfstein and Stein, 1990]. Gale analyzes the robustness of different herd models in terms of different constraints and externalities [Gale, 1996], and Shiller discusses the relation between information, conversation, and herd behavior [Shiller, 1995]. Another well-known social conformity experiment was conducted in Manhattan by Milgram et al. [1969].

Other recent applications of threshold models can be found in [Young, 1988; Watts, 1999, 2002; Valente, 1995, 1996a; Schelling, 1978; Peleg, 1997; Morris, 2000; Macy and Willer, 2002; Macy, 1991; Granovetter, 1976; Berger, 2001]. Bikhchandani et al. [1998] review conformity, fads, and information cascades and describe how observing past human decisions can help explain human behavior. Hirshleifer [1997] provides information cascade examples in many fields, including zoology and finance.

In terms of diffusion models, Robertson [1967] describes the process and Hagerstrand [1967] introduces a model based on the spatial stages of the diffusion of innovations and Monte Carlo simulation models for diffusion of innovations. Bass [1969] discusses a model based on differential equations. Mahajan and Peterson [1978] extend the Bass model.

Instances of external-influence models can be found in [Hamblin et al., 1973; Coleman et al., 1966] and internal-influence models are applied in [Mansfield, 1961; Griliches, 2007; Gray, 2007]. The Gompertz function [Martino, 1983], widely used in forecasting, has a direct relationship with the internal-influence diffusion curve. Mixed-influence model examples include the work of Mahajan and Muller [1982] and Bass model [Bass, 1969].

Midgley and Dowling [1978] introduce the *contingency model*. Abrahamson and Rosenkopf [1993] mathematically analyze the bandwagon effect and diffusion of innovations. Their model predicts whether the bandwagon effect will occur and how many organizations will adopt the innovation. Network models of diffusion and thresholds for diffusion of innovations models are discussed by Valente [1996a,1996b]. Diffusion through blogspace and in general, social networks, has been analyzed by [Gruhl et al., 2004; Leskovec et al., 2007; Yang and Leskovec, 2010; Zafarani, Cole, and Liu, 2010].

For information on different pandemics, refer to [Nohl, 2006; Bell, 1995; Patterson and Runge, 2002; Des Jarlais et al., 1994; Dye and Gay, 2003; Chinese et al., 2004; Guan et al., 2007; Nelson and Holmes, 2007]. To review some early and in-depth analysis of epidemic models, refer to [Bailey et al., 1975; Anderson and May, 1991]. Surveys of epidemics can be found in [Hethcote, 1994, 2000; Hethcote et al., 1981; Dietz, 1967]. Epidemics in networks have been discussed [Newman, 2010; Moore and Newman, 1999; Keeling and Eames, 2005] extensively. Other general sources include [Lewis, 2009; Easley and Kleinberg, 2010; Newman, 2010; Barrat et al., 2008]. A generalized model for contagion is provided by Dodds and Watts [2004] and, in the case of best response dynamics, in Morris [2000].

Other topics related to this chapter include wisdom of crowd models [Golub and Jackson, 2010] and swarm intelligence [Eberhart et al., 2001; Engelbrecht, 2005; Bonabeau et al., 1999; Kennedy, 2006]. One can also analyze *information provenance*, which aims to identify the sources from which information has diffused. Barbier et al. [2013] provide an overview of information provenance in social media in their book.

7.7 Exercises

1. Discuss how different information diffusion modeling techniques differ. Name applications on social media that can make use of methods in each area.

Herd Effect

2. What are the minimum requirements for a herd behavior experiment? Design an experiment of your own.

Diffusion of Innovation

3. Simulate internal-, external-, and mixed-influence models in a program. How are the saturation levels different for each model?
4. Provide a simple example of diffusion of innovations and suggest a specific way of intervention to expedite the diffusion.

Information Cascades

5. Briefly describe the independent cascade model (ICM).
6. What is the objective of cascade maximization? What are the usual constraints?
7. Follow the ICM procedure until it converges for the following graph. Assume that node i activates node j when $i - j \equiv 1 \ (mod\ 3)$ and node 5 is activated at time 0.

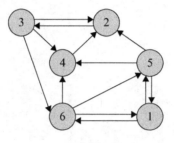

Epidemics

8. Discuss the mathematical relationship between the SIR and the SIS models.
9. Based on our assumptions in the SIR model, the probability that an individual remains infected follows a standard exponential distribution. Describe why this happens.
10. In the SIR model, what is the most likely time to recover based on the value of γ?
11. In the SIRS model, compute the length of time that an infected individual is likely to remain infected before he or she recovers.
12. After the model saturates, how many are infected in the SIS model?

Part III

Applications

8

Influence and Homophily

Social forces connect individuals in different ways. When individuals get connected, one can observe distinguishable patterns in their connectivity networks. One such pattern is *assortativity*, also known as *social similarity*. In networks with assortativity, similar nodes are connected to one another more often than dissimilar nodes. For instance, in social networks, a high similarity between friends is observed. This similarity is exhibited by similar behavior, similar interests, similar activities, and shared attributes such as language, among others. In other words, friendship networks are *assortative*. Investigating assortativity patterns that individuals exhibit on social media helps one better understand user interactions. Assortativity is the most commonly observed pattern among linked individuals. This chapter discusses assortativity along with principal factors that result in assortative networks.

Many social forces induce assortative networks. Three common forces are *influence*, *homophily*, and *confounding*. Influence is the process by which an individual (the influential) affects another individual such that the influenced individual becomes more similar to the influential figure. Homophily is observed in already similar individuals. It is realized when similar individuals become friends due to their high similarity. Confounding is the environment's effect on making individuals similar. For instance, individuals who live in Russia speak Russian fluently because of the environment and are therefore similar in language. The confounding force is an external factor that is independent of inter-individual interactions and is therefore not discussed further.

Note that both influence and homophily social forces give rise to assortative networks. After either of them affects a network, the network exhibits more similar nodes; however, when "friends become similar," we denote that as influence, and when "similar individuals become friends," we call it homophily. Figure 8.1 depicts how both influence and homophily affect social networks.

ASSORTATIVITY

INFLUENCE,
HOMOPHILY,
AND
CONFOUNDING

217

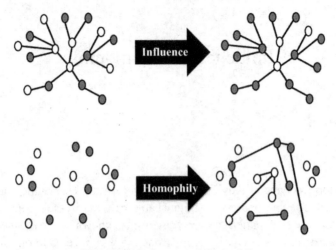

Figure 8.1. Influence and Homophily.

In particular, when discussing influence and homophily in social media, we are interested in asking the following questions:

- How can we measure influence or homophily?
- How can we model influence or homophily?
- How can we distinguish between the two?

Because both processes result in assortative networks, we can quantify their effect on the network by measuring the assortativity of the network.

8.1 Measuring Assortativity

Measuring assortativity helps quantify how much influence and homophily, among other factors, have affected a social network. Assortativity can be quantified by measuring how similar connected nodes are to one another. Figure 8.2 depicts the friendship network in a U.S. high school in 1994.[1] In the figure, races are represented with different colors: whites are white, blacks are gray, Hispanics are light gray, and others are black. As we observe, there is a high assortativity between individuals of the same race, particularly among whites and among blacks. Hispanics have a high tendency to become friends with whites.

To measure assortativity, we measure the number of edges that fall in between the nodes of the same race. This technique works for nominal attributes, such as race, but does not work for ordinal ones such as age.

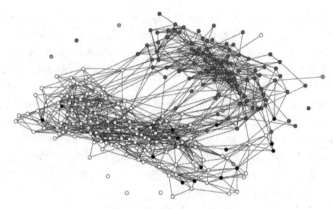

Figure 8.2. A U.S. High School Friendship Network in 1994 between Races. Eighty percent of the links exist between members of the same race (from [Currarini et al., 2009]).

Consider a network where individuals are friends with people of different ages. Unlike races, individuals are more likely to be friends with others close in age, but not necessarily with ones of the exact same age. Hence, we discuss two techniques: one for nominal attributes and one for ordinal attributes.

8.1.1 Measuring Assortativity for Nominal Attributes

Consider a scenario where we have nominal attributes assigned to nodes. As in our example, this attribute could be race or nationality, gender, or the like. One simple technique to measure assortativity is to consider the number of edges that are between nodes of the same type. Let $t(v_i)$ denote the type of node v_i. In an undirected graph[2], $G(V, E)$, with adjacency matrix A, this measure can be computed as follows,

$$\frac{1}{m} \sum_{(v_i,v_j) \in E} \delta(t(v_i), t(v_j)) = \frac{1}{2m} \sum_{ij} A_{ij}\, \delta(t(v_i), t(v_j)), \qquad (8.1)$$

where m is the number of edges in the graph, $\frac{1}{m}$ is applied for normalization, and the factor $\frac{1}{2}$ is added because G is undirected. $\delta(.,.)$ is the Kronecker delta function:

$$\delta(x, y) = \begin{cases} 0, & \text{if } x \neq y; \\ 1, & \text{if } x = y. \end{cases} \qquad (8.2)$$

This measure has its limitations. Consider a school of Hispanic students. Obviously, all connections will be between Hispanics, and assortativity value 1 is not a significant finding. However, consider a school where half the population is white and half the population is Hispanic. It is statistically expected that 50% of the connections will be between members of different race. If connections in this school were only between whites and Hispanics and not within groups, then our observation is significant. To account for this limitation, we can employ a common technique where we measure the *assortativity significance* by subtracting the measured assortativity by the statistically expected assortativity. The higher this value, the more significant the assortativity observed.

ASSORTATIVITY
SIGNIFICANCE

Consider a graph $G(V, E)$, $|E| = m$, where the degrees are known beforehand (how many friends an individual has), but the edges are not. Consider two nodes v_i and v_j, with degrees d_i and d_j, respectively. What is the expected number of edges between these two nodes? Consider node v_i. For any edge going out of v_i randomly, the probability of this edge getting connected to node v_j is $\frac{d_j}{\sum_i d_i} = \frac{d_j}{2m}$. Since the degree for v_i is d_i, we have d_i such edges; hence, the expected number of edges between v_i and v_j is $\frac{d_i d_j}{2m}$. Now, the expected number of edges between v_i and v_j that are of the same type is $\frac{d_i d_j}{2m}\delta(t(v_i), t(v_j))$ and the expected number of edges of the same type in the whole graph is

$$\frac{1}{m} \sum_{(v_i, v_j) \in E} \frac{d_i d_j}{2m} \delta(t(v_i), t(v_j)) = \frac{1}{2m} \sum_{ij} \frac{d_i d_j}{2m} \delta(t(v_i), t(v_j)). \quad (8.3)$$

We are interested in computing the distance between the assortativity observed and the expected assortativity:

$$Q = \frac{1}{2m} \sum_{ij} A_{ij} \, \delta(t(v_i), t(v_j)) - \frac{1}{2m} \sum_{ij} \frac{d_i d_j}{2m} \delta(t(v_i), t(v_j)) \quad (8.4)$$

$$= \frac{1}{2m} \sum_{ij} (A_{ij} - \frac{d_i d_j}{2m}) \delta(t(v_i), t(v_j)). \quad (8.5)$$

MODULARITY

This measure is called *modularity* [Newman, 2006]. The maximum modularity value for a network depends on the number of nodes of the same type and degree. The maximum occurs when all edges are connecting nodes of the same type (i.e., when $A_{ij} = 1$, $\delta(t(v_i), t(v_j)) = 1$). We can normalize modularity by dividing it by the maximum it can take:

$$Q_{\text{normalized}} = \frac{Q}{Q_{\text{max}}} \tag{8.6}$$

$$= \frac{\frac{1}{2m} \sum_{ij} (A_{ij} - \frac{d_i d_j}{2m}) \delta(t(v_i), t(v_j))}{\max[\frac{1}{2m} \sum_{ij} A_{ij} \delta(t(v_i), t(v_j)) - \frac{1}{2m} \sum_{ij} \frac{d_i d_j}{2m} \delta(t(v_i), t(v_j))]} \tag{8.7}$$

$$= \frac{\frac{1}{2m} \sum_{ij} (A_{ij} - \frac{d_i d_j}{2m}) \delta(t(v_i), t(v_j))}{\frac{1}{2m} 2m - \frac{1}{2m} \sum_{ij} \frac{d_i d_j}{2m} \delta(t(v_i), t(v_j))} \tag{8.8}$$

$$= \frac{\sum_{ij} (A_{ij} - \frac{d_i d_j}{2m}) \delta(t(v_i), t(v_j))}{2m - \sum_{ij} \frac{d_i d_j}{2m} \delta(t(v_i), t(v_j))}. \tag{8.9}$$

Modularity can be simplified using a matrix format. Let $\Delta \in \mathbb{R}^{n \times k}$ denote the indicator matrix and let k denote the number of types,

$$\Delta_{x,k} = \begin{cases} 1, & \text{if } t(x) = k; \\ 0, & \text{if } t(x) \neq k \end{cases} \tag{8.10}$$

Note that δ function can be reformulated using the indicator matrix:

$$\delta(t(v_i), t(v_j)) = \sum_k \Delta_{v_i,k} \Delta_{v_j,k}. \tag{8.11}$$

Therefore, $(\Delta \Delta^T)_{i,j} = \delta(t(v_i), t(v_j))$. Let $B = A - \mathbf{d}\mathbf{d}^T/2m$ denote the modularity matrix where $\mathbf{d} \in \mathbb{R}^{n \times 1}$ is the degree vector for all nodes. Given that the trace of multiplication of two matrices X and Y^T is $Tr(XY^T) = \sum_{i,j} X_{i,j} Y_{i,j}$ and $Tr(XY) = Tr(YX)$, modularity can be reformulated as

$$Q = \frac{1}{2m} \sum_{ij} \underbrace{(A_{ij} - \frac{d_i d_j}{2m})}_{B_{ij}} \underbrace{\delta(t(v_i), t(v_j))}_{(\Delta\Delta^T)_{i,j}} = \frac{1}{2m} Tr(B \Delta \Delta^T)$$

$$= \frac{1}{2m} Tr(\Delta^T B \Delta). \tag{8.12}$$

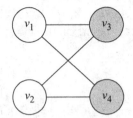

Figure 8.3. A Modularity Example for a Bipartite Graph.

Example 8.1. *Consider the bipartite graph in Figure 8.3. For this bipartite graph,*

$$A = \begin{bmatrix} 0 & 0 & 1 & 1 \\ 0 & 0 & 1 & 1 \\ 1 & 1 & 0 & 0 \\ 1 & 1 & 0 & 0 \end{bmatrix}, \quad \Delta = \begin{bmatrix} 1 & 0 \\ 1 & 0 \\ 0 & 1 \\ 0 & 1 \end{bmatrix}, \quad \mathbf{d} = \begin{bmatrix} 2 \\ 2 \\ 2 \\ 2 \end{bmatrix}, m = 4. \tag{8.13}$$

Therefore, matrix B is

$$B = A - \mathbf{d}\mathbf{d}^T/2m = \begin{bmatrix} -0.5 & -0.5 & 0.5 & 0.5 \\ -0.5 & -0.5 & 0.5 & 0.5 \\ 0.5 & 0.5 & -0.5 & -0.5 \\ 0.5 & 0.5 & -0.5 & -0.5 \end{bmatrix}. \tag{8.14}$$

The modularity value Q is

$$\frac{1}{2m} Tr(\Delta^T B \Delta) = -0.5. \tag{8.15}$$

*In this example, all edges are between nodes of different color. In other words, the number of edges between nodes of the **same color** is less than the expected number of edges between them. Therefore, the modularity value is negative.*

8.1.2 Measuring Assortativity for Ordinal Attributes

COVARIANCE

A common measure for analyzing the relationship between two variables with ordinal values is covariance. Covariance describes how two variables change with respect to each other. In our case, we are interested in how correlated, the attribute values of nodes connected via edges are. Let x_i be the ordinal attribute value associated with node v_i. In Figure 8.4, for node c, the value associated is $x_c = 21$.

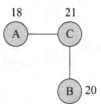

Figure 8.4. A Correlation Example.

We construct two variables X_L and X_R, where for any edge (v_i, v_j) we assume that x_i is observed from variable X_L and x_j is observed from variable X_R. For Figure 8.4,

$$X_L = \begin{bmatrix} 18 \\ 21 \\ 21 \\ 20 \end{bmatrix}, \quad X_R = \begin{bmatrix} 21 \\ 18 \\ 20 \\ 21 \end{bmatrix}. \tag{8.16}$$

In other words, X_L represents the ordinal values associated with the left node of the edges, and X_R represents the values associated with the right node of the edges. Our problem is therefore reduced to computing the covariance between variables X_L and X_R. Note that since we are considering an undirected graph, both edges (v_i, v_j) and (v_j, v_i) exist; therefore, x_i and x_j are observed in both X_L and X_R. Thus, X_L and X_R include the same set of values but in a different order. This implies that X_L and X_R have the same mean and standard deviation.

$$\mathbf{E}(X_L) = \mathbf{E}(X_R), \tag{8.17}$$

$$\sigma(X_L) = \sigma(X_R). \tag{8.18}$$

Since we have m edges and each edge appears twice for the undirected graph, then X_L and X_R have $2m$ elements. Each value x appears d_i times since it appears as endpoints of d_i edges. The covariance between X_L and X_R is

$$\begin{aligned}
\sigma(X_L, X_R) &= \mathbf{E}[(X_L - \mathbf{E}[X_L])(X_R - \mathbf{E}[X_R])] \\
&= \mathbf{E}[X_L X_R - X_L \mathbf{E}[X_R] - \mathbf{E}[X_L]X_R + \mathbf{E}[X_L]\mathbf{E}[X_R]] \\
&= \mathbf{E}[X_L X_R] - \mathbf{E}[X_L]\mathbf{E}[X_R] - \mathbf{E}[X_L]\mathbf{E}[X_R] + \mathbf{E}[X_L]\mathbf{E}[X_R] \\
&= \mathbf{E}[X_L X_R] - \mathbf{E}[X_L]\mathbf{E}[X_R]. \tag{8.19}
\end{aligned}$$

$\mathbf{E}(X_L)$ is the mean (expected value) of variable X_L, and $\mathbf{E}(X_L X_R)$ is the mean of the multiplication of X_L and X_R. In our setting and following

Equation 8.17, these expectations are as follows:

$$E(X_L) = E(X_R) = \frac{\sum_i (X_L)_i}{2m} = \frac{\sum_i d_i x_i}{2m} \qquad (8.20)$$

$$E(X_L X_R) = \frac{1}{2m} \sum_i (X_L)_i (X_R)_i = \frac{\sum_{ij} A_{ij} x_i x_j}{2m}. \qquad (8.21)$$

By plugging Equations 8.20 and 8.21 into Equation 8.19, the covariance between X_L and X_R is

$$\sigma(X_L, X_R) = \mathbf{E}[X_L X_R] - \mathbf{E}[X_L]\mathbf{E}[X_R]$$

$$= \frac{\sum_{ij} A_{ij} x_i x_j}{2m} - \frac{\sum_{ij} d_i d_j x_i x_j}{(2m)^2}$$

$$= \frac{1}{2m} \sum_{ij} \left(A_{ij} - \frac{d_i d_j}{2m} \right) x_i x_j. \qquad (8.22)$$

Similar to modularity (Section 8.1.1), we can normalize covariance. Pearson correlation $\rho(X_L, X_R)$ is the normalized version of covariance:

$$\rho(X_L, X_R) = \frac{\sigma(X_L, X_R)}{\sigma(X_L)\sigma(X_R)}. \qquad (8.23)$$

From Equation 8.18, $\sigma(X_L) = \sigma(X_R)$; thus,

$$\rho(X_L, X_R) = \frac{\sigma(X_L, X_R)}{\sigma(X_L)^2},$$

$$= \frac{\frac{1}{2m} \sum_{ij} \left(A_{ij} - \frac{d_i d_j}{2m} \right) x_i x_j}{\mathbf{E}[(X_L)^2] - (\mathbf{E}[X_L])^2}$$

$$= \frac{\frac{1}{2m} \sum_{ij} \left(A_{ij} - \frac{d_i d_j}{2m} \right) x_i x_j}{\frac{1}{2m} \sum_{ij} A_{ij} x_i^2 - \frac{1}{2m} \sum_{ij} \frac{d_i d_j}{2m} x_i x_j}. \qquad (8.24)$$

Note the similarity between Equations 8.9 and 8.24. Although modularity is used for nominal attributes and correlation for ordinal attributes, the major difference between the two equations is that the δ function in modularity is replaced by $x_i x_j$ in the correlation equation.

Example 8.2. *Consider Figure 8.4 with values demonstrating the attributes associated with each node. Since this graph is undirected, we have the following edges:*

$$E = \{(a, c), (c, a), (c, b), (b, c)\}. \qquad (8.25)$$

The correlation is between the values associated with the endpoints of the edges. Consider X_L as the value of the left end of an edge and X_R as the value of the right end of an edge:

$$X_L = \begin{bmatrix} 18 \\ 21 \\ 21 \\ 20 \end{bmatrix}, \quad X_R = \begin{bmatrix} 21 \\ 18 \\ 20 \\ 21 \end{bmatrix} \tag{8.26}$$

The correlation between these two variables is $\rho(X_L, X_R) = -0.67$.

8.2 Influence

Influence[3] is "the act or power of producing an effect without apparent exertion of force or direct exercise of command." In this section, we discuss influence and, in particular, how we can (1) measure influence in social media and (2) design models that detail how individuals influence one another in social media.

8.2.1 Measuring Influence

Influence can be measured based on (1) *prediction* or (2) *observation*.

Prediction-Based Measures. In prediction-based measurement, we assume that an individual's attribute or the way she is situated in the network predicts how influential she *will be*. For instance, we can assume that the gregariousness (e.g., number of friends) of an individual is correlated with how influential she *will be*. Therefore, it is natural to use any of the centrality measures discussed in Chapter 3 for prediction-based influence measurements. Examples of such centrality measures include PageRank and degree centrality. In fact, many of these centrality measures were introduced as influence-measuring techniques. For instance, on Twitter, in-degree (number of followers) is a common attribute for measuring influence. Since these methods were covered in-depth in that chapter, in this section we focus on observational techniques.

Observation-Based Measures. In observation-based measures, we quantify the influence of an individual by measuring the amount of influence attributed to him. An individual can influence differently in diverse settings,

PREDICTION-BASED INFLUENCE MEASURES

OBSERVATION-BASED INFLUENCE MEASURES

and so, depending on the context, the observation-based measuring of influence changes. We next describe three different settings and how influence can be measured in each.

1. **When an individual is the role model.** This happens in the case of individuals in the fashion industry, teachers, and celebrities. In this case, **the size of the audience that has been influenced** due to that fashion, charisma, or the like could act as an accurate measure. A local grade-school teacher has a tremendous influence over a class of students, whereas Gandhi influenced millions.

2. **When an individual spreads information.** This scenario is more likely when a piece of information, an epidemic, or a product is being spread in a network. In this case, **the size of the cascade** – that is, the number of hops the information traveled – or **the population affected**, or the **rate at which population gets influenced** is considered a measure.

3. **When an individual's participation increases the value of an item or action.** As in the case of diffusion of innovations (see Chapter 7), often when individuals perform actions such as buying a product, they increase the value of the product for other individuals. For example, the first individual who bought a fax machine had no one to send faxes to. The second individual who bought a fax machine increased its value for the first individual. So, the **increase (or rate of increase) in the value of an item or action** (such as buying a product) is often used as a measure.

Case Studies for Measuring Influence in Social Media

This section provides examples of measuring influence in the blogosphere and on the micrologging site Twitter. These techniques can be adapted to other social media sites, as well.

Measuring Social Influence in the Blogosphere

The goal of measuring influence in the blogosphere is to identify influential bloggers. Due to the limited time that individuals have, following the influentials is often necessary for fast access to interesting news. One common measure for quantifying the influence of bloggers is to use in-degree centrality: the number of (in-)links that point to the blog. However, because of the sparsity of in-links, more detailed analysis is required to measure influence in the blogosphere.

In their book, *The Influentials: One American in Ten Tells the Other Nine How to Vote, Where to Eat, and What to Buy*. Keller and Berry [2003] argue that the influentials are individuals who (1) are recognized by others, (2) whose activities result in follow-up activities, (3) have novel perspectives, and (4) are eloquent.

To address these issues, Agarwal et al. [2008] proposed the *iFinder* system to measure influence of blogposts and to identify influential bloggers. In particular, for each one of these four characteristics and a blogpost p, they approximate the characteristic by collecting specific blogpost's attributes:

1. **Recognition**. Recognition for a blogpost can be approximated by the links that point to the blogpost (in-links). Let $\mathcal{I}_p$ denote the set of in-links that point to blogpost p.
2. **Activity Generation**. Activity generated by a blogpost can be estimated using the number of comments that p receives. Let c_p denote the number of comments that blogpost p receives.
3. **Novelty.** The blogpost's novelty is inversely correlated with the number of references a blogpost employs. In particular the more citations a blogpost has, the less novel it is. Let $\mathcal{O}_p$ denote the set of out-links for blogpost p.
4. **Eloquence.** Eloquence can be estimated by the length of the blogpost. Given the informal nature of blogs and the bloggers' tendency to write short blogposts, longer blogposts are commonly believed to be more eloquent. So, the length of a blogpost l_p can be employed as a measure of eloquence.

Given these approximations for each one of these characteristics, we can design a measure of influence for each blogpost. Since the number of out-links inversely affects the influence of a blogpost and the number of in-links increases it, we construct an influence graph, or *i-graph*, where blogposts are nodes and influence flows through the nodes. The amount of this *influence flow* for each post p can be characterized as

INFLUENCE FLOW

$$\mathit{InfluenceFlow}(p) = w_{\text{in}} \sum_{m=1}^{|\mathcal{I}_p|} I(P_m) - w_{\text{out}} \sum_{n=1}^{|\mathcal{O}_p|} I(P_n), \qquad (8.27)$$

where $I(.)$ denotes the influence of a blogpost and w_{in} and w_{out} are the weights that adjust the contribution of in- and out-links, respectively. In this equation, P_m's are blogposts that point to post p, and P_n's are blogposts that are referred to in post p. Influence flow describes a measure that only accounts for in-links (recognition) and out-links (novelty). To account for the other two factors, we design the influence of a blogpost p as

$$I(p) = w_{\text{length}} l_p (w_{\text{comment}} c_p + InfluenceFlow(p)). \qquad (8.28)$$

Here, w_{length} is the weight for the length of blogpost[4] . w_{comment} describes how the number of comments is weighted. Note that the four weights w_{in}, w_{out}, w_{comments}, and w_{length} need to be tuned to make the model more accurate. This tuning can be done by a variety of techniques. For instance, we can use a test system where the influential posts are already known (labeled data) to tune them.[5] Finally, a blogger's influence index (*iIndex*) can be defined as the maximum influence value among all his or her N blogposts,

$$iIndex = \max_{p_n \in N} I(p_n). \qquad (8.29)$$

Computing *iIndex* for a set of bloggers over all their blogposts can help identify and rank influential bloggers in a system.

Measuring Social Influence on Twitter. On Twitter, a microblogging platform, users receive tweets from other users by *following* them. Intuitively, we can think of the number of followers as a measure of influence (in-degree centrality). In particular, three measures are frequently used to quantify influence in Twitter,

1. **In-degree**: the number of users following a person on Twitter. As discussed, the number of individuals who are interested in someone's tweets (i.e., followers) is commonly used as an influence measure on Twitter. In-degree denotes the "audience size" of an individual.
2. **Number of mentions**: the number of times an individual is mentioned in tweets. Mentioning an individual with a `username` handle is performed by including `@username` in a tweet. The number of times an individual is mentioned can be used as an influence measure. The number of mentions denotes the "ability in engaging others in conversation" [Cha et al., 2010].
3. **Number of retweets**: the number of times tweets of a user are retweeted. Individuals on Twitter have the opportunity to forward tweets to a broader audience via the retweet capability. Clearly, the more one's tweets are retweeted, the more likely one is influential. The number of retweets indicates an individual's ability to generate content that is worth being passed along.

Each one of these measures by itself can be used to identify influential users in Twitter. This can be done by utilizing the measure for each individual and then ranking individuals based on their measured influence

Table 8.1. *Rank Correlation between Top 10%*
of Influentials for Different Measures on Twitter

Measures	Correlation Value
In-degree vs. retweets	0.122
In-degree vs. mentions	0.286
Retweets vs. mentions	0.638

value. Contrary to public perception, the number of followers is considered an inaccurate measure compared to the other two. This is shown in [Cha et al., 2010], where the authors ranked individuals on Twitter independently based on these three measures. To see if they are correlated or redundant, they compared ranks of individuals across three measures using rank correlation measures. One such measure is the Spearman's rank correlation coefficient,

$$\rho = 1 - \frac{6\sum_{i=1}^{n}(m_1^i - m_2^i)^2}{n^3 - n}, \qquad (8.30)$$

SPEARMAN'S
RANK
CORRELATION

where m_1^i and m_2^i are ranks of individual i based on measures m_1 and m_2, and n is the total number of users. Spearman's rank correlation is the Pearson correlation coefficient for ordinal variables that represent ranks (i.e., takes values between 1...n); hence, the value is in range $[-1,1]$. Their findings suggest that popular users (users with high in-degree) do not necessarily have high ranks in terms of number of retweets or mentions. This can be observed in Table 8.1, which shows the Spearman's correlation between the top 10% influentials for each measure.

8.2.2 Modeling Influence

In influence modeling, the goal is to design models that can explain how individuals influence one another. Given the nature of social media, it is safe to assume that influence takes place among connected individuals. At times, this network is observable (explicit networks), and at others times, it is unobservable (implicit networks). For instance, in referral networks, where people refer others to join an online service on social media, the network of referrals is often observable. In contrast, people are influenced to buy products, and in most cases, the seller has no information on who referred the buyer, but does have approximate estimates on the number of products sold over time. In the observable (explicit) network, we resort to threshold

LINEAR
THRESHOLD
MODEL (LTM)

models such as the linear threshold model (LTM) to model influence; in implicit networks, we can employ methods such as the linear influence model (LIM) that take the number of individuals who get influenced at different times as input (e.g., the number of buyers per week).

Modeling Influence in Explicit Networks

Threshold models are simple yet effective methods for modeling influence in explicit networks. In these models, nodes make decision based on the number or the fraction (the threshold) of their neighbors (or incoming neighbors in a directed graph) who have already decided to make the same decision. Threshold models were employed in the literature as early as the 1970s in the works of Granovetter [1983] and Schelling [1971]. Using a threshold model, Schelling demonstrated that minor local preferences in having neighbors of the same color leads to global racial segregation.

A *linear threshold model (LTM)* is an example of a threshold model. Assume a weighted directed graph where nodes v_j and v_i are connected with weight $w_{j,i} \geq 0$. This weight denotes how much node v_j can affect node v_i's decision. We also assume

$$\sum_{v_j \in N_{in}(v_i)} w_{j,i} \leq 1, \qquad (8.31)$$

where $N_{in}(v_i)$ denotes the incoming neighbors of node v_i. In a linear threshold model, each node v_i is assigned a threshold θ_i such that when the amount of influence exerted toward v_i by its active incoming neighbors is more than θ_i, then v_i becomes active, if still inactive. Thus, for v_i to become active at time t, we should have

$$\sum_{v_j \in N_{in}(v_i), v_j \in A_{t-1}} w_{j,i} \geq \theta_i, \qquad (8.32)$$

where A_{t-1} denotes the set of active nodes at the end of time $t-1$. The threshold values are generally assigned uniformly at random to nodes from the interval [0,1]. Note that the threshold θ_i defines how resistant to change node v_i is: a very small θ_i value might indicate that a small change in the activity of v_i's neighborhood results in v_i becoming active and a large θ_i shows that v_i resists changes.

Provided a set of initial active nodes A_0 and a graph, the LTM algorithm is shown in Algorithm 8.1. In each step, for all inactive nodes, the condition in Equation 8.32 is checked, and if it is satisfied, the node becomes active. The process ends when no more nodes can be activated. Once θ thresholds

---

Algorithm 8.1 Linear Threshold Model (LTM)

Require: Graph $G(V, E)$, set of initial activated nodes A_0
 1: **return** Final set of activated nodes A_∞
 2: i=0;
 3: Uniformly assign random thresholds θ_v from the interval $[0, 1]$;
 4: **while** $i = 0$ or $(A_{i-1} \neq A_i, i \geq 1)$ **do**
 5:     $A_{i+1} = A_i$
 6:     inactive $= V - A_i$;
 7:     **for all** $v \in$ inactive **do**
 8:         **if** $\sum_{j \text{ connected to } v, j \in A_i} w_{j,v} \geq \theta_v$. **then**
 9:             activate v;
10:             $A_{i+1} = A_{i+1} \cup \{v\}$;
11:         **end if**
12:     **end for**
13:     $i = i + 1$;
14: **end while**
15: $A_\infty = A_i$;
16: Return A_∞;

---

are fixed, the process is deterministic and will always converge to the same state.

Example 8.3. *Consider the graph in Figure 8.5. Values attached to nodes represent the LTM thresholds, and edge values represent the weights. At time 0, node v_1 is activated. At time 2, both nodes v_2 and v_3 receive influence from node v_1. Node v_2 is not activated since $0.5 < 0.8$ and node v_3 is activated since $0.8 > 0.7$. Similarly, the process continues and then stops with five activated nodes.*

Modeling Influence in Implicit Networks

An implicit network is one where the influence spreads over edges in the network; however, unlike the explicit model, we cannot observe the individuals (the influentials) who are responsible for influencing others, but only those who get influenced. In other words, the information available is the set of influenced population $P(t)$ at any time and the time t_u, when each individual u gets initially influenced (activated). We assume that any influenced individual u can influence $I(u, t)$ number of non-influenced (inactive) individuals after t time steps. We call $I(., .)$ the influence function.

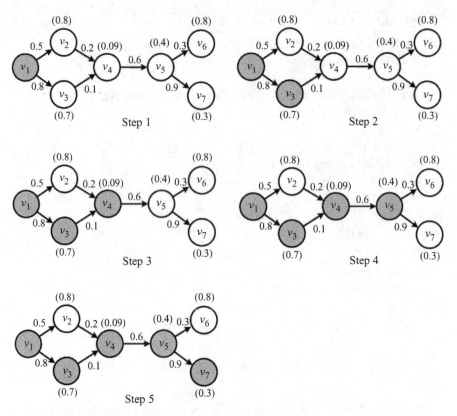

Figure 8.5. Linear Threshold Model (LTM) Simulation. The values attached to nodes denote thresholds θ_i, and the values on the edges represent weights $w_{i,j}$.

Assuming discrete time steps, we can formulate the size of the influenced population $|P(t)|$:

$$|P(t)| = \sum_{u \in P(t)} I(u, t - t_u). \qquad (8.33)$$

Figure 8.6 shows how the model performs. Individuals u, v, and w are activated at time steps t_u, t_v, and t_w, respectively. At time t, the total number of influenced individuals is a summation of influence functions I_u, I_v, and I_w at time steps $t - t_u$, $t - t_v$, and $t - t_w$, respectively. Our goal is to estimate $I(., .)$ given activation times and the number of influenced individuals at all times. A simple approach is to utilize a probability distribution to estimate I function. For instance, we can employ the power-law distribution to estimate influence. In this case, $I(u, t) = c_u(t - t_u)^{-\alpha_u}$, where we estimate

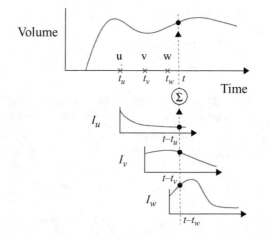

Figure 8.6. The Size of the Influenced Population as a Summation of Individuals Influenced by Activated Individuals (from [Yang and Leskovec, 2010]).

coefficients c_u and α_u for any u by methods such as *maximum likelihood* estimation (see [Myung, 2003] for more details).

This is called the *parametric* estimation, and the method assumes that all users influence others in the same parametric form. A more flexible approach is to assume a nonparametric function and estimate the influence function's form. This approach was first introduced as the linear influence model (LIM) [Yang and Leskovec, 2010].

In LIM, we extend our formulation by assuming that nodes get deactivated over time and then no longer influence others. Let $A(u, t) = 1$ denote that node u is active at time t, and $A(u, t) = 0$ denote that node u is either deactived or still not influenced. Following a network notation and assuming that $|V|$ is the total size of the population and T is the last time step, we can reformulate Equation 8.33 for $|P(t)|$ as

LINEAR
INFLUENCE
MODEL (LIM)

$$|P(t)| = \sum_{u=1}^{|V|} \sum_{t=1}^{T} A(u, t)I(u, t), \qquad (8.34)$$

or equivalently in matrix form,

$$P = AI. \qquad (8.35)$$

It is common to assume that individuals can only activate other individuals and cannot stop others from becoming activated. Hence, negative values for influence do not make sense; therefore, we would like measured influence values to be positive $I \geq 0$,

$$\text{minimize } ||P - AI||_2^2 \tag{8.36}$$

$$\text{subject to } \quad I \geq 0. \tag{8.37}$$

This formulation is similar to regression coefficients computation outlined in Chapter 5, where we compute a least square estimate of I; however, this formulation cannot be solved using regression techniques studied earlier because, in regression, computed I values can become negative. In practice, this formulation can be solved using non-negative least square methods (see [Lawson and Hanson, 1995] for details).

8.3 Homophily

Homophily is the tendency of similar individuals to become friends. It happens on a daily basis in social media and is clearly observable in social networking sites where befriending can explicitly take place. The well-known saying, "birds of a feather flock together," is frequently quoted when discussing homophily. Unlike influence, where an influential influences others, in homophily, **two** similar individuals decide to get connected.

8.3.1 Measuring Homophily

Homophily is the linking of two individuals due to their similarity and leads to assortative networks over time. To measure homophily, we measure how the assortativity of the network has changed over time.[6] Consider two snapshots of a network $G_{t_1}(V, E_{t_1})$ and $G_{t_2}(V, E_{t_2})$ at times t_1 and t_2, respectively, where $t_2 > t_1$. Without loss of generality, we assume that the number of nodes is fixed and only edges connecting these nodes change (i.e., are added or removed).

When dealing with nominal attributes, the homophily index is defined as

$$H = Q^{t_2}_{\text{normalized}} - Q^{t_1}_{\text{normalized}}, \tag{8.38}$$

where $Q_{\text{normalized}}$ is defined in Equation 8.9. Similarly, for ordinal attributes, the homophily index can be defined as the change in the Pearson correlation (Equation 8.24):

$$H = \rho^{t_2} - \rho^{t_1}. \tag{8.39}$$

Algorithm 8.2 Homophily Model

Require: Graph $G(V, E)$, $E = \emptyset$, similarities $sim(v, u)$
1: **return** Set of edges E
2: **for all** $v \in V$ **do**
3:   $\theta_v =$ generate a random number in $[0,1]$;
4:   **for all** $(v, u) \notin E$ **do**
5:     **if** $\theta_v < sim(v, u)$ **then**
6:       $E = E \cup (v, u)$;
7:     **end if**
8:   **end for**
9: **end for**
10: Return E;

8.3.2 Modeling Homophily

Homophily can be modeled using a variation of the independent cascade model discussed in Chapter 7. In this variation, at each time step a single node gets activated, and the activated node gets a chance of getting connected to other nodes due to homophily. In other words, if the activated node finds other nodes in the network similar enough (i.e., their similarity is higher than some tolerance value), it connects to them via an edge. A node once activated has no chance of getting activated again.

Modeling homophily is outlined in Algorithm 8.2. Let $sim(u, v)$ denote the similarity between nodes u and v. When a node gets activated, we generate a random tolerance value for the node v between 0 and 1. Alternatively, we can set this tolerance to some predefined value. The tolerance value defines the minimum similarity that node v tolerates for connecting to other nodes. Then, for any likely edge (v, u) that is still not in the edge set, if the similarity is more than the tolerance: $sim(v, u) > \theta_v$, the edge (v, u) is added. The process continues until all nodes are activated.

The model can be used in two different scenarios. First, given a network in which assortativity is attributed to homophily, we can estimate tolerance values for all nodes. To estimate tolerance values, we can simulate the homophily model in Algorithm 8.2 on the given network (by removing all its edges) with different tolerance values. We can then compare the assortativity of the simulated network and the given network. By finding the simulated network that best fits the given network (i.e., has the closest assortativity value to the given network's assortativity), we can determine the tolerance values for individuals. Second, when a network is given and the source of assortativity is unknown, we can estimate how much of the observed assortativity can be attributed to homophily. To measure assortativity due to homophily, we can simulate homophily on the given network by removing edges. The distance between the assortativity measured on the simulated network and the given network explains how much of the observed assortativity is due to homophily. The smaller this distance, the higher the effect of homophily in generating the observed assortativity.

8.4 Distinguishing Influence and Homophily

We are often interested in understanding which social force (influence or homophily) resulted in an assortative network. To distinguish between an influence-based assortativity or homophily-based one, statistical tests can be used. In this section, we discuss three tests: the shuffle test, the edge-reversal test, and the randomization test. The first two can detect whether influence exists in a network or not, but are incapable of detecting homophily. The last one, however, can distinguish influence and homophily. Note that in all these tests, we assume that several temporal snapshots of the dataset are available (like the LIM model) where we know exactly when each node is activated, when edges are formed, or when attributes are changed.

8.4.1 Shuffle Test

The shuffle test was originally introduced by Anagnostopoulos et al. [2008]. The basic idea behind the shuffle test comes from the fact that influence is temporal. In other words, when u influences v, then v should have been activated after u. So, in the shuffle test, we define a temporal assortativity measure. We assume that if there is no influence, then a shuffling of the activation time stamps should not affect the temporal assortativity measurement.

SOCIAL
CORRELATION
    In this temporal assortativity measure, called *social correlation*, the probability of activating a node v depends on a, the number of already active friends it has. This activation probability is calculated using a logistic function,[7]

$$p(a) = \frac{e^{\alpha a + \beta}}{1 + e^{\alpha a + \beta}},$$

(8.40)

or equivalently,

$$\ln(\frac{p(a)}{1 - p(a)}) = \alpha a + \beta,$$ (8.41)

where α measures the social correlation and β denotes the activation bias. For computing the number of already active nodes of an individual, we need to know the activation time stamps of the nodes.

Let $y_{a,t}$ denote the number of individuals who became activated at time t and had a active friends and let $n_{a,t}$ denote the ones who had a active friends but did not get activated at time t. Let $y_a = \sum_t y_{a,t}$ and $n_a = \sum_t n_{a,t}$. We define the likelihood function as

$$\prod_a p(a)^{y_a}(1 - p(a))^{n_a}.$$ (8.42)

To estimate α and β, we find their values such that the likelihood function denoted in Equation 8.42 is maximized. Unfortunately, there is no closed-form solution, but there exist software packages that can efficiently compute the solution to this optimization.[8]

Let t_u denote the activation time (when a node is first influenced) of node u. When activated node u influences nonactivated node v, and v is activated, then we have $t_u < t_v$. Hence, when temporal information is available about who activated whom, we see that influenced nodes are activated at a later time than those who influenced them. Now, if there is no influence in the network, we can randomly shuffle the activation time stamps, and the predicted α should not change drastically. So, if we shuffle activation time stamps and compute the correlation coefficient α' and its value is close to the α computed in the original unshuffled dataset (i.e., $|\alpha - \alpha'|$ is small), then the network does not exhibit signs of social influence.

8.4.2 Edge-Reversal Test

The edge-reversal test introduced by Christakis and Fowler [2007] follows a similar approach as the shuffle test. If influence resulted in activation, then the direction of edges should be important (who influenced whom). So, we can reverse the direction of edges, and if there is no social influence in the network, then the value of social correlation α, as defined in Section 8.4.1, should not change dramatically.

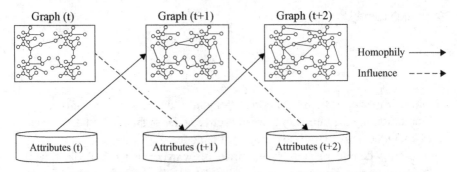

Figure 8.7. The Effect of Influence and Homophily on Attributes and Links over Time (reproduced from [La Fond and Neville, 2010]).

8.4.3 Randomization Test

Unlike the other two tests, the randomization test [La Fond and Neville, 2010] is capable of detecting both influence and homophily in networks. Let X denote the attributes associated with nodes (age, gender, location, etc.) and X_t denote the attributes at time t. Let X^i denote attributes of node v_i. As mentioned before, in influence, individuals already linked to one another change their attributes (e.g., a user changes habits), whereas in homophily, attributes do not change but connections are formed due to similarity. Figure 8.7 demonstrates the effect of influence and homophily in a network over time.

The assumption is that, if influence or homophily happens in a network, then networks become more assortative. Let $A(G_t, X_t)$ denote the assortativity of network G and attributes X at time t. Then, the network becomes more assortative at time $t + 1$ if

$$A(G_{t+1}, X_{t+1}) - A(G_t, X_t) > 0. \tag{8.43}$$

INFLUENCE GAIN AND HOMOPHILY GAIN

Now, we can assume that part of this assortativity is due to influence if the *influence gain* $G_{\text{Influence}}$ is positive,

$$G_{\text{Influence}}(t) = A(G_t, X_{t+1}) - A(G_t, X_t) > 0, \tag{8.44}$$

and part is due to homophily if we have positive *homophily gain* $G_{\text{Homophily}}$:

$$G_{\text{Homophily}}(t) = A(G_{t+1}, X_t) - A(G_t, X_t) > 0. \tag{8.45}$$

Note that X_{t+1} denotes the changes in attributes, and G_{t+1} denotes the changes in links in the network (new friendships formed). In randomization tests, one determines whether changes in $A(G_t, X_{t+1}) - A(G_t, X_t)$

Algorithm 8.3 Influence Significance Test

Require: $G_t, G_{t+1}, X_t, X_{t+1}$, number of randomized runs n, α
1: **return** Significance
2: $g_0 = G_{Influence}(t)$;
3: **for all** $1 \leq i \leq n$ **do**
4:      $XR_{t+1}^i = randomize_I(X_t, X_{t+1})$;
5:      $g_i = A(G_t, XR_{t+1}^i) - A(G_t, X_t)$;
6: **end for**
7: **if** g_0 larger than $(1 - \alpha/2)\%$ of values in $\{g_i\}_{i=1}^n$ **then**
8:      return significant;
9: **else if** g_0 smaller than $\alpha/2\%$ of values in $\{g_i\}_{i=1}^n$ **then**
10:      return significant;
11: **else**
12:      return insignificant;
13: **end if**

(influence), or $A(G_{t+1}, X_t) - A(G_t, X_t)$ (homophily), are significant or not. To detect change significance, we use the influence significance test and homophily significance test algorithms outlined in Algorithms 8.3 and 8.4, respectively. The influence significance algorithm starts with computing influence gain, which is the assortativity difference observed due to influence (g_0). It then forms a random attribute set at time $t + 1$ (null-hypotheses), assuming that attributes changed randomly at $t + 1$ and not due to influence. This random attribute set XR_{t+1}^i is formed from X_{t+1} by making sure that effects of influence in changing attributes are removed.

For instance, assume two users u and v are connected at time t, and u has hobby `movies` at time t and v does not have this hobby listed at time t. Now, assuming there is an influence of u over v, so that at time $t + 1$, v adds `movies` to her set of hobbies. In other words, `movies` $\notin X_t^v$ and `movies` $\in X_{t+1}^v$. To remove this influence, we can construct XR_{t+1}^i by removing `movies` from the hobbies of v at time $t + 1$ and adding some random hobby such as `reading`, which is $\notin X_t^u$ and $\notin X_t^v$, to the list of hobbies of v at time $t + 1$ in XR_{t+1}^i. This guarantees that the randomized XR_{t+1}^i constructed has no sign of influence. We construct this randomized set n times; this set is then used to compute influence gains $\{g_i\}_{i=1}^n$. Obviously, the more distant g_0 is from these gains, the more significant influence is. We can assume that whenever g_0 is smaller than $\alpha/2\%$ (or larger

INFLUENCE SIGNIFICANCE TEST

Algorithm 8.4 Homophily Significance Test

Require: G_t, G_{t+1}, X_t, X_{t+1}, number of randomized runs n, α

1: **return** Significance
2: $g_0 = G_{Homophily}(t)$;
3: **for all** $1 \leq i \leq n$ **do**
4:     $GR^i_{t+1} = randomize_H(G_t, G_{t+1})$;
5:     $g_i = A(GR^i_{t+1}, X_t) - A(G_t, X_t)$;
6: **end for**
7: **if** g_0 larger than $(1 - \alpha/2)\%$ of values in $\{g_i\}_{i=1}^n$ **then**
8:     return significant;
9: **else if** g_0 smaller than $\alpha/2\%$ of values in $\{g_i\}_{i=1}^n$ **then**
10:     return significant;
11: **else**
12:     return insignificant;
13: **end if**

---

than $1 - \alpha/2\%$) of $\{g_i\}_{i=1}^n$ values, it is significant. The value of α is set empirically.

HOMOPHILY
SIGNIFICANCE
TEST
    Similarly, in the homophily significance test, we compute the original homophily gain and construct random graph links GR^i_{t+1} at time $t + 1$, such that no homophily effect is exhibited in how links are formed. To perform this for any two (randomly selected) links e_{ij} and e_{kl} formed in the original G_{t+1} graph, we form edges e_{il} and e_{kj} in GR^i_{t+1}. This is to make sure that the homophily effect is removed and that the degrees in GR^i_{t+1} are equal to that of G_{t+1}.

8.5 Summary

Individuals are driven by different social forces across social media. Two such important forces are influence and homophily.

    In influence, an individual's actions induce her friends to act in a similar fashion. In other words, influence makes friends more similar. Homophily is the tendency for similar individuals to befriend each other. Both influence and homophily result in networks where similar individuals are connected to each other. These are assortative networks. To estimate the assortativity of networks, we use different measures depending on the attribute type that is tested for similarity. We discussed modularity for nominal attributes and correlation for ordinal ones.

Influence can be quantified via different measures. Some are prediction-based, where the measure assumes that some attributes can accurately predict how influential an individual will be, such as with in-degree. Others are observation-based, where the influence score is assigned to an individual based on some history, such as how many individuals he or she has influenced. We also presented case studies for measuring influence in the blogosphere and on Twitter.

Influence is modeled differently depending on the visibility of the network. When network information is available, we employ threshold models such as the linear threshold model (LTM), and when network information is not available, we estimate influence rates using the linear influence model (LIM). Similarly, homophily can be measured by computing the assortativity difference in time and modeled using a variant of independent cascade models.

Finally, to determine the source of assortativity in social networks, we described three statistical tests: the shuffle test, the edge-reversal test, and the randomization test. The first two can determine if influence is present in the data, and the last one can determine both influence and homophily. All tests require temporal data, where activation times and changes in attributes and links are available.

8.6 Bibliographic Notes

Indications of assortativity observed in the real world can be found in Currarini et al. [2009]. General reviews of the assortativity measuring methods discussed in this chapter can be found in [Newman, 2002a, 2010; Newman and Girvan, 2003].

Influence and homophily are extensively discussed in the social sciences literature (see [Cialdini and Trost, 1998; McPherson et al., 2001]). Interesting experiments in this area can be found in Milgram's seminal experiment on obedience to authority [Milgram, 2009]. In his controversial study, Milgram showed many individuals, because of fear or their desire to appear cooperative, are willing to perform acts that are against their better judgment. He recruited participants in what seemingly looked like a learning experiment. Participants were told to administer increasingly severe electric shocks to another individual ("the learner") if he answered questions incorrectly. These shocks were from 15–450 volts (lethal level). In reality, the learner was an actor, a confederate of Milgram, and never received any shocks. However, the actor shouted loudly to demonstrate the painfulness of the shocks. Milgram found that 65% of participants in his experiments were willing to give lethal electric shocks up to 450 volts to the learner, after being given assurance statements such as "Although the shocks may be painful, there is no permanent tissue damage, so please go on," or given direct orders, such as "the experiment *requires* that you continue." Another study is the 32-year longitudinal study on the spread of obesity in social networks [Christakis and Fowler, 2007]. In this study, Christakis et al. analyzed a population of 12,067 individuals. The body mass index for these individuals was available from 1971–2003. They showed that an individual's likelihood of becoming obese over time increased by almost 60% if he or she had an obese friend. This likelihood decreased to around 40% for those with an obese sibling or spouse.

The analysis of influence and homophily is also an active topic in social media mining. For studies regarding influence and homophily online, refer to [Watts and Dodds, 2007; Shalizi and Thomas, 2010; Currarini et al., 2009; Onnela and Reed-Tsochas, 2010; Weng et al., 2010; Bakshy et al., 2001]. The effect of influence and homophily on the social network has also been used for prediction purposes. For instance, Tang et al. [2013a] use the effect of homophily for trust prediction.

Modeling influence is challenging. For a review of threshold models, similar techniques, and challenges, see [Goyal et al., 2010; Watts, 2002; Granovetter, 1976; Kempe et al., 2003].

In addition to tests discussed for identifying influence or homophily, we refer readers to the works of Aral et al. [2009] and Snijders et al. [2006].

8.7 Exercises

1. State two common factors that explain why connected people are similar or vice versa.

Measuring Assortativity

2. • What is the range $[\alpha_1, \alpha_2]$ for modularity Q values? Provide examples for both extreme values of the range, as well as cases where modularity becomes zero.
   • What are the limitations for modularity?
   • Compute modularity in the following graph. Assume that $\{a_i\}_{i=0}^{4}$ nodes are category a, $\{b_i\}_{i=0}^{4}$ nodes are category b, and $\{c_i\}_{i=0}^{4}$ nodes are category c.

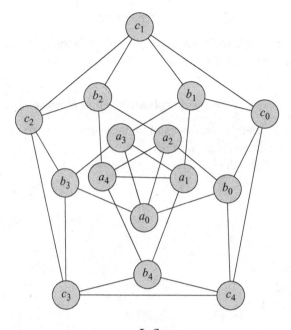

Influence

3. Does the linear threshold model (LTM) converge? Why?
4. Follow the LTM procedure until convergence for the following graph. Assume all the thresholds are 0.5 and node v_1 is activated at time 0.

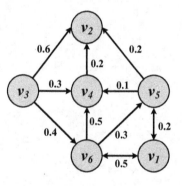

5. Discuss a methodology for identifying the influentials given multiple influence measures using the following scenario: on Twitter, one can use in-degree and number of retweets as two independent influence measures. How can you find the influentials by employing both measures?

Homophily

6. Design a measure for homophily that takes into account assortativity changes due to influence.

Distinguishing Influence and Homophily

7. What is a shuffle test designed for in the context of social influence? Describe how it is performed.
8. Describe how the edge-reversal test works. What is it used for?

9

Recommendation in Social Media

Individuals in social media make a variety of decisions on a daily basis. These decisions are about buying a product, purchasing a service, adding a friend, and renting a movie, among others. The individual often faces many options to choose from. These diverse options, the pursuit of optimality, and the limited knowledge that each individual has create a desire for external help. At times, we resort to search engines for recommendations; however, the results in search engines are rarely tailored to our particular tastes and are query-dependent, independent of the individuals who search for them.

Applications and algorithms are developed to help individuals decide easily, rapidly, and more accurately. These algorithms are tailored to individuals' tastes such that customized recommendations are available for them. These algorithms are called *recommendation algorithms* or *recommender systems*.

Recommender systems are commonly used for product recommendation. Their goal is to recommend products that would be interesting to individuals. Formally, a recommendation algorithm takes a set of users U and a set of items I and learns a function f such that

$$f : U \times I \to \mathbb{R} \qquad (9.1)$$

In other words, the algorithm learns a function that assigns a real value to each user-item pair (u, i), where this value indicates how interested user u is in item i. This value denotes the *rating* given by user u to item i. The recommendation algorithm is not limited to item recommendation and can be generalized to recommending people and material, such as, ads or content.

Recommendation vs. Search

When individuals seek recommendations, they often use web search engines. However, search engines are rarely tailored to individuals' needs and often retrieve the same results as long as the search query stays the same. To receive accurate recommendation from a search engine, one needs to send accurate keywords to the search engine. For instance, the query ''best 2013 movie to watch'' issued by an 8-year old and an adult will result in the same set of movies, whereas their individual tastes dictate different movies.

Recommendation systems are designed to recommend individual-based choices. Thus, the same query issued by different individuals should result in different recommendations. These systems commonly employ browsing history, product purchases, user profile information, and friends information to make customized recommendations. As simple as this process may look, a recommendation system algorithm actually has to deal with many challenges.

9.1 Challenges

Recommendation systems face many challenges, some of which are presented next:

- **Cold-Start Problem.** Many recommendation systems use historical data or information provided by the user to recommend items, products, and the like. However, when individuals first join sites, they have not yet bought any product: they have no history. This makes it hard to infer what they are going to like when they start on a site. The problem is referred to as the *cold-start* problem. As an example, consider an online movie rental store. This store has no idea what recently joined users prefer to watch and therefore cannot recommend something close to their tastes. To address this issue, these sites often ask users to rate a couple of movies before they begin recommend others to them. Other sites ask users to fill in profile information, such as interests. This information serves as an input to the recommendation algorithm.
- **Data Sparsity.** Similar to the cold-start problem, data sparsity occurs when not enough historical or prior information is available. Unlike the cold-start problem, data sparsity relates to the system as a whole and is not specific to an individual. In general, data sparsity occurs when a few individuals rate many items while many other individuals rate only a few items. Recommender systems often use information provided by other users to help offer better recommendations to an individual. When this information is not reasonably available, then it is said that a *data sparsity* problem exists. The problem is more prominent in sites that are recently launched or ones that are not popular.

- **Attacks.** The recommender system may be attacked to recommend items otherwise not recommended. For instance, consider a system that recommends items based on similarity between ratings (e.g., lens A is recommended for camera B because they both have rating 4). Now, an attacker that has knowledge of the recommendation algorithm can create a set of fake user accounts and rate lens C (which is not as good as lens A) highly such that it can get rating 4. This way the recommendation system will recommend C with camera B as well as A. This attack is called a *push attack*, because it pushes the ratings up such that the system starts recommending items that would otherwise not be recommended. Other attacks such as *nuke* attacks attempt to stop the whole recommendation system algorithm and make it unstable. A recommendation system should have the means to stop such attacks.

  NUKE ATTACK AND PUSH ATTACK

- **Privacy.** The more information a recommender system has about the users, the better the recommendations it provides to the users. However, users often avoid revealing information about themselves due to privacy concerns. Recommender systems should address this challenge while protecting individuals' privacy.
- **Explanation.** Recommendation systems often recommend items without having an explanation why they did so. For instance, when several items are bought together by many users, the system recommends these to new users items together. However, the system does not know why these items are bought together. Individuals may prefer some reasons for buying items; therefore, recommendation algorithms should provide explanation when possible.

9.2 Classical Recommendation Algorithms

Classical recommendation algorithms have a long history on the web. In recent years, with the emergence of social media sites, these algorithms have been provided new information, such as friendship information, interactions, and so on. We review these algorithms in this section.

9.2.1 Content-Based Methods

Content-based recommendation systems are based on the fact that a user's interest should match the description of the items that are recommended by the system. In other words, the more similar the item's description to the user's interest, the higher the likelihood that the user is going to find the item's recommendation interesting. *Content-based* recommender systems

---

Algorithm 9.1 Content-based recommendation

Require: User i's Profile Information, Item descriptions for items $j \in \{1, 2, \ldots, n\}$, k keywords, r number of recommendations.

1: **return** r recommended items.
2: $U_i = (u_1, u_2, \ldots, u_k) = $ user i's profile vector;
3: $\{I_j\}_{j=1}^n = \{(i_{j,1}, i_{j,2}, \ldots, i_{j,k}) = $ item j's description vector$\}_{j=1}^n$;
4: $s_{i,j} = sim(U_i, I_j), 1 \leq j \leq n$;
5: Return top r items with maximum similarity $s_{i,j}$.

---

implement this idea by measuring the similarity between an item's description and the user's profile information. The higher this similarity, the higher the chance that the item is recommended.

To formalize a content-based method, we first represent both user profiles and item descriptions by vectorizing (see Chapter 5) them using a set of k keywords. After vectorization, item j can be represented as a k-dimensional vector $I_j = (i_{j,1}, i_{j,2}, \ldots, i_{j,k})$ and user i as $U_i = (u_{i,1}, u_{i,2}, \ldots, u_{i,k})$. To compute the similarity between user i and item j, we can use cosine similarity between the two vectors U_i and I_j:

$$sim(U_i, I_j) = cos(U_i, I_j) = \frac{\sum_{l=1}^k u_{i,l} i_{j,l}}{\sqrt{\sum_{l=1}^k u_{i,l}^2} \sqrt{\sum_{l=1}^k i_{j,l}^2}} \tag{9.2}$$

In content-based recommendation, we compute the topmost similar items to a user j and then recommend these items in the order of similarity. Algorithm 9.1 shows the main steps of content-based recommendation.

9.2.2 Collaborative Filtering (CF)

Collaborative filtering is another set of classical recommendation techniques. In collaborative filtering, one is commonly given a user-item matrix where each entry is either unknown or is the rating assigned by the user to an item. Table 9.1 is an user-item matrix where ratings for some cartoons are known and unknown for others (question marks). For instance, on a review scale of 5, where 5 is the best and 0 is the worst, if an entry (i, j) in the user-item matrix is 4, that means that user i liked item j.

In collaborative filtering, one aims to predict the missing ratings and possibly recommend the cartoon with the highest predicted rating to the user. This prediction can be performed directly by using previous ratings in the matrix. This approach is called *memory-based* collaborative filtering

Table 9.1. *User-Item Matrix*

	Lion King	Aladdin	Mulan	Anastasia
John	3	0	3	3
Joe	5	4	0	2
Jill	1	2	4	2
Jane	3	?	1	0
Jorge	2	2	0	1

because it employs historical data available in the matrix. Alternatively, one can assume that an underlying model (hypothesis) governs the way users rate items. This model can be approximated and learned. After the model is learned, one can use it to predict other ratings. The second approach is called *model-based* collaborative filtering.

Memory-Based Collaborative Filtering

In memory-based collaborative filtering, one assumes one of the following (or both) to be true:

- Users with similar **previous** ratings for items are likely to rate future items similarly.
- Items that have received similar ratings **previously** from users are likely to receive similar ratings from future users.

If one follows the first assumption, the memory-based technique is a *user-based* CF algorithm, and if one follows the latter, it is an *item-based* CF algorithm. In both cases, users (or items) collaboratively help filter out irrelevant content (dissimilar users or items). To determine similarity between users or items, in collaborative filtering, two commonly used similarity measures are cosine similarity and Pearson correlation. Let $r_{u,i}$ denote the rating that user u assigns to item i, let $\bar{r}_u$ denote the average rating for user u, and let $\bar{r}_i$ be the average rating for item i. Cosine similarity between users u and v is

$$sim(U_u, U_v) = cos(U_u, U_v) = \frac{U_u \cdot U_v}{||U_u|| \, ||U_v||} = \frac{\sum_i r_{u,i} r_{v,i}}{\sqrt{\sum_i r_{u,i}^2} \sqrt{\sum_i r_{v,i}^2}}. \tag{9.3}$$

And the Pearson correlation coefficient is defined as

$$sim(U_u, U_v) = \frac{\sum_i (r_{u,i} - \bar{r}_u)(r_{v,i} - \bar{r}_v)}{\sqrt{\sum_i (r_{u,i} - \bar{r}_u)^2} \sqrt{\sum_i (r_{v,i} - \bar{r}_v)^2}}. \tag{9.4}$$

Next, we discuss user- and item-based collaborative filtering.

User-Based Collaborative Filtering. In this method, we predict the rating of user u for item i by (1) finding users most similar to u and (2) using a combination of the ratings of these users for item i as the predicted rating of user u for item i. To remove noise and reduce computation, we often limit the number of similar users to some fixed number. These most similar users NEIGHBORHOOD are called the *neighborhood* for user u, $N(u)$. In user-based collaborative filtering, the rating of user u for item i is calculated as

$$r_{u,i} = \bar{r}_u + \frac{\sum_{v \in N(u)} sim(u, v)(r_{v,i} - \bar{r}_v)}{\sum_{v \in N(u)} sim(u, v)}, \tag{9.5}$$

where the number of members of $N(u)$ is predetermined (e.g., top 10 most similar members).

Example 9.1. *In Table 9.1, $r_{Jane,Aladdin}$ is missing. The average ratings are the following:*

$$\bar{r}_{John} = \frac{3 + 3 + 0 + 3}{4} = 2.25 \tag{9.6}$$

$$\bar{r}_{Joe} = \frac{5 + 4 + 0 + 2}{4} = 2.75 \tag{9.7}$$

$$\bar{r}_{Jill} = \frac{1 + 2 + 4 + 2}{4} = 2.25 \tag{9.8}$$

$$\bar{r}_{Jane} = \frac{3 + 1 + 0}{3} = 1.33 \tag{9.9}$$

$$\bar{r}_{Jorge} = \frac{2 + 2 + 0 + 1}{4} = 1.25. \tag{9.10}$$

Using cosine similarity (or Pearson correlation), the similarity between Jane and others can be computed:

$$sim(Jane, John) = \frac{3 \times 3 + 1 \times 3 + 0 \times 3}{\sqrt{10}\sqrt{27}} = 0.73 \tag{9.11}$$

$$sim(Jane, Joe) = \frac{3 \times 5 + 1 \times 0 + 0 \times 2}{\sqrt{10}\sqrt{29}} = 0.88 \tag{9.12}$$

$$sim(Jane, Jill) = \frac{3 \times 1 + 1 \times 4 + 0 \times 2}{\sqrt{10}\sqrt{21}} = 0.48 \tag{9.13}$$

$$sim(Jane, Jorge) = \frac{3 \times 2 + 1 \times 0 + 0 \times 1}{\sqrt{10}\sqrt{5}} = 0.84. \tag{9.14}$$

Now, assuming that the neighborhood size is 2, then Jorge and Joe are the two most similar neighbors. Then, Jane's rating for Aladdin computed from user-based collaborative filtering is

$$r_{Jane,Aladdin} = \bar{r}_{Jane} + \frac{sim(Jane, Joe)(r_{Joe,Aladdin} - \bar{r}_{Joe})}{sim(Jane, Joe) + sim(Jane, Jorge)}$$

$$+ \frac{sim(Jane, Jorge)(r_{Jorge,Aladdin} - \bar{r}_{Jorge})}{sim(Jane, Joe) + sim(Jane, Jorge)}$$

$$= 1.33 + \frac{0.88(4 - 2.75) + 0.84(2 - 1.25)}{0.88 + 0.84} = 2.33 \quad (9.15)$$

Item-based Collaborative Filtering. In user-based collaborative filtering, we compute the average rating for different users and find the most similar users to the users for whom we are seeking recommendations. Unfortunately, in most online systems, users do not have many ratings; therefore, the averages and similarities may be unreliable. This often results in a different set of similar users when new ratings are added to the system. On the other hand, products usually have many ratings and their average and the similarity between them are more stable. In item-based CF, we perform collaborative filtering by finding the most similar items. The rating of user u for item i is calculated as

$$r_{u,i} = \bar{r}_i + \frac{\sum_{j \in N(i)} sim(i, j)(r_{u,j} - \bar{r}_j)}{\sum_{j \in N(i)} sim(i, j)}, \quad (9.16)$$

where $\bar{r}_i$ and $\bar{r}_j$ are the average ratings for items i and j, respectively.

Example 9.2. *In Table 9.1, $r_{Jane,Aladdin}$ is missing. The average ratings for items are*

$$\bar{r}_{Lion\ King} = \frac{3 + 5 + 1 + 3 + 2}{5} = 2.8. \quad (9.17)$$

$$\bar{r}_{Aladdin} = \frac{0 + 4 + 2 + 2}{4} = 2. \quad (9.18)$$

$$\bar{r}_{Mulan} = \frac{3 + 0 + 4 + 1 + 0}{5} = 1.6. \quad (9.19)$$

$$\bar{r}_{Anastasia} = \frac{3 + 2 + 2 + 0 + 1}{5} = 1.6. \quad (9.20)$$

Using cosine similarity (or Pearson correlation), the similarity between Aladdin and others can be computed:

$$sim(Aladdin, Lion King) = \frac{0 \times 3 + 4 \times 5 + 2 \times 1 + 2 \times 2}{\sqrt{24}\sqrt{39}} = 0.84.$$

$$(9.21)$$

$$sim(Aladdin, Mulan) = \frac{0 \times 3 + 4 \times 0 + 2 \times 4 + 2 \times 0}{\sqrt{24}\sqrt{25}} = 0.32.$$

$$(9.22)$$

$$sim(Aladdin, Anastasia) = \frac{0 \times 3 + 4 \times 2 + 2 \times 2 + 2 \times 1}{\sqrt{24}\sqrt{18}} = 0.67.$$

$$(9.23)$$

Now, assuming that the neighborhood size is 2, then Lion King and Anastasia are the two most similar neighbors. Then, Jane's rating for Aladdin computed from item-based collaborative filtering is

$$
\begin{aligned}
r_{Jane,Aladdin} = \bar{r}_{Aladdin} &+ \frac{sim(Aladdin, Lion King)(r_{Jane,Lion King} - \bar{r}_{Lion King})}{sim(Aladdin, Lion King) + sim(Aladdin, Anastasia)} \\
&+ \frac{sim(Aladdin, Anastasia)(r_{Jane,Anastasia} - \bar{r}_{Anastasia})}{sim(Aladdin, Lion King) + sim(Aladdin, Anastasia)} \\
&= 2 + \frac{0.84(3 - 2.8) + 0.67(0 - 1.6)}{0.84 + 0.67} = 1.40. \quad (9.24)
\end{aligned}
$$

Model-Based Collaborative Filtering

In memory-based methods (either item-based or user-based), one aims to predict the missing ratings based on similarities between users or items. In model-based collaborative filtering, one assumes that an underlying model governs the way users rate. We aim to learn that model and then use that model to predict the missing ratings. Among a variety of model-based techniques, we focus on a well-established model-based technique that is

SINGULAR based on singular value decomposition (SVD).

VALUE   SVD is a linear algebra technique that, given a real matrix $X \in \mathbb{R}^{m \times n}$,

DECOMPOSITION $m \geq n$, factorizes it into three matrices,

$$X = U\Sigma V^T, \quad (9.25)$$

LOSSLESS where $U \in \mathbb{R}^{m \times m}$ and $V \in \mathbb{R}^{n \times n}$ are orthogonal matrices and $\Sigma \in \mathbb{R}^{m \times n}$ is

MATRIX a diagonal matrix. The product of these matrices is equivalent to the original

FACTORIZATION matrix; therefore, no information is lost. Hence, the process is *lossless*.

Let $\|X\|_F = \sqrt{\sum_{i=1}^{m}\sum_{j=1}^{n}X_{ij}^2}$ denote the Frobenius norm of matrix X. A low-rank matrix approximation of matrix X is another matrix $C \in \mathbb{R}^{m \times n}$. C approximates X, and C's rank (the maximum number of linearly independent columns) is a fixed number $k \ll min(m, n)$:

FROBENIUS NORM

$$rank(C) = k. \tag{9.26}$$

The best low-rank matrix approximation is a matrix C that minimizes $\|X - C\|_F$. Low-rank approximations of matrices remove noise by assuming that the matrix is not generated at random and has an underlying structure. SVD can help remove noise by computing a low-rank approximation of a matrix. Consider the following matrix X_k, which we construct from matrix X after computing the SVD of $X = U \Sigma V^T$:

1. Create Σ_k from Σ by keeping only the first k elements on the diagonal. This way, $\Sigma_k \in \mathbb{R}^{k \times k}$.
2. Keep only the first k columns of U and denote it as $U_k \in \mathbb{R}^{m \times k}$, and keep only the first k rows of V^T and denote it as $V_k^T \in \mathbb{R}^{k \times n}$.
3. Let $X_k = U_k \Sigma_k V_k^T$, $X_k \in \mathbb{R}^{m \times n}$.

As it turns out, X_k is the *best low-rank approximation* of a matrix X. The following Eckart-Young-Mirsky theorem outlines this result.

ECKART-YOUNG-MIRSKY THEOREM

Theorem 9.1 (Eckart-Young-Mirsky Low-Rank Matrix Approximation). *Let X be a matrix and C be the best low-rank approximation of X; if $\|X - C\|_F$ is minimized, and $rank(C) = k$, then $C = X_k$.*

To summarize, the best rank-k approximation of the matrix can be easily computed by calculating the SVD of the matrix and then taking the first k columns of U, truncating Σ to the the first k entries, and taking the first k rows of V^T.

As mentioned, low-rank approximation helps remove noise from a matrix by assuming that the matrix is low rank. In low-rank approximation using SVD, if $X \in \mathbb{R}^{m \times n}$, then $U_k \in \mathbb{R}^{m \times k}$, $\Sigma_k \in \mathbb{R}^{k \times k}$, and $V_k^T \in \mathbb{R}^{k \times n}$. Hence, U_k has the same number of rows as X, but in a k-dimensional space. Therefore, U_k represents rows of X, but in a transformed k-dimensional space. The same holds for V_k^T because it has the same number of columns as X, but in a k-dimensional space. To summarize, U_k and V_k^T can be thought of as k-dimensional representations of rows and columns of X. In this k-dimensional space, noise is removed and more similar points should be closer.

Now, given the user-item matrix X, we can remove its noise by computing X_k from X and getting the new k-dimensional user space U_k or the

Table 9.2. *An User-Item Matrix*

	Lion King	Aladdin	Mulan
John	3	0	3
Joe	5	4	0
Jill	1	2	4
Jorge	2	2	0

k-dimensional item space V_k^T. This way, we can compute the most similar neighbors based on distances in this k-dimensional space. The similarity in the k-dimensional space can be computed using cosine similarity or Pearson correlation. We demonstrate this via Example 9.3.

Example 9.3. *Consider the user-item matrix, in Table 9.2. Assuming this matrix is X, then by computing the SVD of $X = U \Sigma V^T$,[1] we have*

$$U = \begin{bmatrix} -0.4151 & -0.4754 & -0.7679 & 0.1093 \\ -0.7437 & 0.5278 & 0.0169 & -0.4099 \\ -0.4110 & -0.6626 & 0.6207 & -0.0820 \\ -0.3251 & 0.2373 & 0.1572 & 0.9018 \end{bmatrix} \tag{9.27}$$

$$\Sigma = \begin{bmatrix} 8.0265 & 0 & 0 \\ 0 & 4.3886 & 0 \\ 0 & 0 & 2.0777 \\ 0 & 0 & 0 \end{bmatrix} \tag{9.28}$$

$$V^T = \begin{bmatrix} -0.7506 & -0.5540 & -0.3600 \\ 0.2335 & 0.2872 & -0.9290 \\ -0.6181 & 0.7814 & 0.0863 \end{bmatrix} \tag{9.29}$$

Considering a rank 2 approximation (i.e., $k = 2$), we truncate all three matrices:

$$U_k = \begin{bmatrix} -0.4151 & -0.4754 \\ -0.7437 & 0.5278 \\ -0.4110 & -0.6626 \\ -0.3251 & 0.2373 \end{bmatrix} \tag{9.30}$$

$$\Sigma_k = \begin{bmatrix} 8.0265 & 0 \\ 0 & 4.3886 \end{bmatrix} \tag{9.31}$$

$$V_k^T = \begin{bmatrix} -0.7506 & -0.5540 & -0.3600 \\ 0.2335 & 0.2872 & -0.9290 \end{bmatrix}. \tag{9.32}$$

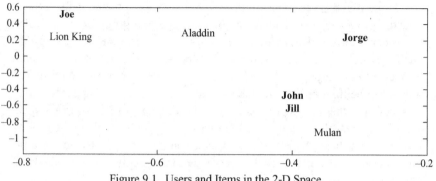

Figure 9.1. Users and Items in the 2-D Space.

The rows of U_k represent users. Similarly the columns of V_k^T (or rows of V_k) represent items. Thus, we can plot users and items in a 2-D figure. By plotting user rows or item columns, we avoid computing distances between them and can visually inspect items or users that are most similar to one another. Figure 9.1 depicts users and items depicted in a 2-D space. As shown, to recommend for Jill, John is the most similar individual to her. Similarly, the most similar item to Lion King is Aladdin.

After most similar items or users are found in the lower k-dimensional space, one can follow the same process outlined in user-based or item-based collaborative filtering to find the ratings for an unknown item. For instance, we showed in Example 9.3 (see Figure 9.1) that if we are predicting the rating $r_{Jill, Lion King}$ and assume that neighborhood size is 1, item-based CF uses $r_{Jill, Aladdin}$, because Aladdin is closest to Lion King. Similarly, user-based collaborative filtering uses $r_{John, Lion King}$, because John is the closest user to Jill.

9.2.3 Extending Individual Recommendation to Groups of Individuals

All methods discussed thus far are used to predict a rating for item i for an individual u. Advertisements that individuals receive via email marketing are examples of this type of recommendation on social media. However, consider ads displayed on the starting page of a social media site. These ads are shown to a large population of individuals. The goal when showing these ads is to ensure that they are interesting to the individuals who observe them. In other words, the site is advertising to a group of individuals.

Our goal in this section is to formalize how existing methods for recommending to a single individual can be extended to a group of individuals. Consider a group of individuals $G = \{u_1, u_2, \ldots, u_n\}$ and a set of products $I = \{i_1, i_2, \ldots, i_m\}$. From the products in I, we aim to recommend products to our group of individuals G such the recommendation satisfies the group being recommended to as much as possible. One approach is to first consider the ratings predicted for each individual in the group and then devise methods that can aggregate ratings for the individuals in the group. Products that have the highest aggregated ratings are selected for recommendation. Next, we discuss these aggregation strategies for individuals in the group.

Aggregation Strategies for a Group of Individuals

We discuss three major aggregation strategies for individuals in the group. Each aggregation strategy considers an assumption based on which ratings are aggregated. Let $r_{u,i}$ denote the rating of user $u \in G$ for item $i \in I$. Denote R_i as the group-aggregated rating for item i.

Maximizing Average Satisfaction. We assume that products that satisfy each member of the group on average are the best to be recommended to the group. Then, R_i group rating based on the maximizing average satisfaction strategy is given as

$$R_i = \frac{1}{n} \sum_{u \in G} r_{u,i}. \tag{9.33}$$

After we compute R_i for all items $i \in I$, we recommend the items that have the highest R_i's to members of the group.

Least Misery. This strategy combines ratings by taking the minimum of them. In other words, we want to guarantee that no individuals is being recommended an item that he or she strongly dislikes. In least misery, the aggregated rating R_i of an item is given as

$$R_i = \min_{u \in G} r_{u,i}. \tag{9.34}$$

Similar to the previous strategy, we compute R_i for all items $i \in I$ and recommend the items with the highest R_i values. In other words, we prefer recommending items to the group such that no member of the group strongly dislikes them.

Most Pleasure. Unlike the least misery strategy, in the most pleasure approach, we take the maximum rating in the group as the group rating:

$$R_i = \max_{u \in G} r_{u,i}. \tag{9.35}$$

Since we recommend items that have the highest R_i values, this strategy guarantees that the items that are being recommended to the group are enjoyed the most by at least one member of the group.

Example 9.4. *Consider the user-item matrix in Table 9.3. Consider group* $G = \{John, Jill, Juan\}$. *For this group, the aggregated ratings for all products using average satisfaction, least misery, and most pleasure are as follows.*

Table 9.3. *User-Item Matrix*

	Soda	Water	Tea	Coffee
John	1	3	1	1
Joe	4	3	1	2
Jill	2	2	4	2
Jorge	1	1	3	5
Juan	3	3	4	5

Average Satisfaction:

$$R_{Soda} = \frac{1+2+3}{3} = 2. \tag{9.36}$$

$$R_{Water} = \frac{3+2+3}{3} = 2.66. \tag{9.37}$$

$$R_{Tea} = \frac{1+4+4}{3} = 3. \tag{9.38}$$

$$R_{Coffee} = \frac{1+2+5}{3} = 2.66. \tag{9.39}$$

Least Misery:

$$R_{Soda} = \min\{1, 2, 3\} = 1. \tag{9.40}$$

$$R_{Water} = \min\{3, 2, 3\} = 2. \tag{9.41}$$

$$R_{Tea} = \min\{1, 4, 4\} = 1. \tag{9.42}$$

$$R_{Coffee} = \min\{1, 2, 5\} = 1. \tag{9.43}$$

Most Pleasure:

$$R_{Soda} = \max\{1, 2, 3\} = 3. \tag{9.44}$$

$$R_{Water} = \max\{3, 2, 3\} = 3. \tag{9.45}$$

$$R_{Tea} = \max\{1, 4, 4\} = 4. \tag{9.46}$$

$$R_{Coffee} = \max\{1, 2, 5\} = 5. \tag{9.47}$$

Thus, the first recommended items are tea, water, and coffee based on average satisfaction, least misery, and most pleasure, respectively.

9.3 Recommendation Using Social Context

In social media, in addition to ratings of products, there is additional information available, such as the friendship network among individuals. This information can be used to improve recommendations, based on the assumption that an individual's friends have an impact on the ratings ascribed to the individual. This impact can be due to homophily, influence, or confounding, discussed in Chapter 8. When utilizing this social information (i.e., *social context*) we can (1) use friendship information alone, (2) use social information in addition to ratings, or (3) constrain recommendations using social information. Figure 9.2 compactly represents these three approaches.

9.3.1 Using Social Context Alone

Consider a network of friendships for which no user-item rating matrix is provided. In this network, we can still recommend users from the network to other users for friendship. This is an example of *friend recommendation* in social networks. For instance, in social networking sites, users are often provided with a list of individuals they may know and are asked if they wish to befriend them. How can we recommend such friends?

There are many methods that can be used to recommend friends in social networks. One such method is *link prediction*, which we discuss in detail in Chapter 10. We can also use the structure of the network to recommend friends. For example, it is well known that individuals often form triads of friendships on social networks. In other words, two friends of an individual are often friends with one another. A triad of three individuals a, b, and c consists of three edges $e(a, b)$, $e(b, c)$, and $e(c, a)$. A triad that is missing one of these edges is denoted as an *open triad*. To recommend friends, we

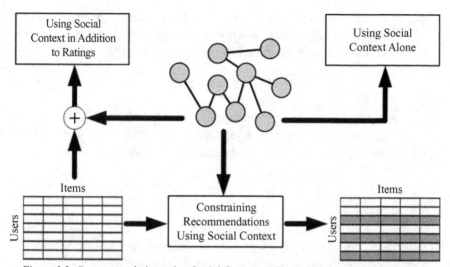

Figure 9.2. Recommendation using Social Context. When utilizing social information, we can 1) utilize this information independently, 2) add it to user-rating matrix, or 3) constrain recommendations with it.

can find open triads and recommend individuals who are not connected as friends to one another.

9.3.2 Extending Classical Methods with Social Context

Social information can also be used in addition to a user-item rating matrix to improve recommendation. Addition of social information can be performed by assuming that users that are connected (i.e., friends) have similar tastes in rating items. We can model the taste of user U_i using a k-dimensional vector $U_i \in \mathbb{R}^{k \times 1}$. We can also model items in the k-dimensional space. Let $V_j \in \mathbb{R}^{k \times 1}$ denote the item representation in k-dimensional space. We can assume that rating R_{ij} given by user i to item j can be computed as

$$R_{ij} = U_i^T V_i. \tag{9.48}$$

To compute U_i and V_i, we can use matrix factorization. We can rewrite Equation 9.48 in matrix format as

$$R = U^T V, \tag{9.49}$$

where $R \in \mathbb{R}^{n \times m}$, $U \in \mathbb{R}^{k \times n}$, $V \in \mathbb{R}^{k \times m}$, n is the number of users, and m is the number of items. Similar to model-based CF discussed in Section 9.2.2, matrix factorization methods can be used to find U and V, given user-item rating matrix R. In mathematical terms, in this matrix factorization, we are finding U and V by solving the following optimization problem:

$$\min_{U,V} \frac{1}{2}||R - U^T V||_F^2. \tag{9.50}$$

Users often have only a few ratings for items; therefore, the R matrix is very sparse and has many missing values. Since we compute U and V only for nonmissing ratings, we can change Equation 9.50 to

$$\min_{U,V} \frac{1}{2}\sum_{i=1}^{n}\sum_{j=1}^{m} I_{ij}(R_{ij} - U_i^T V_j)^2, \tag{9.51}$$

where $I_{ij} \in \{0, 1\}$ and $I_{ij} = 1$ when user i has rated item j and is equal to 0 otherwise. This ensures that nonrated items do not contribute to the summations being minimized in Equation 9.51. Often, when solving this optimization problem, the computed U and V can estimate ratings for the **already rated** items accurately, but fail at predicting ratings for unrated

OVERFITTING items. This is known as the *overfitting problem*. The overfitting problem can be mitigated by allowing both U and V to only consider important features required to represent the data. In mathematical terms, this is equivalent to both U and V having small matrix norms. Thus, we can change Equation 9.51 to

$$\frac{1}{2}\sum_{i=1}^{n}\sum_{j=1}^{m} I_{ij}(R_{ij} - U_i^T V_j)^2 + \frac{\lambda_1}{2}||U||_F^2 + \frac{\lambda_2}{2}||V||_F^2, \tag{9.52}$$

where $\lambda_1, \lambda_2 > 0$ are predetermined constants that control the effects of matrix norms. The terms $\frac{\lambda_1}{2}||U||_F^2$ and $\frac{\lambda_2}{2}||V||_F^2$ are denoted as *regularization* terms. Note that to minimize Equation 9.52, we need to minimize all

REGULARIZATION TERM terms in the equation, including the regularization terms. Thus, whenever one needs to minimize some other constraint, it can be introduced as a new additive term in Equation 9.52. Equation 9.52 lacks a term that incorporates the social network of users. For that, we can add another regularization term,

$$\sum_{i=1}^{n}\sum_{j\in F(i)} sim(i, j)||U_i - U_j||_F^2, \tag{9.53}$$

where $sim(i, j)$ denotes the similarity between user i and j (e.g., cosine similarity or Pearson correlation between their ratings) and $F(i)$ denotes the friends of i. When this term is minimized, it ensures that the taste for user i is close to that of all his friends $j \in F(i)$. As we did with previous regularization terms, we can add this term to Equation 9.51. Hence, our final goal is to solve the following optimization problem:

$$
\min_{U,V} \frac{1}{2} \sum_{i=1}^{n} \sum_{j=1}^{m} I_{ij}(R_{ij} - U_i^T V_j)^2 + \beta \sum_{i=1}^{n} \sum_{j \in F(i)} sim(i, j) \|U_i - U_j\|_F^2
$$

$$
+ \frac{\lambda_1}{2} \|U\|_F^2 + \frac{\lambda_2}{2} \|V\|_F^2, \tag{9.54}
$$

where β is the constant that controls the effect of social network regularization. A local minimum for this optimization problem can be obtained using gradient-descent-based approaches. To solve this problem, we can compute the gradient with respect to U_i's and V_i's and perform a gradient-descent-based method.

9.3.3 Recommendation Constrained by Social Context

In classical recommendation, to estimate ratings of an item, one determines similar users or items. In other words, *any user* similar to the individual can contribute to the predicted ratings for the individual. We can limit the set of individuals that can contribute to the ratings of a user to the set of friends of the user. For instance, in user-based collaborative filtering, we determine a neighborhood of most similar individuals. We can take the intersection of this neighborhood with the set of friends of the individual to attract recommendations only from friends who are *similar enough*:

$$
r_{u,i} = \bar{r}_u + \frac{\sum_{v \in N(u) \cap F(u)} sim(u, v)(r_{v,i} - \bar{r}_v)}{\sum_{v \in N(u) \cap F(u)} sim(u, v)}. \tag{9.55}
$$

This approach has its own shortcomings. When there is no intersection between the set of friends and the neighborhood of most similar individuals, the ratings cannot be computed. To mitigate this, one can use the set of k *most similar* friends of an individual $S(i)$ to predict the ratings,

$$
r_{u,i} = \bar{r}_u + \frac{\sum_{v \in S(u)} sim(u, v)(r_{v,i} - \bar{r}_v)}{\sum_{v \in S(u)} sim(u, v)}. \tag{9.56}
$$

Similarly, when friends are not very similar to the individual, the predicted rating can be different from the rating predicted using most similar users. Depending on the context, both equations can be utilized.

Table 9.4. *User-Item Matrix*

	Lion King	Aladdin	Mulan	Anastasia
John	4	3	2	2
Joe	5	2	1	5
Jill	2	5	?	0
Jane	1	3	4	3
Jorge	3	1	1	2

Example 9.5. *Consider the user-item matrix in Table 9.4 and the following adjacency matrix denoting the friendship among these individuals.*

$$
A = \begin{array}{c} \\ John \\ Joe \\ Jill \\ Jane \\ Jorge \end{array}
\begin{array}{ccccc} John & Joe & Jill & Jane & Jorge \\
\left[\begin{array}{ccccc} 0 & 1 & 0 & 0 & 1 \\ 1 & 0 & 1 & 0 & 0 \\ 0 & 1 & 0 & 1 & 1 \\ 0 & 0 & 1 & 0 & 0 \\ 1 & 0 & 1 & 0 & 0 \end{array}\right] \end{array}, \tag{9.57}
$$

We wish to predict $r_{Jill,Mulan}$. We compute the average ratings and similarity between Jill and other individuals using cosine similarity:

$$
\bar{r}_{John} = \frac{4+3+2+2}{4} = 2.75. \tag{9.58}
$$

$$
\bar{r}_{Joe} = \frac{5+2+1+5}{4} = 3.25. \tag{9.59}
$$

$$
\bar{r}_{Jill} = \frac{2+5+0}{3} = 2.33. \tag{9.60}
$$

$$
\bar{r}_{Jane} = \frac{1+3+4+3}{4} = 2.75. \tag{9.61}
$$

$$
\bar{r}_{Jorge} = \frac{3+1+1+2}{4} = 1.75. \tag{9.62}
$$

The similarities are

$$
sim(Jill, John) = \frac{2 \times 4 + 5 \times 3 + 0 \times 2}{\sqrt{29}\sqrt{29}} = 0.79. \tag{9.63}
$$

$$
sim(Jill, Joe) = \frac{2 \times 5 + 5 \times 2 + 0 \times 5}{\sqrt{29}\sqrt{54}} = 0.50. \tag{9.64}
$$

$$
sim(Jill, Jane) = \frac{2 \times 1 + 5 \times 3 + 0 \times 3}{\sqrt{29}\sqrt{19}} = 0.72. \tag{9.65}
$$

$$
sim(Jill, Jorge) = \frac{2 \times 3 + 5 \times 1 + 0 \times 2}{\sqrt{29}\sqrt{14}} = 0.54. \tag{9.66}
$$

Considering a neighborhood of size 2, the most similar users to Jill are John and Jane:

$$N(Jill) = \{John, Jane\}. \tag{9.67}$$

We also know that friends of Jill are

$$F(Jill) = \{Joe, Jane, Jorge\}. \tag{9.68}$$

We can use Equation 9.55 to predict the missing rating by taking the intersection of friends and neighbors:

$$r_{Jill,Mulan} = \bar{r}_{Jill} + \frac{sim(Jill, Jane)(r_{Jane,Mulan} - \bar{r}_{Jane})}{sim(Jill, Jane)}$$

$$= 2.33 + (4 - 2.75) = 3.58. \tag{9.69}$$

Similarly, we can utilize Equation 9.56 to compute the missing rating. Here, we take Jill's two most similar neighbors: Jane and Jorge.

$$r_{Jill,Mulan} = \bar{r}_{Jill} + \frac{sim(Jill, Jane)(r_{Jane,Mulan} - \bar{r}_{Jane})}{sim(Jill, Jane) + sim(Jill, Jorge)}$$

$$+ \frac{sim(Jill, Jorge)(r_{Jorge,Mulan} - \bar{r}_{Jorge})}{sim(Jill, Jane) + sim(Jill, Jorge)}$$

$$= 2.33 + \frac{0.72(4 - 2.75) + 0.54(1 - 1.75)}{0.72 + 0.54} = 2.72 \tag{9.70}$$

9.4 Evaluating Recommendations

When a recommendation algorithm predicts ratings for items, one must evaluate how accurate its recommendations are. One can evaluate the (1) accuracy of predictions, (2) relevancy of recommendations, or (3) rankings of recommendations.

9.4.1 Evaluating Accuracy of Predictions

When evaluating the accuracy of predictions, we measure how close predicted ratings are to the true ratings. Similar to the evaluation of supervised learning, we often predict the ratings of some items with known ratings (i.e., true ratings) and compute how close the predictions are to the true ratings. One of the simplest methods, mean absolute error (MAE), computes the average absolute difference between the predicted ratings and true ratings,

$$MAE = \frac{\sum_{ij} |\hat{r}_{ij} - r_{ij}|}{n}, \tag{9.71}$$

where n is the number of predicted ratings, $\hat{r}_{ij}$ is the predicted rating, and r_{ij} is the true rating. Normalized mean absolute error (NMAE) normalizes MAE by dividing it by the range ratings can take,

$$NMAE = \frac{MAE}{r_{max} - r_{min}}, \tag{9.72}$$

where r_{max} is the maximum rating items can take and r_{min} is the minimum. In MAE, error linearly contributes to the MAE value. We can increase this contribution by considering the summation of squared errors in the root mean squared error (RMSE):

$$RMSE = \sqrt{\frac{1}{n}\sum_{i,j}(\hat{r}_{ij} - r_{ij})^2}. \tag{9.73}$$

Example 9.6. *Consider the following table with both the predicted ratings and true ratings of five items:*

Item	Predicted Rating	True Rating
1	1	3
2	2	5
3	3	3
4	4	2
5	4	1

The MAE, NMAE, and RMSE values are

$$MAE = \frac{|1-3| + |2-5| + |3-3| + |4-2| + |4-1|}{5} = 2. \tag{9.74}$$

$$NMAE = \frac{MAE}{5-1} = 0.5. \tag{9.75}$$

$$RMSE = \sqrt{\frac{(1-3)^2 + (2-5)^2 + (3-3)^2 + (4-2)^2 + (4-1)^2}{5}}. \tag{9.76}$$

$$= 2.28.$$

9.4.2 Evaluating Relevancy of Recommendations

When evaluating recommendations based on relevancy, we ask users if they find the recommended items relevant to their interests. Given a set of recommendations to a user, the user describes each recommendation as

Table 9.5. *Partitioning of Items with Respect to Their Selection for Recommendation and Their Relevancy*

	Selected	Not Selected	Total
Relevant	N_{rs}	N_{rn}	N_r
Irrelevant	N_{is}	N_{in}	N_i
Total	N_s	N_n	N

relevant or *irrelevant*. Based on the selection of items for recommendations and their relevancy, we can have the four types of items outlined in Table 9.5. Given this table, we can define measures that use relevancy information provided by users. *Precision* is one such measure. It defines the fraction of relevant items among recommended items:

$$P = \frac{N_{rs}}{N_s}. \tag{9.77}$$

Similarly, we can use *recall* to evaluate a recommender algorithm, which provides the probability of selecting a relevant item for recommendation:

$$R = \frac{N_{rs}}{N_r}. \tag{9.78}$$

We can also combine both precision and recall by taking their harmonic mean in the *F-measure*:

$$F = \frac{2PR}{P + R}. \tag{9.79}$$

Example 9.7. *Consider the following recommendation relevancy matrix for a set of 40 items. For this table, the precision, recall, and F-measure values are*

	Selected	Not Selected	Total
Relevant	9	15	24
Irrelevant	3	13	16
Total	12	28	40

$$P = \frac{9}{12} = 0.75. \tag{9.80}$$

$$R = \frac{9}{24} = 0.375. \tag{9.81}$$

$$F = \frac{2 \times 0.75 \times 0.375}{0.75 + 0.375} = 0.5. \tag{9.82}$$

9.4.3 Evaluating Ranking of Recommendations

Often, we predict ratings for multiple products for a user. Based on the predicted ratings, we can rank products based on their levels of interestingness to the user and then evaluate this ranking. Given the true ranking of interestingness of items, we can compare this ranking with it and report a value. Rank correlation measures the correlation between the predicted ranking and the true ranking. One such technique is the Spearman's rank correlation discussed in Chapter 8. Let x_i, $1 \leq x_i \leq n$, denote the rank predicted for item i, $1 \leq i \leq n$. Similarly, let y_i, $1 \leq y_i \leq n$, denote the true rank of item i from the user's perspective. Spearman's rank correlation is defined as

$$\rho = 1 - \frac{6 \sum_{i=1}^{n}(x_i - y_i)^2}{n^3 - n},$$
(9.83)

where n is the total number of items.

Here, we discuss another rank correlation measure: Kendall's tau. We KENDALL'S say that the pair of items (i, j) are *concordant* if their ranks $\{x_i, y_i\}$ and TAU $\{x_j, y_j\}$ are in order:

$$x_i > x_j, \quad y_i > y_j \quad \text{or} \quad x_i < x_j, \quad y_i < y_j.$$
(9.84)

A pair of items is *discordant* if their corresponding ranks are not in order:

$$x_i > x_j, \quad y_i < y_j \quad \text{or} \quad x_i < x_j, \quad y_i > y_j.$$
(9.85)

When $x_i = x_j$ or $y_i = y_j$, the pair is neither concordant nor discordant. Let c denote the total number of concordant item pairs and d the total number of discordant item pairs. Kendall's tau computes the difference between the two, normalized by the total number of item pairs $\binom{n}{2}$:

$$\tau = \frac{c - d}{\binom{n}{2}}.$$
(9.86)

Kendall's tau takes value in range $[-1, 1]$. When the ranks completely agree, all pairs are concordant and Kendall's tau takes value 1, and when the ranks completely disagree, all pairs are discordant and Kendall's tau takes value -1.

Example 9.8. *Consider a set of four items* $I = \{i_1, i_2, i_3, i_4\}$ *for which the predicted and true rankings are as follows:*

	Predicted Rank	True Rank
i_1	1	1
i_2	2	4
i_3	3	2
i_4	4	3

The pair of items and their status {concordant/discordant} are

$$(i_1, i_2) : concordant \tag{9.87}$$

$$(i_1, i_3) : concordant \tag{9.88}$$

$$(i_1, i_4) : concordant \tag{9.89}$$

$$(i_2, i_3) : discordant \tag{9.90}$$

$$(i_2, i_4) : discordant \tag{9.91}$$

$$(i_3, i_4) : concordant \tag{9.92}$$

Thus, Kendall's tau for the rankings is

$$\tau = \frac{4 - 2}{6} = 0.33. \tag{9.93}$$

9.5 Summary

In social media, recommendations are constantly being provided. Friend recommendation, product recommendation, and video recommendation, among others, are all examples of recommendations taking place in social media. Unlike web search, recommendation is tailored to individuals' interests and can help recommend more relevant items. Recommendation is challenging due to the cold-start problem, data sparsity, attacks on these systems, privacy concerns, and the need for an explanation for why items are being recommended.

In social media, sites often resort to classical recommendation algorithms to recommend items or products. These techniques can be divided into content-based methods and collaborative filtering techniques. In content-based methods, we use the similarity between the content (e.g., item description) of items and user profiles to recommend items. In collaborative filtering (CF), we use historical ratings of individuals in the form of a user-item matrix to recommend items. CF methods can be categorized into memory-based and model-based techniques. In memory-based techniques, we use the similarity between users (user-based) or items (item-based) to predict missing ratings. In model-based techniques, we assume that an underlying model describes how users rate items. Using matrix factorization techniques we approximate this model to predict missing ratings. Classical recommendation algorithms often predict ratings for individuals. We discussed ways to extend these techniques to groups of individuals.

In social media, we can also use friendship information to give recommendations. These friendships alone can help recommend (e.g., friend recommendation), can be added as complementary information to classical techniques, or can be used to constrain the recommendations provided by classical techniques.

Finally, we discussed the evaluation of recommendation techniques. Evaluation can be performed in terms of accuracy, relevancy, and rank of recommended items. We discussed MAE, NMAE, and RMSE as methods that evaluate accuracy, precision, recall, and F-measure from relevancy-based methods, and Kendall's tau from rank-based methods.

9.6 Bibliographic Notes

General references for the content provided in this chapter can be found in [Jannach et al., 2010; Resnick and Varian, 1997; Schafer et al., 1999; Adomavicius and Tuzhilin, 2005]. In social media, recommendation is utilized for various items, including blogs [Arguello et al., 2008], news [Liu et al., 2010; Das et al., 2007], videos [Davidson et al., 2010], and tags [Sigurbjörnsson and Van Zwol, 2008]. For example, YouTube video recommendation system employs co-visitation counts to compute the similarity between videos (items). To perform recommendations, videos with high similarity to a seed set of videos are recommended to the user. The seed set consists of the videos that users watched on YouTube (beyond a certain threshold), as well as videos that are explicitly favorited, "liked," rated, or added to playlists.

Among classical techniques, more on content-based recommendation can be found in [Palla et al., 2007], and more on collaborative filtering can be found in [Su and Khoshgoftaar, 2009; Sarwar et al., 2001; Schafer et al., 2007]. Content-based and CF methods can be combined into *hybrid* methods, which are not discussed in this chapter. A survey of hybrid methods is available in [Burke, 2002]. More details on extending classical techniques to groups are provided in [Jameson and Smyth, 2007].

When making recommendations using social context, we can use additional information such as tags [Guy et al., 2010; Sen et al., 2009] or trust [Golbeck and Hendler, 2006; O'Donovan and Smyth, 2005; Massa and Avesani, 2004; Ma et al., 2009]. For instance, in [Tang, Gao, and Liu, 2012b], the authors discern multiple facets of trust and apply multifaceted trust in social recommendation. In another work, Tang et al. [2012a] exploit the evolution of both rating and trust relations for social recommendation. Users in the physical world are likely to ask for suggestions from their local friends while they also tend to seek suggestions from users with high global reputations (e.g., reviews by vine voice reviewers of Amazon.com). Therefore, in addition to friends, one can also use global network information for better recommendations. In [Tang et al., 2013b], the authors exploit both local and global social relations for recommendation.

When recommending people (potential friends), we can use all these types of information. A comparison of different people recommendation techniques can be found in the work of Chen et al. [2009]. Methods that extend classical techniques with social context are discussed in [Ma et al., 2008, 2011; Konstas et al., 2009].

9.7 Exercises

Classical Recommendation Algorithm

1. Discuss one difference between content-based recommendation and collaborative filtering.

2. Compute the missing rating in this table using user-based collaborative filtering (CF). Use cosine similarity to find the nearest neighbors.

	God	Le Cercle Rouge	Cidade de Deu	Rashomon	La vita e bella	$\bar{r}_u$
Newton	3	0	3	3	2	
Einstein	5	4	0	2	3	
Gauss	1	2	4	2	0	
Aristotle	3	?	1	0	2	1.5
Euclid	2	2	0	1	5	

Assuming that you have computed similarity values in the following table, calculate Aristotle's rating by completing these four tasks:

	Newton	Einstein	Gauss	Euclid
Aristotle	0.76	?	0.40	0.78

- Calculate the similarity value between Aristotle and Einstein.
- Identify Aristotle's two nearest neighbors.
- Calculate $\bar{r}_u$ values for everyone (Aristotle's is given).
- Calculate Aristotle's rating for *Le Cercle Rouge*.

3. In an item-based CF recommendation, describe how the recommender finds and recommends items to the given user.

Recommendation Using Social Context

4. Provide two examples where social context can help improve classical recommendation algorithms in social media.

5. In Equation 9.54, the term $\beta \sum_{i=1}^{n} \sum_{j \in F(i)} sim(i, j) \|U_i - U_j\|_F^2$ is added to model the similarity between friends' tastes. Let $T \in \mathbb{R}^{n \times n}$ denote the pairwise trust matrix, in which $0 \leq T_{ij} \leq 1$ denotes how much user i trusts user j. Using your intuition on how trustworthiness of individuals should affect recommendations received from them, modify Equation 9.54 using trust matrix T.

Evaluating Recommendation Algorithms

6. What does "high precision" mean? Why is precision alone insufficient to measure performance under normal circumstances? Provide an example to show that both precision and recall are important.

7. When is Kendall's tau equal to -1? In other words, how is the predicted ranking different from the true ranking?

10

Behavior Analytics

What motivates individuals to join an online group? When individuals abandon social media sites, where do they migrate to? Can we predict box office revenues for movies from tweets posted by individuals? These questions are a few of many whose answers require us to analyze or predict behaviors on social media.

Individuals exhibit different behaviors in social media: as individuals or as part of a broader *collective behavior*. When discussing *individual behavior*, our focus is on one individual. *Collective behavior* emerges when a population of individuals behave in a similar way with or without coordination or planning.

In this chapter we provide examples of individual and collective behaviors and elaborate techniques used to *analyze*, *model*, and *predict* these behaviors.

10.1 Individual Behavior

We read online news; comment on posts, blogs, and videos; write reviews for products; post; like; share; tweet; rate; recommend; listen to music; and watch videos, among many other daily behaviors that we exhibit on social media. What are the types of individual behavior that leave a trace on social media?

We can generally categorize individual online behavior into three categories (shown in Figure 10.1):

1. **User-User Behavior.** This is the behavior individuals exhibit with respect to other individuals. For instance, when befriending someone, sending a message to another individual, playing games, following, inviting, blocking, subscribing, or chatting, we are demonstrating a user-user behavior.

271

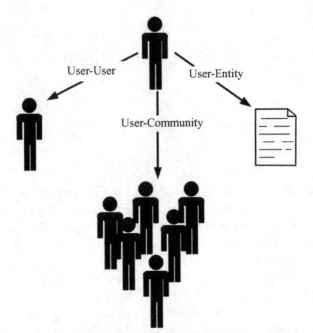

Figure 10.1. Individual Behavior.

2. **User-Community Behavior.** The target of this type of behavior is a community. For example, joining or leaving a community, becoming a fan of a community, or participating in its discussions are forms of user-community behavior.
3. **User-Entity Behavior.** The target of this behavior is an entity in social media. For instance, it includes writing a blogpost or review or uploading a photo to a social media site.

As we know, *link data* and *content data* are frequently available on social media. Link data represents the interactions users have with other users, and content data is generated by users when using social media. One can think of *user-user* behavior as users linking to other users and *user-entity* behavior as users generating and consuming content. Users interacting with communities is a blend of linking and content-generation behavior, in which one can simply join a community (linking), read or write content for a community (content consumption and generation), or can do a mix of both activities. *Link analysis* and *link prediction* are commonly used to analyze links, and *text analysis* is designed to analyze content. We use these techniques to analyze, model, and predict individual behavior.

10.1.1 Individual Behavior Analysis

Individual behavior analysis aims to understand how different factors affect individual behaviors observed online. It aims to correlate those behaviors (or their intensity) with other measurable characteristics of users, sites, or contents that could have possibly resulted in those behaviors.

First we discuss an example of behavior analysis on social media and demonstrate how this behavior can be analyzed. After that, we outline the process that can be followed to analyze any behavior on social media.

Community Membership in Social Media

Users often join different communities in social media; the act of becoming a community member is an example of user-community behavior. Why do users join communities? In other words, what factors affect the community-joining behavior of individuals?

To analyze community-joining behavior, we can observe users who join communities and determine the factors that are common among them. Hence, we require a population of users $U = \{u_1, u_2, \ldots, u_n\}$, a community C, and community membership information (i.e., users $u_i \in U$ who are members of C). The community need not be explicitly defined. For instance, one can think of individuals buying a product as a community, and people buying the product for the first time as individuals joining the community. To distinguish between users who have already joined the community and those who are now joining it, we need community memberships at two different times: t_1 and t_2, with $t_2 > t_1$. At t_2, we determine users such as u who are currently members of the community, but were not members at t_1. These new users form the subpopulation that is analyzed for community-joining behavior.

To determine factors that affect community-joining behavior, we can design hypotheses based on different factors that describe when community-joining behavior takes place. We can verify these hypotheses by using data available on social media. The factors used in the validated hypotheses describe the behavior under study most accurately.

One such hypothesis is that individuals are inclined toward an activity when their friends are engaged in the same activity. Thus, if the hypothesis is valid, a factor that plays a role in users joining a community is the number of their friends who are already members of the community. In data mining terms, this translates to using the number of friends of an individual in a community as a feature to predict whether the individual joins the

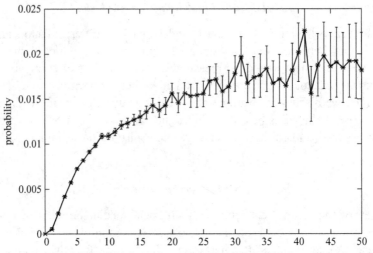

Figure 10.2. Probability of Joining a Community (with Error Bars) as a Function of the Number of Friends *m* Already in the Community (from Backstrom et al. [2006]).

community (i.e., class attribute). Figure 10.2 depicts the probability of joining a community with respect to the number of friends an individual has who are already members of the community. The probability increases as more friends are in a community, but a *diminishing returns* property is also observed, meaning that when enough friends are inside the community, more friends have no or only marginal effects on the likelihood of the individual's act of joining the community.

DIMINISHING RETURNS

Thus far we have defined only one feature. However, one can go beyond a single feature. Figure 10.3 lists the comprehensive features that can be used to analyze community-joining behavior.

As discussed, these features may or may not affect the joining behavior; thus, a validation procedure is required to understand their effect on the joining behavior. Which one of these features is more relevant to the joining behavior? In other words, which feature can help best determine whether individuals will join or not?

To answer this question, we can use any *feature selection* algorithm. Feature selection algorithms determine features that contribute the most to the prediction of the class attribute. Alternatively, we can use a classification algorithm, such as decision tree learning, to identify the relationship between features and the class attribute (i.e., joined={Yes, No}). The earlier a feature is selected in the learned tree (i.e., is closer to the root of the tree), the more important to the prediction of the class attribute value.

Feature Set	Feature
Features related to the community, C. (Edges between only members of the community are $E_C \subseteq E$.)	Number of members ($|C|$).
	Number of individuals with a friend in C (the *fringe* of C) .
	Number of edges with one end in the community and the other in the fringe.
	Number of edges with both ends in the community, $|E_C|$.
	The number of open triads: $\|\{(u, v, w)\|(u, v) \in E_C \wedge (v, w) \in E_C \wedge (u, w) \notin E_C \wedge u \neq w\}\|$.
	The number of closed triads: $\|\{(u, v, w)\|(u, v) \in E_C \wedge (v, w) \in E_C \wedge (u, w) \in E_C\}\|$.
	The ratio of closed to open triads.
	The fraction of individuals in the fringe with at least k friends in the community for $2 \leq k \leq 19$.
	The number of posts and responses made by members of the community.
	The number of members of the community with at least one post or response.
	The number of responses per post.
Features related to an individual u, and her set S of friends in community C.	Number of friends in community ($|S|$).
	Number of adjacent pairs in S ($\|\{(u, v)\|u, v \in S \wedge (u, v) \in E_C\}\|$).
	Number of pairs in S connected via a path in E_C.
	Average distance between friends connected via a path in E_C.
	Number of community members reachable from S using edges in E_C.
	Average distance from S to reachable community members using edges in E_C.
	The number of posts and response made by individuals in S.
	The number of individuals in S with at least 1 post or response.

Figure 10.3. User Community-Joining Behavior Features (from Backstrom et al. [2006]).

By performing decision tree learning for a large dataset of users and the features listed in Figure 10.3, one finds that not only the number of friends inside a community but also how these friends are connected to each other affect the joining probability. In particular, the denser the subgraph of friends inside a community, the higher the likelihood of a user joining the community. Let S denote the set of friends inside community C, and let E_S denote the set of edges between these $|S|$ friends. The maximum number of edges between these S friends is $\binom{|S|}{2}$. So, the edge density is $\phi(S) = E_s/\binom{|S|}{2}$. One finds that the higher this density, the more likely that one is going to join a community. Figure 10.4 shows the first two levels of the decision tree learned for this task using features described in Figure 10.3. Higher level features are more discriminative in decision tree learning, and in our case, the most important feature is the density of edges for the friends subgraph inside the community.

To analyze community-joining behavior, one can design features that are likely to be related to community joining behavior. Decision tree learning can help identify which features are more predictive than others. However, how can we evaluate if these features are designed well and whether other features are not required to accurately predict joining behavior? Since classification is used to learn the relation between features and behaviors one can always use classification evaluation metrics such as accuracy to evaluate the performance of the learned model. An accurate model translates to an accurate learning of feature-behavior association.

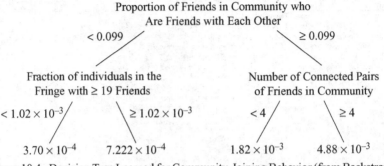

Figure 10.4. Decision Tree Learned for Community-Joining Behavior (from Backstrom et al. [2006]).

A Behavior Analysis Methodology

The analysis of community-joining behavior can be summarized via a four-step methodology for behavioral analysis. The same approach can be followed as a general guideline for analyzing other behaviors in social media.

Commonly, to perform behavioral analysis, one needs the following four components:

1. **An observable behavior.** The behavior that is analyzed needs to be observable. For instance, to analyze community-joining behavior, it is necessary to be able to accurately observe the joining of individuals (and possibly their joining times).
2. **Features.** One needs to construct relevant data features (covariates) that may or may not affect (or be affected by) the behavior. Anthropologists and sociologists can help design these features. The intrinsic relation between these features and the behavior should be clear from the domain expert's point of view. In community-joining behavior, we used the number of friends inside the community as one feature.
3. **Feature-Behavior Association.** This step aims to find the relationship between features and behavior, which describes how changes in features result in the behavior (or changes its intensity). We used decision tree learning to find features that are most correlated with community-joining behavior.
4. **Evaluation Strategy.** The final step evaluates the findings. This evaluation guarantees that the findings are due to the features defined and not to externalities. We use classification accuracy to verify the quality of features in community-joining behavior. Various evaluation techniques can be used, such as randomization tests discussed in Chapter 8. In randomization tests, we measure a phenomenon in a dataset and then randomly generate subsamples from the dataset in

which the phenomenon is guaranteed to be removed. We assume
the phenomenon has happened when the measurements on the subsamples are different from the ones on the original dataset. Another
approach is to use *causality testing* methods. Causality testing methods measure how a feature can affect a phenomenon. A well-known
causality detection technique is called *granger causality* due to Clive
W. J. Granger, the Nobel laureate in economics.

Definition 10.1. Granger Causality. *Assume we are given
two temporal variables* $X = \{X_1, X_2, \ldots, X_t, X_{t+1}, \ldots\}$ *and* $Y = \{Y_1, Y_2, \ldots, Y_t, Y_{t+1}, \ldots\}$. *Variable X "Granger causes" variable Y
when historical values of X can help better predict Y than just using
the historical values of Y.*

Consider a linear regression model outlined in Chapter 5. We can predict Y_{t+1} by using either $Y_1, \ldots, Y_t$ or a combination of $X_1, \ldots, X_t$
and $Y_1, \ldots, Y_t$.

$$Y_{t+1} = \sum_{i=1}^{t} a_i Y_i + \epsilon_1, \tag{10.1}$$

$$Y_{t+1} = \sum_{i=1}^{t} a_i Y_i + \sum_{i=1}^{t} b_i X_i + \epsilon_2, \tag{10.2}$$

where ϵ_1 and ϵ_2 are the regression model errors. Now, if $\epsilon_2 < \epsilon_1$, it
indicates that using X helps reduce the error. In this case, X Granger
causes Y.

10.1.2 Individual Behavior Modeling

Similar to network models, models of individual behavior can help concretely describe why specific individual behaviors are observed in social
media. In addition, they allow for controlled experiments and simulations
that can help study individuals in social media.

As with other modeling approaches (see Chapter 4), in behavior modeling, one must make a set of assumptions. Behavior modeling can be
performed via a variety of techniques, including those from economics,
game theory, or network science. We discussed some of these techniques in
earlier chapters. We review them briefly here, and refer interested readers
to the respective chapters for more details.

- **Threshold models (Chapter 8).** When a behavior diffuses in a network, such as the behavior of individuals buying a product and
  referring it to others, one can use threshold models. In threshold

models, the parameters that need to be learned are the node activation threshold θ_i and the influence probabilities w_{ij}. Consider the following methodology for learning these values. Consider a merchandise store where the store knows the connections between individuals and their transaction history (e.g., the items that they have bought). Then, w_{ij} can be defined as the

fraction of times user i buys a product and

user j buys the same product **soon** after that

The definition of "soon" requires clarification and can be set based on a site's preference and the average time between friends buying the same product. Similarly, θ_i can be estimated by taking into account the average number of friends who need to buy a product before user i decides to buy it. Of course, this is only true when the products bought by user i are also bought by her friends. When this is not the case, methods from collaborative filtering (see Chapter 9) can be used to find out the average number of **similar** items that are bought by user i's friends before user i decides to buy a product.

- **Cascade Models (Chapter 7).** Cascade models are examples of scenarios where an innovation, product, or information cascades through a network. The discussion with respect to cascade models is similar, to the threshold models with the exception that cascade models are sender-centric. That is, the sender decides to activate the receiver, whereas threshold models are receiver-centric, in which receivers get activated by multiple senders. Therefore, the computation of the ICM parameters needs to be done from the sender's point of view in cascade models. Note that both threshold and cascade models are examples of individual behavior modeling.

10.1.3 Individual Behavior Prediction

As discussed previously, most behaviors result in newly formed links in social media. It can be a link to a user, as in befriending behavior; a link to an entity, as in buying behavior; or a link to a community, as in joining behavior. Hence, one can formulate many of these behaviors as a link prediction problem. Next, we discuss link prediction in social media.

Link Prediction

Link prediction assumes a graph $G(V, E)$. Let $e(u, v) \in E$ represent an interaction (edge) between nodes u and v, and let $t(e)$ denote the time of the interaction. Let $G[t_1, t_2]$ represent the subgraph of G such that all edges are created between t_1 and t_2 (i.e., for all edges e in this subgraph, $t_1 < t(e) < t_2$). Now given four time stamps $t_1 < t'_1 < t_2 < t'_2$, a link prediction algorithm is given the subgraph $G[t_1, t'_1]$ (training interval) and is expected to predict edges in $G[t_2, t'_2]$ (testing interval). Note that, just like new edges, new nodes can be introduced in social networks; therefore, $G[t_2, t'_2]$ may contain nodes not present in $G[t_1, t'_1]$. Hence, a link prediction algorithm is generally constrained to predict edges only for pairs of nodes that are present during the training period. One can add extra constraints such as predicting links only for nodes that are incident to at least k edges (i.e., have degree greater or equal to k) during both testing and training intervals.

Let $G(V_{train}, E_{train})$ be our training graph. Then, a link prediction algorithm generates a sorted list of most probable edges in $V_{train} \times V_{train} - E_{train}$. The first edge in this list is the one the algorithm considers the most likely to soon appear in the graph. The link prediction algorithm assigns a score $\sigma(x, y)$ to every edge $e(x, y)$ in $V_{train} \times V_{train} - E_{train}$. Edges sorted by this value in decreasing order will create our ranked list of predictions. $\sigma(x, y)$ can be predicted based on different techniques. Note that any similarity measure between two nodes can be used for link prediction; therefore, methods discussed in Chapter 3 are of practical use here. We outline some of the most well-established techniques for computing $\sigma(x, y)$ here.

Node Neighborhood-Based Methods

The following methods take advantage of neighborhood information to compute the similarity between two nodes.

- **Common Neighbors**. In this method, one assumes that the more common neighbors that two nodes share, the more similar they are. Let $N(x)$ denote the set of neighbors of node x. This method is formulated as

$$\sigma(x, y) = |N(x) \cap N(y)|. \tag{10.3}$$

- **Jaccard Similarity**. This commonly used measure calculates the likelihood of a node that is a neighbor of either x **or** y to be a common neighbor. It can be formulated as the number of common neighbors divided by the total number of neighbors of either x or y:

$$\sigma(x, y) = \frac{|N(x) \cap N(y)|}{|N(x) \cup N(y)|}. \tag{10.4}$$

- **Adamic and Adar Measure**. A similar measure to Jaccard, this measure was introduced by Lada Adamic and Eytan Adar [2003]. The intuition behind it measure is that if two individuals share a neighbor and that neighbor is a *rare* neighbor, it should have a higher impact on their similarity. For instance, we can define the rareness of a node based on its degree (i.e., the smaller the node's degree, the higher its rareness). The original version of the measure is defined based on webpage features. A modified version based on neighborhood information is

$$\sigma(x, y) = \sum_{z \in N(x) \cap N(y)} \frac{1}{\log |N(z)|}. \qquad (10.5)$$

- **Preferential Attachment**. In the preferential attachment model discussed in Chapter 4, one assumes that nodes of higher degree have a higher chance of getting connected to incoming nodes. Therefore, in terms of connection probability, higher degree nodes are similar. The preferential attachment measure is defined to capture this similarity:

$$\sigma(x, y) = |N(x)| \cdot |N(y)|. \qquad (10.6)$$

Example 10.1. *For the graph depicted in Figure 10.5, the similarity between nodes 5 and 7 based on different neighborhood-based techniques is*

$$(\textit{Common Neighbor}) \ \sigma(5, 7) = |\{4, 6\} \cap \{4\}| = 1 \qquad (10.7)$$

$$(\textit{Jaccard}) \ \sigma(5, 7) = \frac{|\{4, 6\} \cap \{4\}|}{|\{4, 6\} \cup \{4\}|} = \frac{1}{2} \qquad (10.8)$$

$$(\textit{Adamic and Adar}) \ \sigma(5, 7) = \frac{1}{\log |\{5, 6, 7\}|} = \frac{1}{\log 3} \qquad (10.9)$$

$$(\textit{Preferential Attachment}) \ \sigma(5, 7) = |\{4\}| \cdot |\{4, 6\}| = 1 \times 2 = 2 \quad (10.10)$$

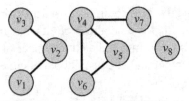

Figure 10.5. Neighborhood-Based Link Prediction Example.

Table 10.1. *A Comparison between Link Prediction Methods*

	First edge	Second edge	Third edge
Common Neighbors	$\sigma(6,7)=1$	$\sigma(1,3)=1$	$\sigma(5,7)=1$
Jaccard Similarity	$\sigma(1,3)=1$	$\sigma(6,7)=1/2$	$\sigma(5,7)=1/2$
Adamic and Adar	$\sigma(1,3)=1/\log 2$	$\sigma(6,7)=1/\log 3$	$\sigma(5,7)=1/\log 3$
Preferential Attachment	$\sigma(2,4)=6$	$\sigma(2,5)=4$	$\sigma(2,6)=4$

In Figure 10.5, there are eight nodes; therefore, we can have a maximum of $\binom{8}{2}=28$ edges. We already have six edges in the graph; hence, there are $28-6=22$ other edges that are not in the graph. For all these edges, we can compute the similarity between their endpoints using the aforementioned neighborhood-based techniques and identify the top three most likely edges that are going to appear in the graph based on each technique. Table 10.1 shows the top three edges based on each technique and the corresponding values for each edge. As shown in this table, different methods predict different edges to be most important; therefore, the method of choice depends on the application.

Methods Based on Paths between Nodes

Similarity between nodes can simply be computed from the shortest path distance between them. The closer the nodes are, the higher their similarity. This similarity measure can be extended by considering multiple paths between nodes and their neighbors. The following measures can be used to calculate similarity.

- **Katz measure.** Similar to the Katz centrality defined in Chapter 3, one can define the similarity between nodes x and y as

$$\sigma(x,y)=\sum_{l=1}^{\infty}\beta^l|paths_{x,y}^{<l>}|, \qquad (10.11)$$

where $|paths_{x,y}^{<l>}|$ denotes the number of paths of length l between x and y. β is a constant that exponentially damps longer paths. Note that a very small β results in a common neighbor measure (see Exercises). Similar to our finding in Chapter 3, one can find the Katz similarity measure in a closed form by $(I-\beta A)^{-1}-I$. The Katz measure can also be weighted or unweighted. In the unweighted format, $|paths_{x,y}^{<1>}|=1$ if there is an edge between x and y. The weighted version is more suitable for multigraphs, where multiple edges can exist between the same pair of nodes. For example, consider two authors x and y who have collaborated c times. In this case, $|paths_{x,y}^{<1>}| = c$.

- **Hitting and Commute Time**. Consider a random walk that starts at node x and moves to adjacent nodes uniformly. Hitting time $H_{x,y}$ is the expected number of random walk steps needed to reach y starting from x. This is a distance measure. In fact, a smaller hitting time implies a higher similarity; therefore, a negation can turn it into a similarity measure:

$$\sigma(x, y) = -H_{x,y}. \qquad (10.12)$$

Note that if node y is highly connected to other nodes in the network (i.e., has a high stationary probability π_y), then a random walk starting from any x likely ends up visiting y early. Hence, all hitting times to y are very short, and all nodes become similar to y. To account for this, one can normalize hitting time by multiplying it with the stationary probability π_y:

$$\sigma(x, y) = -H_{x,y}\pi_y. \qquad (10.13)$$

Hitting time is not symmetric, and in general, $H_{x,y} \neq H_{y,x}$. Thus, one can introduce the *commute* time to mitigate this issue:

$$\sigma(x, y) = -(H_{x,y} + H_{y,x}). \qquad (10.14)$$

Similarly, commute time can also be normalized,

$$\sigma(x, y) = -(H_{x,y}\pi_y + H_{y,x}\pi_x). \qquad (10.15)$$

- **Rooted PageRank**. A modified version of the PageRank algorithm can be used to measure similarity between two nodes x and y. In rooted PageRank, we measure the stationary probability of y: π_y given the condition that during each random walk step, we jump to x with probability α or a random neighbor with probability $1 - \alpha$. The matrix format discussed in Chapter 3 can be used to solve this problem.
- **SimRank**. One can define similarity between two nodes recursively based on the similarity between their neighbors. In other words, similar nodes have similar neighbors. SimRank performs the following:

$$\sigma(x, y) = \gamma \cdot \frac{\sum_{x' \in N(x)} \sum_{y' \in N(y)} \sigma(x', y')}{|N(x)||N(y)|}, \qquad (10.16)$$

where y is some value in range $[0, 1]$. We set $\sigma(x, x) = 1$, and by finding the fixed point of this equation, we can find the similarity between node x and node y

After one of the aforementioned measures is selected, a list of the top most similar pairs of nodes are selected. These pairs of nodes denote edges predicted to be the most likely to soon appear in the network. Performance (precision, recall, or accuracy) can be evaluated using the testing graph and by comparing the number of the testing graph's edges that the link prediction algorithm successfully reveals. Note that the performance is usually very low, since many edges are created due to reasons not solely available in a social network graph. So, a common baseline is to compare the performance with random edge predictors and report the factor improvements over random prediction.

10.2 Collective Behavior

Collective behavior, first defined by sociologist Robert Park, refers to a population of individuals behaving in a similar way. This similar behavior can be planned and coordinated, but is often spontaneous and unplanned. For instance, individuals stand in line for a new product release, rush into stores for a sale event, and post messages online to support their cause or show their support for an individual. These events, though formed by independent individuals, are observed as a collective behavior by outsiders.

10.2.1 Collective Behavior Analysis

Collective behavior analysis is often performed by analyzing individuals performing the behavior. In other words, one can divide collective behavior into many individual behaviors and analyze them independently. The result, however, when all these analyses are put together would be an *expected* behavior for a large population. The user migration behavior we discuss in this section is an example of this type of analysis of collective behavior.

One can also analyze the population as a whole. In this case, an individual's opinion or behavior is rarely important. In general, the approach is the same as analyzing an individual, with the difference that the content and links are now considered for a large community. For instance, if we are analyzing 1,000 nodes, one can combine these nodes and edges into one hyper-node, where the hyper-node is connected to all other nodes in the graph to which its members are connected and has an internal structure (subgraph) that details the interaction among its members. This approach is unpopular for **analyzing** collective behavior because it does not consider specific individuals and at times, interactions within the population. Interested readers can refer to the bibliographic notes for further references that use this approach to analyze collective behavior. On the contrary, this approach is often considered when **predicting** collective behavior, which is discussed later in this chapter.

User Migration in Social Media

Users often migrate from one site to another for different reasons. The main rationale behind it is that users have to select some sites over others due to their limited time and resources. Moreover, social media's networking often dictates that one cannot freely choose a site to join or stay. An individual's decision is heavily influenced by his or her friends, and vice versa. Sites are often interested in keeping their users, because they are valuable assets that help contribute to their growth and generate revenue by increased traffic. There are two types of migration that take place in social media sites: *site migration* and *attention migration*.

1. **Site Migration.** For any user who is a member of two sites s_1 and s_2 at time t_i, and is only a member of s_2 at time $t_j > t_i$, then the user is said to have migrated from site s_1 to site s_2.
2. **Attention Migration.** For any user who is a member of two sites s_1 and s_2 and is active at both at time t_i, if the user becomes inactive on s_1 and remains active on s_2 at time $t_j > t_i$, then the user's attention is said to have migrated away from site s_1 and toward site s_2.

Activity (or inactivity) of a user can be determined by observing the user's actions performed on the site. For instance, we can consider a user active in interval $[t_i, t_i + \delta]$, if the user has performed at least one action on the site during this interval. Otherwise, the user is considered inactive.

The interval δ could be measured at different granularity, such as *days*, *weeks*, *months*, and *years*. It is common to set $\delta = 1$ month. To analyze the migration of populations across sites, we can analyze migrations of individuals and then measure the rate at which the population of these individuals is migrating across sites. Since this method analyzes migrations at the individual level, we can use the methodology outlined in Section 10.1.1 for individual behavior analysis as follows.

The Observable Behavior

Site migration is rarely observed since users often abandon their accounts rather than closing them. A more observable behavior is attention migration, which is clearly observable on most social media sites. Moreover, when a user commits site migration, it is often too late to perform preventive measures. However, when attention migration is detected, it is still possible to take actions to retain the user or expedite his or her attention migration to guarantee site migration. Thus, we focus on individuals whose attention has migrated.

To observe attention migrations, several steps need to be taken. First, users are required to be identified on multiple networks so that their activity on multiple sites can be monitored simultaneously. For instance, username huan.liu1 on Facebook is username liuhuan on Twitter. This identification can be done by collecting information from sites where individuals list their multiple identities on social media sites. On social networking sites such as Google+ or Facebook, this happens regularly. The second step is collecting multiple snapshots of social media sites. At least two snapshots are required to observe migrations. After these two steps, we can observe whether attention migrations have taken place or not. In other words, we can observe if users have become inactive on one of the sites over time. Figure 10.6 depicts these migrations for some well-known social media sites. In this figure, each radar chart shows migrations *from* a site to multiple sites. Each target site is shown as a vertex, and the longer the spokes toward that site, the larger the migrating population to it.

Features

Three general features can be considered for user migration: (1) *user activity* on one site, (2) *user network size*, and (3) *user rank*. User activity is important, because we can conjecture that a more active user on one site is less likely to migrate. User network size is important, because a user with more social ties (i.e., friends) in a social network is less likely to move. Finally, user rank is important. The rank is the value of a user as perceived by others. A user with high status in a network is less likely to move to a new one where he or she must spend more time getting established.

User activity can be measured differently for different sites. On Twitter, it can be the number of tweets posted by the user; on Flickr, the number photos uploaded by the user; and on YouTube, the number of videos the user has uploaded. One can normalize this value by its maximum in the site (e.g.,

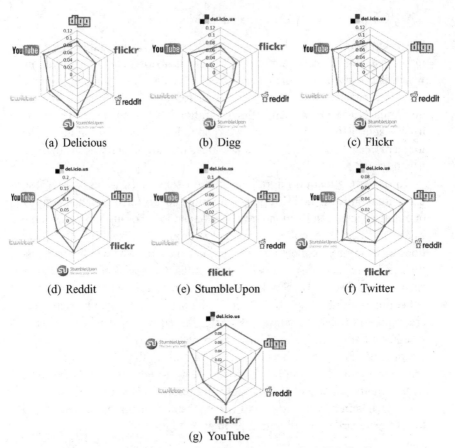

(a) Delicious   (b) Digg   (c) Flickr

(d) Reddit   (e) StumbleUpon   (f) Twitter

(g) YouTube

Figure 10.6. Pairwise Attention Migration among Social Media Sites.

the maximum number of videos any user has uploaded) to get an activity measure in the range [0,1]. If a user is allowed to have multiple activities on a site, as in posting comments and liking videos, then a linear combination of these measures can be used to describe user activity on a site.

User network size can be easily measured by taking the number of friends a user has on the site. It is common for social media sites to facilitate the addition of friends. The number of friends can be normalized in the range [0,1] by the maximum number of friends one can have on the site.

Finally, user rank is how important a user is on the site. Some sites explicitly provide their users' prestige rank list (e.g., top 100 bloggers), whereas for others, one needs to approximate a user's rank. One way of approximating it is to count the number of citations (in-links) an individual is receiving from others. A practical technique is to perform this via web search engines. For instance, user `test` on StumbleUpon has `http://test.stumpleupon.com` as his profile page. A Google search for `link:http://test.stumbleupon.com` provides us with the number of in-links to the profile on StumbleUpon and can be considered as a ranking measure for user `test`.

These three features are correlated with the site attention migration behavior and one expects changes in them when migrations happen.

Feature-Behavior Association

Given two snapshots of a network, we know if users migrated or not. We can also compute the values for the aforementioned features. Hence, we can determine the correlation between features and migration behavior.

Let vector $Y \in \mathbb{R}^n$ indicate whether any of our n users have migrated or not. Let $X_t \in \mathbb{R}^{3 \times n}$ be the features collected (activity, friends, rank) for any one of these users at time stamp t. Then, the correlation between features X_t and labels Y can be computed via logistic regression. How can we verify that this correlation is not random? Next, we discuss how we verify that this correlation is statistically significant.

Evaluation Strategy

To verify if the correlation between features and the migration behavior is not random, we can construct a random set of migrating users and compute X_{Random} and Y_{Random} for them as well. This can be obtained by shuffling the rows of the original X_t and Y. Then, we perform logistic regression on these new variables. This approach is very similar to the shuffle test presented in Chapter 8. The idea is that if some behavior creates a change in features, then other random behaviors should not create that drastic a change. So, the observed correlation between features and the behavior should be significantly different in both cases. The correlation can be described in terms of logistic regression coefficients, and the significance can be measured via any significance testing methodology. For instance, we can employ the χ^2-*statistic*,

χ^2-STATISTIC

$$\chi^2 = \sum_{i=1}^{n} \frac{(A_i - R_i)^2}{R_i},$$

(10.17)

where n is the number of logistic regression coefficients, A_i's are the coefficients determined using the original dataset, and R_i's are the coefficients obtained from the random dataset.

10.2.2 Collective Behavior Modeling

Consider a hypothetical model that can simulate voters who cast ballots in elections. This effective model can help predict an election's turnout rate as an outcome of the collective behavior of voting and help governments prepare logistics accordingly. This is an example of collective behavior modeling, which improves our understanding of the collective behaviors that take place by providing concrete explanations.

Collective behavior can be conveniently modeled using some of the techniques discussed in Chapter 4, "Network Models". Similar to collective behavior, in network models, we express models in terms of characteristics observable in the population. For instance, when a power-law degree distribution is required, the preferential attachment model is preferred, and when the small average shortest path is desired, the small-world model is the method of choice. In network models, node properties rarely play a role; therefore, they are reasonable for modeling collective behavior.

10.2.3 Collective Behavior Prediction

Collective behavior can be predicted using methods we discussed in Chapters 7 and 8. For instance, epidemics can predict the effect of a disease on a population and the behavior that the population will exhibit over time. Similarly, implicit influence models such as the LIM model discussed in Chapter 8 can estimate the influence of individuals based on collective behavior attributes, such as the size of the population adopting an innovation at any time.

As noted earlier, collective behavior can be analyzed either in terms of individuals performing the collective behavior or based on the population as a whole. When predicting collective behavior, it is more common to consider the population as a whole and aim to predict some phenomenon. This simplifies the challenges and reduces the computation dramatically, since the number of individuals who perform a collective behavior is often large and analyzing them one at a time is cumbersome.

In general, when predicting collective behavior, we are interested in predicting the intensity of a phenomenon, which is due to the collective behavior of the population (e.g., how many of them will vote?) To perform this prediction, we utilize a data mining approach where features that describe the population well are used to predict a response variable (i.e., the intensity of the phenomenon). A training-testing framework or correlation analysis is used to determine the generalization and the accuracy of the predictions. We discuss this collective behavior prediction strategy through the following example. This example demonstrates how the collective behavior of individuals on social media can be utilized to predict real-world outcomes.

Predicting Box Office Revenue for Movies

Can we predict opening-weekend revenue for a movie from its prerelease chatter among fans? This tempting goal of *predicting the future* has been around for many years. The goal is to predict the collective behavior of watching a movie by a large population, which in turn determines the revenue for the movie. One can design a methodology to predict box office revenue for movies that uses Twitter and the aforementioned collective behavior prediction strategy. To summarize, the strategy is as follows:

1. Set the target variable that is being predicted. In this case, it is the revenue that a movie produces. Note that the revenue is the direct result of the collective behavior of going to the theater to watch the movie.
2. Determine the features in the population that may affect the target variable.
3. Predict the target variable using a supervised learning approach, utilizing the features determined in step 2.
4. Measure performance using supervised learning evaluation.

One can use the population that is discussing the movie on Twitter before its release to predict its opening-weekend revenue. The target variable is the amount of revenue. In fact, utilizing only eight features, one can predict the revenue with high accuracy. These features are the average hourly number of tweets related to the movie for each of the seven days prior to the movie opening (seven features) and the number of opening theaters for the movie (one feature). Using only these eight features, training data for some movies (their seven-day tweet rates, their number of opening theaters, and their revenue), and a linear regression model, one can predict the movie opening-weekend revenue with high correlation. It has been shown by researchers (see Bibliographic Notes) that the predictions using this approach are closer to reality than that of the Hollywood Stock Exchange (HSX), which is the gold standard for predicting revenues for movies.

This simple model for predicting movie revenue can be easily extended to other domains. For instance, assume we are planning to predict another collective behavior outcome, such as the number of individuals who aim to buy a product. In this case, the target variable y is the number of individuals who will buy the product. Similar to tweet rate, we require some feature A that denotes the attention the product is receiving. We also need to model the publicity of the product P. In our example, this was the number of theaters for the movie; for a product, it could represent the number of stores that sell it. A simple linear regression model can help learn the relation between these features and the target variable:

$$y = w_1 A + w_2 P + \epsilon, \tag{10.18}$$

where ϵ is the regression error. Similar to our movie example, one attempts to extract the values for A and P from social media.

10.3 Summary

Individuals exhibit different behaviors in social media, which can be categorized into individual and collective behavior. Individual behavior is the behavior that an individual targets toward (1) another individual (*individual-individual behavior*), (2) an entity (*individual-entity behavior*), or (3) a community (*individual-community behavior*). We discussed how to analyze and predict individual behavior. To analyze individual behavior, there is a four-step procedure, outlined as a guideline. First, the behavior observed should be clearly observable on social media. Second, one needs to design meaningful features that are correlated with the behavior taking place in social media. The third step aims to find correlations and relationships between features and the behavior. The final step is to verify these relationships that are found. We discussed community joining as an example of individual behavior. Modeling individual behavior can be performed via cascade or threshold models. Behaviors commonly result in interactions in the form of links; therefore, link prediction techniques are highly efficient in predicting behavior. We discussed neighborhood-based and path based techniques for link prediction.

Collective behavior is when a group of individuals with or without coordination act in an aligned manner. Collective behavior analysis is either done via individual behavior analysis and then averaged or analyzed collectively. When analyzed collectively, one commonly looks at the general patterns of the population. We discussed user migrations in social media as an example of collective behavior analysis. Modeling collective behavior can be performed via network models, and prediction is possible by using population properties to predict an outcome. Predicting movie box-office revenues was given as an example, which uses population properties such as the rate at which individuals are tweeting to demonstrate the effectiveness of this approach.

It is important to evaluate behavior analytics findings to ensure that these finding are not due to externalities. We discussed causality testing, randomization tests, and supervised learning evaluation techniques for evaluating behavior analytics findings. However, depending on the context, researchers may need to devise other informative techniques to ensure the validity of the outcomes.

10.4 Bibliographic Notes

In addition to methods discussed in this chapter, game theory and theories from economics can be used to analyze human behavior [Easley and Kleinberg, 2010]. Community-joining behavior analysis was first introduced by [Backstrom et al., 2006]. The approach discussed in this chapter is a brief summary of their approach for analyzing community-joining behavior. Among other individual behaviors, tie formation is analyzed in detail. In [Wang et al., 2009], the authors analyze tie formation behavior on Facebook and investigate how visual cues influence individuals with no prior interaction to form ties. The features used are gender (i.e., male or female), and visual conditions (attractive, nonattractive, and no photo). Their analyses show that individuals have a tendency to connect to attractive opposite-sex individuals when no other information is available. Analyzing individual information-sharing behavior helps understand how individuals disseminate information on social media. Gundecha et al. [2011] analyze how the information-sharing behavior of individuals results in vulnerabilties and how one can exploit such vulnerabilities to secure user privacy on a social networking site. Finally, most social media mining research is dedicated to analyzing a single site; however, users are often members of different sites and hence, current studies need to be generalized to cover multiple sites. Zafarani and Liu [2009a, 2013] were the first to design methods that help connect user identities across social media sites using behavioral modeling. A study of user tagging behavior across sites is available in [Wang et al., 2011].

General surveys on link prediction can be found in [Adamic and Adar, 2003; Liben-Nowell and Kleinberg, 2003; Al Hasan et al., 2006; Lü and Zhou, 2011]. Individual behavior prediction is an active area of research.

Location prediction is an active area of individual behavior analysis that has been widely studied over a long period in the realm of mobile computing. Researchers analyze human mobility patterns to improve location prediction services, thereby exploiting their potential power on various applications such as mobile marketing [Barwise and Strong, 2002; Barnes and Scornavacca, 2004], traffic planning [Ben-Akiva et al., 1998; Dia, 2001], and even disaster relief [Gao et al., 2011a,b; Goodchild and Glennon, 2010; Gao et al., 2012a; Wang and Huang, 2010; Barbier et al., 2012; Kumar et al., 2013]. Other general references can be found in [Backstrom et al., 2010; Monreale et al., 2009; Spaccapietra et al., 2008; Thanh and Phuong, 2007; Scellato et al., 2011; Gao et al., 2012b,c].

Kumar et al. [2011] first analyzed migration in social media. Other collective behavior analyses can be found in Leskovec et al. [2009]. The movie revenue prediction was first discussed by Asur and Huberman [2010]. Another example of collective behavior prediction can be found in the work of O'Connor et al. [2010], which proposed using Twitter data for opinion polls. Their results are highly correlated with Gallup opinion polls for presidential job approval. In [Abbasi et al., 2012], the authors analyzed collective social media data and show that by carefully selecting data from social media, it is possible to use social media as a lens to analyze and even predict real-world events.

10.5 Exercises

Individual Behavior

1. • Name five real-world behaviors that are commonly difficult to observe in social media (e.g., your daily schedule or where you eat lunch are rarely available in social media).
    • Select one behavior that is most likely to leave traces online. Can you think of a methodology for identifying that behavior using these traces?

2. Consider the "commenting under a blogpost" behavior in social media. Follow the four steps of behavior analysis to analyze this behavior.

3. We emphasized selecting meaningful features for analyzing a behavior. Discuss a methodology to verify if the selected features carry enough information with respect to the behavior being analyzed.

4. Correlation does not imply causality. Discuss how this fact relates to most of the datasets discussed in this chapter being temporal.

5. Using a neighborhood-based link prediction method compute the top two most likely edges for the following figure.

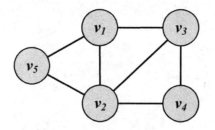

6. Compute the most likely edge for the following figure for each path-based link prediction technique.

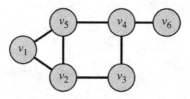

7. In a link prediction problem, show that for small β, the *Katz* similarity measure $(\sigma(u,v) = \Sigma_{\ell=1}^{\infty} \beta^{\ell} \cdot |path_{u,v}^{<\ell>}|)$ becomes *Common neighbors* $(\sigma(u,v) = |N(u) \cap N(v)|)$.

8. Provide the matrix format for rooted PageRank and SimRank techniques.

Collective Behavior

9. Recent research has shown that social media can help replicate survey results for elections and ultimately predict presidential election outcomes. Discuss what possible features can help predict a presidential election.

Notes

Chapter 1

1. The data has a power-law distribution and more often than not, data is not independent and identically distributed (i.i.d.) as generally assumed in data mining.

Chapter 2

1. This is similar to plotting the probability mass function for degrees.
2. Instead of W in weighted networks, C is used to clearly represent capacities.
3. This edge is often called the *weak link*.
4. The proof is omitted here and is a direct result from the minimum-cut/maximum flow theorem not discussed in this chapter.

Chapter 3

1. This constraint is optional and can be lifted based on the context.
2. When $\det(\mathbf{I} - \alpha A^T) = 0$, it can be rearranged as $\det(A^T - \alpha^{-1}I) = 0$, which is basically the characteristic equation. This equation first becomes zero when the largest eigenvalue equals α^{-1}, or equivalently $\alpha = 1/\lambda$.
3. When $d_j^{\text{out}} = 0$, we know that since the out-degree is zero, $\forall i, A_{j,i} = 0$. This makes the term inside the summation $\frac{0}{0}$. We can fix this problem by setting $d_j^{\text{out}} = 1$ since the node will not contribute any centrality to any other nodes.
4. Here, we start from v_1 and follow the edges. One can start from a different node, and the result should remain the same.
5. HITS stands for hypertext-induced topic search.

Chapter 4

1. For a more detailed approach refer to [Clauset et al., 2009].
2. Note that for $c = 1$, the component size is stable, and in the limit, no growth will be observed. The phase transition happens exactly at $c = 1$.
3. Hint: The proof is similar to the proof provided for the likelihood of observing m edges (Proposition 4.3).

Chapter 5

1. See [Zafarani, Cole, and Liu, 2010] for a repository of network data.
2. One can use all unique words in all documents (D) or a more frequent subset of words in the documents for vectorization.
3. Note that in our example, the class attribute can take two values; therefore, the initial guess of $P(y_i = 1 | N(v_i)) = \frac{1}{2} = 0.5$ is reasonable. When a class attribute takes n values, we can set our initial guess to $P(y_i = 1 | N(v_i)) = \frac{1}{n}$.

Chapter 6

1. For more details refer to [Chung, 1996].
2. See [Kossinets and Watts, 2006] for details.
3. Let X be the solution to spectral clustering. Consider an orthogonal matrix Q (i.e., $QQ^T = I$). Let $Y = XQ$. In spectral clustering, we are maximizing $Tr(X^T LX) = Tr(X^T LXQQ^T) = Tr(Q^T X^T LXQ) = Tr((XQ)^T L(XQ)) = Tr(Y^T LY)$. In other words, Y is another answer to our trace-maximization problem. This proves that the solution X to spectral clustering is non-unique under orthogonal transformations Q.
4. http://www.mturk.com.

Chapter 7

1. This assumption can be lifted [Kempe et al., 2003].
2. See [Gruhl et al., 2004] for an application in the blogosphere.
3. Formally, assuming $P \neq NP$, there is no polynomial time algorithm for this problem.
4. The internal-influence model is similar to the SI model discussed later in the section on epidemics. For the sake of completeness, we provide solutions to both. Readers are encouraged to refer to that model in Section 7.4 for further insight.
5. A generalization of these techniques over networks can be found in [Hethcote et al., 1981; Hethcote, 2000; Newman, 2010].

Chapter 8

1. From ADD health data: http://www.cpc.unc.edu/projects/addhealth.
2. The directed case is left to the reader.
3. As defined by the Merriam-Webster dictionary.
4. In the original paper, the authors utilize a weight function instead. Here, for clarity, we use coefficients for all parameters.
5. Note that Equation 8.28 is defined recursively, because $I(p)$ depends on *InfluenceFlow* and that, in turn, depends on $I(p)$ (Equation 8.27). Therefore, to estimate $I(p)$, we can use iterative methods where we start with an initial value for $I(p)$ and compute until convergence.
6. Note that we have assumed that homophily is the leading social force in the network and that it leads to its assortativity change. This assumption is often strong for social networks because other social forces act in these networks.

7. In the original paper, instead of a, the authors use $\ln(a + 1)$ as the variable. This helps remove the effect of a power-law distribution in the number of activated friends. Here, for simplicity, we use the nonlogarithmic form.

8. Note that maximizing this term is equivalent to maximizing the logarithm; this is where Equation 8.41 comes into play.

Chapter 9

1. In Matlab, this can be performed using the svd command.

Bibliography

Abbasi, Mohammad-Ali, Chai, Sun-Ki, Liu, Huan, and Sagoo, Kiran. 2012. Real-World behavior analysis through a social media lens. In: *Social computing, behavioral-cultural modeling and prediction.* Springer, pp. 18–26.

Abello, J., Resende, M., and Sudarsky, S. 2002. Massive quasi-clique detection. *LATIN 2002: Theoretical Informatics.*

Adamic, L.A., and Adar, E. 2003. Friends and neighbors on the web. *Social networks,* **25**(3).

Abrahamson, E. and Rosenkopf, L. 1993. Institutional and competitive bandwagons: Using mathematical modeling as a tool to explore innovation diffusion. *Academy of Management Review,* JSTOR, 487–517.

Adomavicius, Gediminas, and Tuzhilin, Alexander. 2005. Toward the next generation of recommender systems: a survey of the state-of-the-art and possible extensions. *IEEE Transactions on Knowledge and Data Engineering,* **17**(6), 734–749.

Agarwal, N., Liu, H., Tang, L., and Yu, P.S. 2008. Identifying the influential bloggers in a community. In: *Proceedings of the International Conference on Web Search and Web Data Mining.* ACM.

Ahuja, R.K., Magnanti, T.L., Orlin, J.B., and Weihe, K. 1993. *Network flows: theory, algorithms and applications.* Prentice-Hall, **41**(3).

Albert, R., and Barabási, A.L. 2000. Topology of evolving networks: local events and universality. *Physical review letters,* **85**(24).

Al Hasan, Mohammad, Chaoji, Vineet, Salem, Saeed, and Zaki, Mohammed. 2006. Link prediction using supervised learning. In: *SDM'06: Workshop on Link Analysis, Counter-terrorism and Security.*

Anagnostopoulos, A., Kumar, R., and Mahdian, M. 2008. Influence and correlation in social networks. In: *Proceedings of the 14th ACM SIGKDD international conference on Knowledge Discovery and Data Mining.* ACM.

Anderson, L.R., and Holt, C.A. 1996. Classroom games: information cascades. *Journal of Economic Perspectives,* **10**(4).

Anderson, L.R., and Holt, C.A. 1997. Information cascades in the laboratory. *American Economic Review.*

Anderson, R.M., and May, R.M. *Infectious diseases of humans: dynamics and control.* Oxford University Press.

Ankerst, M., Breunig, M.M., Kriegel, H.P., and Sander, J. 1999. OPTICS: ordering points to identify the clustering structure. *Proceedings of the 1999 ACM SIGMOD international conference on Management of Data.*

Aral, S., Muchnik, L., and Sundararajan, A. 2009. Distinguishing influence-based contagion from homophily-driven diffusion in dynamic networks. *Proceedings of the National Academy of Sciences*, **106**(51).

Arguello, Jaime, Elsas, Jonathan, Callan, Jamie, and Carbonell, Jaime. 2008. Document representation and query expansion models for blog recommendation. In: *Proceedings of the second international conference on Weblogs and Social Media (ICWSM)*.

Asch, S.E. 1956. Studies of independence and conformity: I. A minority of one against a unanimous majority. *Psychological Monographs: General and Applied*, **70**(9).

Asur, Sitaram, and Huberman, Bernardo A. 2010. Predicting the future with social media. IEEE international conference on *Web Intelligence and Intelligent Agent Technology*, **1**: 492–499. IEEE.

Backstrom, L., Huttenlocher, D., Kleinberg, J.M., and Lan, X. 2006. Group formation in large social networks: membership, growth, and evolution. In: *Proceedings of the 12th ACM SIGKDD international conference on Knowledge Discovery and Data Mining*. ACM.

Backstrom, L., Sun, E., and Marlow, C. 2010. Find me if you can: improving geographical prediction with social and spatial proximity. In: *Proceedings of the 19th international conference on the World Wide Web*. ACM, pp. 61–70.

Bailey, N.T.J. 1975. *The mathematical theory of infectious diseases and its applications*. Charles Griffin & Company.

Bakshy, E., Hofman, J.M., Mason, W.A., and Watts, D.J. 2001. Everyone's an influencer: quantifying influence on Twitter. In: *Proceedings of the fourth ACM international conference on Web Search and Data Mining*. ACM.

Banerjee, A.V. 1992. A simple model of herd behavior. *The Quarterly Journal of Economics*, **107**(3).

Barabási, A.L., and Albert, R. 1999. Emergence of scaling in random networks. *Science*, **286**(5439).

Barbier, Geoffrey, Zafarani, Reza, Gao, Huiji, Fung, Gabriel, and Liu, Huan. 2012. Maximizing benefits from crowdsourced data. *Computational and Mathematical Organization Theory*, **18**(3), 257–279.

Barbier, Geoffrey, Feng, Zhuo, Gundecha, Pritam, and Liu, Huan. 2013. *Provenance data in social media*. Morgan & Claypool Publishers.

Barnes, S.J., and Scornavacca, E. 2004. Mobile marketing: the role of permission and acceptance. *International Journal of Mobile Communications*, **2**(2), 128–139.

Barrat, Alain, Barthelemy, Marc, and Vespignani, Alessandro. 2008. *Dynamical processes on complex networks*. Vol. 1. Cambridge University Press.

Barwise, P., and Strong, C. 2002. Permission-based mobile advertising. *Journal of interactive Marketing*, **16**(1), 14–24.

Bass, F. 1969. A new product growth model for product diffusion. *Management Science*, **15**, 215–227.

Bell, W.G. 1995. The Great Plague in London in 1665. *Bracken Books*.

Bellma, R. 1956. On a routing problem. *Notes*, **16**(1).

Ben-Akiva, M., Bierlaire, M., Koutsopoulos, H., and Mishalani, R. 1998. DynaMIT: a simulation-based system for traffic prediction. In: *DACCORS Short Term Forecasting Workshop, The Netherlands*.

Berger, E. 2001. Dynamic monopolies of constant size. *Journal of Combinatorial Theory, Series B*, **83**(2).

Berkhin, P. 2006. A survey of clustering data mining techniques. *Grouping Multidimensional Data*.

Bernard, H. Russell. 2012. *Social research methods: qualitative and quantitative approaches*. Sage.

Bikhchandani, S., and Sharma, S. 2001. Herd behavior in financial markets. *IMF Staff Papers*.

Bikhchandani, S., Hirshleifer, D., and Welch, I. 1992. A theory of fads, fashion, custom, and cultural change as informational cascades. *Journal of Political Economy*, **5**.

Bikhchandani, S., Hirshleifer, D., and Welch, I. 1998. Learning from the behavior of others: conformity, fads, and informational cascades. *Journal of Economic Perspectives*, **12**(3).

Bishop, C.M. 1995. Neural networks for pattern recognition. Oxford University Press.

Bishop, C.M. 2006. *Pattern recognition and machine learning*. Vol. 4. Springer.

Bollobás, B. 2001. *Random graphs*. Vol. 73. Cambridge University Press.

Bonabeau, E., Dorigo, M., and Theraulaz, G. 1999. *Swarm intelligence: from natural to artificial systems*. Oxford University Press.

Bondy, J.A., and Murty, U.S.R. 1976. *Graph theory with applications*. Vol. 290. MacMillan, **5**.

Boyd, Stephen Poythress, and Vandenberghe, Lieven. 2004. *Convex optimization*. Cambridge University Press.

Brandes, Ulrik. 2001. A faster algorithm for betweenness centrality. *Journal of Mathematical Sociology*, **25**(2), 163–177.

Broder, Andrei, Kumar, Ravi, Maghoul, Farzin, Raghavan, Prabhakar, Rajagopalan, Sridhar, Stata, Raymie, Tomkins, Andrew, and Wiener, Janet. 2000. Graph structure in the web. *Computer Networks*, **33**(1), 309–320.

Bryman, Alan. 2012. *Social research methods*. Oxford University Press.

Burke, Robin. 2002. Hybrid recommender systems: Survey and experiments. *User Modeling and User-Adapted Interaction*, **12**(4), 331–370.

Candan, K. Selçuk, and Sapino, Maria Luisa. 2010. *Data management for multimedia retrieval*. Cambridge University Press.

Cha, M., Haddadi, H., Benevenuto, F., and Gummadi, K.P. 2010. Measuring user influence in twitter: the million follower fallacy. In: *AAAI Conference on Weblogs and Social Media*, **14**, 8.

Chakrabarti, Soumen. 2003. *Mining the Web: discovering knowledge from hypertext data*. Morgan Kaufmann.

Chen, Jilin, Geyer, Werner, Dugan, Casey, Muller, Michael, and Guy, Ido. 2009. Make new friends, but keep the old: recommending people on social networking sites. In: *Proceedings of the SIGCHI Conference on Human Factors in Computing Systems*. ACM, pp. 201–210.

Chinese, S., et al. 2004. Molecular evolution of the SARS coronavirus during the course of the SARS epidemic in China. *Science*, **303**(5664), 1666.

Christakis, Nicholas A., and James H. Fowler. 2009. Connected: The surprising power of our social networks and how they shape our lives. Hachette Digital, Inc.

Christakis, N.A., and Fowler, J.H. 2007. The spread of obesity in a large social network over 32 years. *New England Journal of Medicine*, **357**(4), 370–379.

Chung, F.R.K. 1996. *Spectral graph theory*. *Journal of the American Mathematical Society*.

Cialdini, R. B., and M. R. Trost. 1998. Social influence: Social norms, conformity and compliance. In: *The handbook of social psychology*. 4th ed. Vol. 2, McGraw-Hill, pp. 151–192.

Clauset, Aaron, Shalizi, Cosma Rohilla, and Newman, Mark EJ. 2009. Power-law distributions in empirical data. *SIAM review*, **51**(4): 661–703.

Coleman, J.S., Katz, E., Menzel, H. 1966. *Medical innovation: a diffusion study*. Bobbs-Merrill.

Cont, R., and Bouchaud, J.P. 2000. Herd behavior and aggregate fluctuations in financial markets. *Macroeconomic Dynamics*, **4**(02).

Cormen, Thomas H., Leiserson, Charles E., Rivest, Ronald L., and Stein, Clifford. 2009. *Introduction to algorithms*. MIT Press.

Currarini, S., Jackson, M.O., and Pin, P. 2009. An Economic Model of Friendship: Homophily, Minorities, and Segregation. *Econometrica*, **77**(4), 1003–1045.

Das, Abhinandan S., Datar, Mayur, Garg, Ashutosh, and Rajaram, Shyam. 2007. Google news personalization: scalable online collaborative filtering. In: *Proceedings of the 16th international conference on the World Wide Web*. ACM, pp. 271–280.

Dash, Manoranjan, and Liu, Huan. 1997. Feature selection for classification. *Intelligent Data Analysis*, **1**(3), 131–156.

Dash, Manoranjan, and Liu, Huan. 2000. Feature selection for clustering. In: *Knowledge Discovery and Data Mining. Current Issues and New Applications*. Springer, pp. 110–121.

Davidson, James, Liebald, Benjamin, Liu, Junning, Nandy, Palash, Van Vleet, Taylor, Gargi, Ullas, Gupta, Sujoy, He, Yu, Lambert, Mike, Livingston, Blake, et al. 2010. The YouTube video recommendation system. In: *Proceedings of the fourth ACM conference on Recommender Systems*. ACM, pp. 293–296.

Davies, D.L., and Bouldin, D.W. 1979. A cluster separation measure. *IEEE Transactions on Pattern Analysis and Machine Intelligence*.

De, I., Pool, S., and Kochen, M. 1978. Contacts and influence. *Social Networks*, **1**, 148.

de Solla Price, D.J. 1965. Networks of scientific papers. *Science*, **149**(3683).

Des Jarlais, D.C., Friedman, S.R., Sotheran, J.L., Wenston, J., Marmor, M. Yancovitz, S.R., Frank, B., Beatrice, S., and Mildvan, D. 1994. Continuity and change within an HIV epidemic. *JAMA*, **271**(2).

Devenow, A., and Welch, I. 1996. Rational herding in financial economics. *European Economic Review*, **40**(3).

Dia, H. 2001. An object-oriented neural network approach to short-term traffic forecasting. *European Journal of Operational Research*, **131**(2), 253–261.

Diestel, R. 2005. Graph theory. 2005. *Graduate Texts in Math.*

Dietz, K. 1967. Epidemics and rumours: a survey. *Journal of the Royal Statistical Society. Series A (General)*.

Dijkstra, E.W. 1959. A note on two problems in connexion with graphs. *Numerische Mathematik*, **1**(1).

Dodds, P.S., and Watts, D.J. 2004. Universal behavior in a generalized model of contagion. *Physical Review Letters*, **92**(21).

Drehmann, M., Oechssler, J., and Roider, A. 2005. Herding and contrarian behavior in financial markets – an internet experiment. *American Economic Review*, **95**.

Duda, Richard O., Hart, Peter E., and Stork, David G. 2012. *Pattern classification*. Wiley-interscience.

Dunn, J.C. 1974. Well-separated clusters and optimal fuzzy partitions. *Journal of Cybernetics*, **4**(1).

Dye, C., and Gay, N. 2003. Modeling the SARS epidemic. *Science*, **300**(5627).

Easley, D., and Kleinberg, J.M. 2010. *Networks, crowds, and markets*. Cambridge Univesity Press.

Eberhart, R.C., Shi, Y., and Kennedy, J. 2001. *Swarm intelligence*. Morgan Kaufmann.

Edmonds, J., and Karp, R.M. 1972. Theoretical improvements in algorithmic efficiency for network flow problems. *Journal of the ACM (JACM)*, **19**(2).

Ellison, Nicole B., et al. 2007. Social network sites: definition, history, and scholarship. *Journal of Computer-Mediated Communication*, **13**(1), 210–230.

Engelbrecht, A.P. 2005. Fundamentals of computational swarm intelligence. *Recherche*, **67**(2).

Erdős, P., and Rényi, A. 1960. *On the evolution of random graphs*. Akademie Kiadó.

Erdős, P., and Rényi, A. 1961. On the strength of connectedness of a random graph. *Acta Mathematica Hungarica*, **12**(1).

Erdős, P., and Rényi, A. 1959. On random graphs. *Publicationes Mathematicae Debrecen*, **6**, 290–297.

Ester, M., Kriegel, H.P., Sander, J., and Xu, X. 1996. A density-based algorithm for discovering clusters in large spatial databases with noise. *Proceedings of the second international conference on Knowledge Discovery and Data Mining, AAAI Press*, 226–231.

Faloutsos, M., Faloutsos, P., and Faloutsos, C. 1999. On power-law relationships of the internet topology. In: *ACM SIGCOMM Computer Communication Review*, **29**.

Fisher, D. 1987. Improving inference through conceptual clustering. *Proceedings of the 1987 AAAI conference*, 461–465.

Floyd, R.W. 1962. Algorithm 97: shortest path. *Communications of the ACM*, **5**(6).

Ford, L.R., and Fulkerson, D.R. 1956. Maximal flow through a network. *Canadian Journal of Mathematics*, **8**(3), 399–404.

Fortunato, S. 2009. Community detection in graphs. *Physics Reports*, **486**(3–5).

Friedman, J., Hastie, T., and Tibshirani, R. 2009. *The elements of statistical learning*. Vol. 1. Springer Series in Statistics.

Gale, D. 1996. What have we learned from social learning? *European Economic Review*, **40**(3).

Gao, Huiji, Wang, Xufei, Barbier, Geoffrey, and Liu, Huan. 2011a. Promoting coordination for disaster relief – from crowdsourcing to coordination. In: *Social computing, behavioral-cultural modeling and prediction*. Springer, pp. 197–204.

Gao, H., Barbier, G., and Goolsby, R. 2011b. Harnessing the Crowdsourcing Power of Social Media for Disaster Relief. *Intelligent Systems, IEEE*, **26**(3), 10–14.

Gao, H., Tang, J., and Liu, H. 2012a. Exploring Social-Historical Ties on Location-Based Social Networks. In: *Proceedings of the sixth international conference on Weblogs and Social Media*.

Gao, H., Tang, J., and Liu, H. 2012b. Mobile Location Prediction in Spatio-Temporal Context. *Nokia Mobile Data Challenge Workshop*.

Gao, Huiji, Tang, Jiliang, and Liu, Huan. 2012c. gSCorr: modeling geo-social correlations for new check-ins on location-based social networks. In: *Proceedings of the 21st ACM international conference on Information and Knowledge Management*. ACM, pp. 1582–1586.

Gibson, D., Kumar, R., and Tomkins, A. 2005. Discovering large dense subgraphs in massive graphs. In: *Proceedings of the 31st international conference on Very Large Data Bases*. VLDB Endowment.

Gilbert, E.N. 1959. Random graphs. *Annals of Mathematical Statistics*, **30**(4).

Girvan, M., and Newman, M.E.J. 2002. Community structure in social and biological networks. *Proceedings of the National Academy of Sciences*, **99**(12).

Golbeck, Jennifer, and Hendler, James. 2006. Filmtrust: movie recommendations using trust in web-based social networks. In: *Proceedings of the IEEE Consumer Communications and Networking Conference*, **96**.

Goldberg, A.V., and Tarjan, R.E. 1988. A new approach to the maximum-flow problem. *Journal of the ACM (JACM)*, **35**(4).

Golub, B., and Jackson, M.O. 2010. Naive learning in social networks and the wisdom of crowds. *American Economic Journal: Microeconomics*, **2**(1).

Goodchild, M.F., and Glennon, J.A. 2010. Crowdsourcing geographic information for disaster response: a research frontier. *International Journal of Digital Earth*, **3**(3), 231–241.

Goodman, L., and Kruskal, W. 1954. Measures of associations for cross-validations. *Journal of the Amerian Statistical Association*, **49**, 732–764.

Goyal, A., Bonchi, F., and Lakshmanan, L.V.S. 2010. Learning influence probabilities in social networks. In: *Proceedings of the Third ACM international conference on Web Search and Data Mining*. ACM.

Granovetter, M. 1976. Threshold models of collective behavior. *American Journal of Sociology*.

Granovetter, M.S. 1983. The strength of weak ties. *American Journal of Sociology*, **1**.

Gray, V. 2007. Innovation in the states: a diffusion study. *American Political Science Review*, **67**(4).

Griliches, Z. 2007. Hybrid corn: an exploration in the economics of technological change. *Econometrica, Journal of the Econometric Society*, **132**.

Gruhl, D., Guha, R., Liben-Nowell, D., and Tomkins, A. 2004. Information diffusion through blogspace. In: *Proceedings of the 13th international conference on the World Wide Web*. ACM.

Guan, Y., Chen, H., Li, K.S., Riley, S., Leung, G.M., Webster, R., Peiris, J.S.M., and Yuen, K.Y. 2007. A model to control the epidemic of H5N1 influenza at the source. *BMC Infectious Diseases*, **7**(1).

Gundecha, Pritam, and Liu, Huan. 2012. Mining Social Media: a Brief Introduction. *Tutorials in Operations Research*, **1**(4).

Gundecha, Pritam, Barbier, Geoffrey, and Liu, Huan. 2011. Exploiting Vulnerability to Secure User Privacy on a Social Networking Site. In: *Proceedings of the 17th ACM SIGKDD international conference on Knowledge Discovery and Data Mining*. KDD, pp. 511–519.

Guy, Ido, Zwerdling, Naama, Ronen, Inbal, Carmel, David, and Uziel, Erel. 2010. Social media recommendation based on people and tags. In: *Proceedings of the 33rd international ACM SIGIR conference on Research and Development in Information Retrieval*. ACM, pp. 194–201.

Guyon, Isabelle. 2006. *Feature extraction: foundations and applications*. Vol. 207. Springer.

Hagerstrand, T., et al. 1967. *Innovation diffusion as a spatial process*. University of Chicago Press.

Hamblin, R.L., Jacobsen, R.B., and Miller, J.L.L. 1973. *A mathematical theory of social change*. Wiley.

Han, Jiawei, Kamber, Micheline, and Pei, Jian. 2006. *Data mining: concepts and techniques*. Morgan Kaufmann.

Handcock, M.S., Raftery, A.E., and Tantrum, J.M. 2007. Model-based clustering for social networks. *Journal of the Royal Statistical Society: Series A (Statistics in Society)*, **170**(2).

Hart, P.E., Nilsson, N.J., and Raphael, B. 2003. A formal basis for the heuristic determination of minimum cost paths. *IEEE Transactions on Systems Science and Cybernetics*, **4**(2).

Haykin, Simon. 1994. Neural networks: a comprehensive foundation. Prentice Hall.

Hethcote, H.W. 1994. A thousand and one epidemic models. *Lecture Notes in Biomathematics*, Springer.

Hethcote, H.W. 2000. The mathematics of infectious diseases. *SIAM Review*, **42**.

Hethcote, H.W., Stech, H.W., and van den Driessche, P. 1981. Periodicity and stability in epidemic models: a survey. In: *Differential equations and applications in ecology, epidemics and population problems (S.N. Busenberg and K.L. Cooke, eds.)*, 65–82.

Hirschman, E.C. 1980. Innovativeness, novelty seeking, and consumer creativity. *Journal of Consumer Research*, **7**.

Hirshleifer, D. 1997. Informational cascades and social conventions. University of Michigan Business School Working Paper No. 9705-10.

Hoff, P.D., Raftery, A.E., and Handcock, M.S. 2002. Latent space approaches to social network analysis. *Journal of the American Statistical Association*, **97**(460).

Hopcroft, J., and Tarjan, R. 1971. Algorithm 447: efficient algorithms for graph manipulation. *Communications of the ACM*, **16**(6).

Hu, Xia, Tang, Jiliang, Gao, Huiji, and Liu, Huan. 2013a. Unsupervised Sentiment Analysis with Emotional Signals. In: *Proceedings of the 22nd international conference on the World Wide Web*. WWW'13. ACM.

Hu, Xia, Tang, Lei, Tang, Jiliang, and Liu, Huan. 2013b. Exploiting Social Relations for Sentiment Analysis in Microblogging. In: *Proceedings of the sixth ACM international conference on Web Search and Data Mining*.

Jaccard, P. 1901. *Distribution de la Flore Alpine: dans le Bassin des dranses et dans quelques régions voisines*. Rouge.

Jackson, M.O. 2010. *Social and economic networks*. Princeton University Press.

Jain, A.K., and Dubes, R.C. 1999. *Algorithms for clustering data*. Prentice-Hall.

Jain, A.K., Murty, M.N., and Flynn, P.J. 1999. Data clustering: a review. *ACM Computing Surveys (CSUR)*, **31**(3).

Jameson, Anthony, and Smyth, Barry. 2007. Recommendation to groups. In: *The adaptive web*. Springer, pp. 596–627.

Jannach, Dietmar, Zanker, Markus, Felfernig, Alexander, and Friedrich, Gerhard. 2010. *Recommender systems: an introduction*. Cambridge University Press.

Jensen, T.R., and Toft, B. 1994. *Graph coloring problems*. Vol. 39. Wiley-Interscience.

Kadushin, Charles. 2012. *Understanding Social Networks: theories, concepts, and findings: theories, concepts, and findings*. Oxford University Press.

Kaplan, Andreas M., and Haenlein, Michael. 2010. Users of the world, unite! The challenges and opportunities of Social Media. *Business Horizons*, **53**(1), 59–68.

Karinthy, F. 1929. *Chains: Everything is Different*, Vintage Press.

Karypis, G., Han, E.H., and Kumar, V. 1999. Chameleon: hierarchical clustering using dynamic modeling. *Computer*, **32**(8), 68–75.

Katz, E., and Lazarsfeld, P.F. 2005. *Personal influence: the part played by people in the flow of mass communications*. Transaction Publication.

Keeling, M.J., and Eames, K.T.D. 2005. Networks and epidemic models. *Journal of the Royal Society Interface*, **2**(4).

Keller, E., and Berry, J. 2003. *The influentials: One American in ten tells the other nine how to vote, where to eat, and what to buy*. Free Press.

Kempe, D., Kleinberg, J.M., and Tardos, É. 2003. Maximizing the spread of influence through a social network. In: *Proceedings of the ninth ACM SIGKDD international conference on Knowledge discovery and data mining*. ACM.

Kennedy, J. 2006. Swarm intelligence. In: *Handbook of Nature-Inspired and Innovative Computing*.

Kermack, W.O., and McKendrick, A.G. 1932. Contributions to the mathematical theory of epidemics. II. The problem of endemicity. *Proceedings of the Royal Society of London. Series A*, **138**(834).

Kietzmann, Jan H., Hermkens, Kristopher, McCarthy, Ian P., and Silvestre, Bruno S. 2011. Social media? Get serious! Understanding the functional building blocks of social media. *Business Horizons*, **54**(3), 241–251.

Kleinberg, J.M. 1998. Authoritative sources in a hyperlinked environment. *Journal of the ACM (JACM)*, **46**(5).

Kleinberg, J.M. 2007. Challenges in mining social network data: processes, privacy, and paradoxes. In: *Proceedings of the 13th ACM SIGKDD international conference on Knowledge Discovery and Data Mining*. ACM, pp. 4–5.

Kleinberg, Jon, and Tardos, Éva. 2005. Algorithm Design. Addison Wesley.

Konstas, Ioannis, Stathopoulos, Vassilios, and Jose, Joemon M. 2009. On social networks and collaborative recommendation. In: *Proceedings of the 32nd international ACM SIGIR conference on Research and Development in Information Retrieval*. ACM, pp. 195–202.

Kosala, R., and Blockeel, H. 2000. Web mining research: a survey. *ACM Sigkdd Explorations Newsletter*, **2**(1).

Kossinets, G., and Watts, D.J. 2006. Empirical analysis of an evolving social network. *Science*, **311**(5757).

Krapivsky, P.L., Redner, S., and Leyvraz, F. 2000. Connectivity of growing random networks. *Physical Review Letters*, **85**(21).

Kruskal, J.B. 1956. On the shortest spanning subtree of a graph and the traveling salesman problem. *Proceedings of the American Mathematical Society*, **7**(1), 48–50.

Kumar, R., Novak, J., and Tomkins, A. 2010. Structure and evolution of online social networks. In: *Link Mining: Models, Algorithms, and Applications*, Springer.

Kumar, R., Raghavan, P., Rajagopalan, S., and Tomkins, A. 1999. Trawling the Web for emerging cyber-communities. *Computer Networks*, **31**(11–16).

Kumar, S., Zafarani, R., and Liu, H. 2011. Understanding User Migration Patterns in Social Media. In: *25th AAAI Conference on Artificial Intelligence*.

Kumar, Shamanth, Zafarani, Reza, and Liu, Huan. 2013. Whom Should I Follow? Identifying Relevant Users During Crises. In: *Proceedings of the 24th ACM Conference on Hypertext and Social Media*.

La Fond, T., and Neville, J. 2010. Randomization tests for distinguishing social influence and homophily effects. In: *Proceedings of the 19th international conference on the World Wide Web*. ACM.

Lancichinetti, A., and Fortunato, S. 2009. Community detection algorithms: a comparative analysis. *Physical Review E*, **80**(5).

Langley, P. 1995. *Elements of machine learning*. Morgan Kaufmann.

Lawson, Charles L., and Hanson, Richard J. 1995. *Solving least squares problems*, **15**. SIAM.

Leibenstein, H. 1950. Bandwagon, snob, and Veblen effects in the theory of consumers' demand. *Quarterly Journal of Economics*, **64**(2).

Leicht, E.A., Holme, P., and Newman, M.E.J. 2005. Vertex similarity in networks. *Physical Review E*, **73**(2).

Leskovec, J., Kleinberg, J.M., and Faloutsos, C. 2005. Graphs over time: densification laws, shrinking diameters and possible explanations. In: *Proceedings of the 11th ACM SIGKDD international conference on Knowledge Discovery in Data Mining*. ACM.

Leskovec, J., Lang, K.J., and Mahoney, M. 2010. Empirical comparison of algorithms for network community detection. In: *Proceedings of the 19th international conference on the World Wide Web*. ACM.

Leskovec, J., McGlohon, M., Faloutsos, C., Glance, N., and Hurst, M. 2007. Cascading behavior in large blog graphs. *Arxiv preprint arXiv:0704.2803*.

Leskovec, Jure, Backstrom, Lars, and Kleinberg, Jon. 2009. Meme-tracking and the dynamics of the news cycle. In: *Proceedings of the 15th ACM SIGKDD international conference on Knowledge Discovery and Data Mining*. ACM, pp. 497–506.

Lewis, T.G. 2009. *Network Science: theory and Applications*. Wiley.

Liben-Nowell, D., and Kleinberg, J.M. 2003. The link-prediction problem for social networks. *Journal of the American Society for Information Science and Technology*, **58**(7).

Lietsala, Katri, and Sirkkunen, Esa. 2008. Social media. Introduction to the tools and processes of participatory economy, Tampere University.

Liu, B. 2007. *Web data mining: exploring hyperlinks, contents, and usage data*. Springer Verlag.

Liu, Huan, and Motoda, Hiroshi. 1998. *Feature extraction, construction and selection: a data mining perspective*. Springer.

Liu, Huan, and Yu, Lei. 2005. Toward integrating feature selection algorithms for classification and clustering. *IEEE Transactions on Knowledge and Data Engineering*, **17**(4), 491–502.

Liu, Jiahui, Dolan, Peter, and Pedersen, Elin Rønby. 2010. Personalized news recommendation based on click behavior. In: *Proceedings of the 15th international conference on Intelligent User Interfaces*. ACM, pp. 31–40.

Lorrain, F., and White, H.C. 1971. Structural equivalence of individuals in social networks. *Journal of Mathematical Sociology*, **1**(1).

Lü, Linyuan, and Zhou, Tao. 2011. Link prediction in complex networks: a survey. *Physica A: Statistical Mechanics and its Applications*, **390**(6), 1150–1170.

Ma, Hao, Yang, Haixuan, Lyu, Michael R., and King, Irwin. 2008. Sorec: social recommendation using probabilistic matrix factorization. In: *Proceedings of the 17th ACM conference on Information and Knowledge Management*. ACM, pp. 931–940.

Ma, Hao, Lyu, Michael R., and King, Irwin. 2009. Learning to recommend with trust and distrust relationships. In: *Proceedings of the third ACM conference on Recommender Systems*. ACM, pp. 189–196.

Ma, Hao, Zhou, Dengyong, Liu, Chao, Lyu, Michael R., and King, Irwin. 2011. Recommender systems with social regularization. In: *Proceedings of the fourth ACM international conference on Web Search and Data Mining*. ACM, pp. 287–296.

Macy, M.W. 1991. Chains of cooperation: threshold effects in collective action. *American Sociological Review*, **56**.

Macy, M.W., and Willer, R. 2002. From factors to actors: computational sociology and agent-based modeling. *Annual Review of Sociology*, **28**.

Mahajan, V. 1985. *Models for innovation diffusion*. Sage Publications.

Mahajan, V., and Muller, E. 1982. Innovative behavior and repeat purchase diffusion models. In: *Proceedings of the American Marketing Educators Conference*, **456**, 460.

Mahajan, V., and Peterson, R.A. 1978. Innovation diffusion in a dynamic potential adopter population. *Management Science*, **24**.

Mansfield, E. 1961. Technical change and the rate of imitation. *Econometrica: Journal of the Econometric Society*, **29**.

Martino, J.P. 1983. *Technological forecasting for decision making*. McGraw-Hill.

Massa, Paolo, and Avesani, Paolo. 2004. Trust-aware collaborative filtering for recommender systems. In: *On the move to meaningful internet systems 2004: CoopIS, DOA, and ODBASE*. Springer, pp. 492–508.

McKay, B.D. 1980. Practical Graph Isomorphism. In: *Proceedings of the 10th Manitoba Conference on Numerical Mathematics and Computing, October 1–4, 1980*, vol. 1. Utilitas Mathematica.

McPherson, M., Smith-Lovin, L., and Cook, J.M. 2001. Birds of a feather: homophily in social networks. *Annual Review of Sociology*, **27**.

Midgley, D.F., and Dowling, G.R. 1978. Innovativeness: the concept and its measurement. *Journal of Consumer Research*, **4**.

Milgram, S. 2009. *Obedience to authority: an experimental view*. Harper Perennial Modern Classics.

Milgram, S., Bickman, L., and Berkowitz, L. 1969. Note on the drawing power of crowds of different size. *Journal of Personality and Social Psychology*, **13**(2).

Milligan, G.W., and Cooper, M.C. 1985. An examination of procedures for determining the number of clusters in a data set. *Psychometrika*, **50**(2).

Mirkin, B.G. 2005. *Clustering for data mining: a data recovery approach*. Chapman & Hall/CRC.

Mislove, Alan, Marcon, Massimiliano, Gummadi, Krishna P., Druschel, Peter, and Bhattacharjee, Bobby. 2007. Measurement and analysis of online social networks. In: *Proceedings of the seventh ACM SIGCOMM conference on Internet Measurement*. ACM, pp. 29–42.

Mitchell, T.M. 1997. Machine learning. WCB. *MacGraw Hill*.

Monreale, A., Pinelli, F., Trasarti, R., and Giannotti, F. 2009. WhereNext: a location predictor on trajectory pattern mining. In: *Proceedings of the 15th ACM SIGKDD international conference on Knowledge Discovery and Data Mining*. ACM, pp. 637–646.

Moore, C., and Newman, M.E.J. 1999. Epidemics and percolation in small-world networks. *Physical Review E*, **61**(5).

Morris, S. 2000. Contagion. *Review of Economic Studies*, **67**(1).

Morstatter, Fred, Pfeffer, Jurgen, Liu, Huan, and Carley, Kathleen M. 2013. Is the sample good enough? Comparing data from Twitter's streaming API with Twitter's firehose. *Proceedings of ICWSM*.

Motwani, R., and Raghavan, P. 1995. *Randomized algorithms*. Chapman & Hall/CRC.

Myung, I.J. 2003. Tutorial on maximum likelihood estimation. *Journal of Mathematical Psychology*, **47**(1), 90–100.

Nelson, M.I., and Holmes, E.C. 2007. The evolution of epidemic influenza. *Nature Reviews Genetics*, **8**(3).

Nemhauser, George L., and Wolsey, Laurence A. 1988. *Integer and combinatorial optimization*. Vol. 18. Wiley.

Neter, John, Wasserman, William, Kutner, Michael H., et al. 1996. *Applied linear statistical models*. Vol. 4. Irwin.

Newman, M.E.J. 2002a. Mixing patterns in networks. *Physical Review E*, **67**(2).

Newman, M.E.J. 2002b. Random graphs as models of networks. In: *Handbook of graphs and networks*, Wiley.

Newman, M.E.J. 2006. Modularity and community structure in networks. *Proceedings of the National Academy of Sciences*, **103**(23).

Newman, M.E.J. 2010. *Networks: an introduction*. Oxford University Press.

Newman, M.E.J., and Girvan, M. 2003. Mixing patterns and community structure in networks. *Statistical Mechanics of Complex Networks*, **625**.

Newman, M.E.J., Forrest, S., and Balthrop, J. 2002. Email networks and the spread of computer viruses. *Physical Review E*, **66**(3).

Newman, M.E.J., Watts, D.J., and Strogatz, S.H. 2002. Random graph models of social networks. *Proceedings of the National Academy of Sciences*, **99**(Suppl. 1).

Newman, M.E.J., Strogatz, S.H., and Watts, D.J. 2000. Random graphs with arbitrary degree distributions and their applications. *Physical Review E*, **64**.

Newman, M.E.J., Barabasi, A.L., and Watts, D.J. 2006. *The structure and dynamics of networks*. Princeton University Press.

Ng, R.T., and Han, J. 1994. Efficient and Effective Clustering Methods for Spatial Data Mining. *Proceedings of the 20th international conference on Very Large Data Bases*, 144–155.

Nocedal, Jorge, and Wright, S. 2006. Numerical optimization, series in operations research and financial engineering. *Springer*.

Nohl, J., Clarke, C.H., et al. 2006. *The Black Death. A Chronicle of the Plague*. Westholme.

O'Connor, Brendan, Balasubramanyan, Ramnath, Routledge, Bryan R., and Smith, Noah A. 2010. From tweets to polls: linking text sentiment to public opinion time series. In: *Proceedings of the international AAAI conference on Weblogs and Social Media*, pp. 122–129.

O'Donovan, John, and Smyth, Barry. 2005. Trust in recommender systems. In: *Proceedings of the 10th international conference on Intelligent User Interfaces*. ACM, pp. 167–174.

Onnela, J.P., and Reed-Tsochas, F. 2010. Spontaneous emergence of social influence in online systems. *Proceedings of the National Academy of Sciences*, **107**(43).

Page, L., Brin, S., Motwani, R., and Winograd, T. 1999. *The PageRank citation ranking: bringing order to the web*, Stanford.

Palla, G., Derényi, I., Farkas, I., and Vicsek, T. 2005. Uncovering the overlapping community structure of complex networks in nature and society. *Nature*, **435** (7043).

Palla, Gergely, Barabási, Albert-László, and Vicsek, Tamás. 2007. Quantifying social group evolution. *Nature*, **446**(7136), 664–667.

Pang, Bo, and Lee, Lillian. 2008. Opinion mining and sentiment analysis. *Foundations and Trends in Information Retrieval*, **2**(1–2), 1–135.

Papadimitriou, Christos H., and Steiglitz, Kenneth. 1998. *Combinatorial optimization: algorithms and complexity*. Courier Dover Publications.

Pastor-Satorras, R., and Vespignani, A. 2001. Epidemic spreading in scale-free networks. *Physical Review Letters*, **86**(14).

Patterson, K.B., and Runge, T. 2002. Smallpox and the Native American. *American Journal of the Medical Sciences*, **323**(4), 216.

Pattillo, J., Youssef, N., and Butenko, S. 2012. Clique Relaxation Models in Social Network Analysis. In: *Handbook of Optimization in Complex Networks*, Springer.

Pazzani, Michael J, and Billsus, Daniel. 2007. Content-based recommendation systems. In: *The adaptive web*. Springer, pp. 325–341.

Peleg, D. 1997. Local majority voting, small coalitions and controlling monopolies in graphs: A review. In: *Proceedings of the third Colloquium on Structural Information and Communication Complexity*, pp. 152–169.

Poli, R., Kennedy, J., and Blackwell, T. 2007. Particle swarm optimization. *Swarm Intelligence*, **1**(1).

Price, D.S. 1976. A general theory of bibliometric and other cumulative advantage processes. *Journal of the American Society for Information Science*, **27**(5).

Prim, R.C. 1957. Shortest connection networks and some generalizations. *Bell System Technical Journal*, **36**(6), 1389–1401.

Quinlan, J.R. 1986. Induction of decision trees. *Machine learning*, **1**(1).

Quinlan, J.R. 1993. *C4. 5: programs for machine learning*. Morgan Kaufmann.

Rand, W.M. 1971. Objective criteria for the evaluation of clustering methods. *Journal of the American Statistical Association*, **66**.

Resnick, Paul, and Varian, Hal, R. 1997. Recommender systems. *Communications of the ACM*, **40**(3), 56–58.

Robertson, T.S. 1967. The process of innovation and the diffusion of innovation. *Journal of Marketing*, **31**.

Rogers, E.M. 2003. *Diffusion of innovations*. Free Press.

Rohlfs, J.H., and Varian, H.R. 2003. *Bandwagon effects in high-technology industries*. The MIT Press.

Rousseeuw, P.J. 1987. Silhouettes: a graphical aid to the interpretation and validation of cluster analysis. *Journal of Computational and Applied Mathematics*, **20**.

Ryan, B., and Gross, N.C. 1943. The diffusion of hybrid seed corn in two Iowa communities. *Rural Sociology*, **8**(1), 15–24.

Salton, G., Wong, A., and Yang, C.S. 1975. A vector space model for automatic indexing. *Communications of the ACM*, **18**(11).

Salton, Gerard, and McGill, Michael, J. 1986. Introduction to modern information retrieval, McGraw-Hill.

Sander, J., Ester, M., Kriegel, H.P., and Xu, X. 1998. Density-based clustering in spatial databases: the algorithm GDBSCAN and its applications. *Data Mining and Knowledge Discovery*, **2**(2).

Sarwar, Badrul, Karypis, George, Konstan, Joseph, and Riedl, John. 2001. Item-based collaborative filtering recommendation algorithms. In: *Proceedings of the 10th international conference on the World Wide Web*. ACM, pp. 285–295.

Scellato, S., Musolesi, M., Mascolo, C., Latora, V., and Campbell, A. 2011. Nextplace: a spatio-temporal prediction framework for pervasive systems. *Pervasive Computing*, 152–169.

Schafer, Ben, J., Konstan, Joseph, and Riedi, John. 1999. Recommender systems in e-commerce. In: *Proceedings of the First ACM conference on Electronic Commerce*. ACM, pp. 158–166.

Schafer, J Ben, Frankowski, Dan, Herlocker, Jon, and Sen, Shilad. 2007. Collaborative filtering recommender systems. In: *The adaptive web*. Springer, pp. 291–324.

Scharfstein, D.S., and Stein, J.C. 1990. Herd behavior and investment. *American Economic Review*.

Schelling, T.C. 1971. Dynamic models of segregation. *Journal of Mathematical Sociology*, **1**(2).

Schelling, T.C. 1978. *Micromotives and macrobehavior*. Norton & Company.

Scott, John. 1988. Social network analysis. *Sociology*, **22**(1), 109–127.

Sen, Shilad, Vig, Jesse, and Riedl, John. 2009. Tagommenders: connecting users to items through tags. In: *Proceedings of the 18th international conference on the World Wide Web*. ACM, pp. 671–680.

Shalizi, C.R., and Thomas, A.C. 2010. Homophily and contagion are generically confounded in observational social network studies. *Sociological Methods & Research*, **40**(2).

Shiller, R.J. 1995. Conversation, information, and herd behavior. *American Economic Review*, **85**(2).

Sigurbjörnsson, Börkur, and Van Zwol, Roelof. 2008. Flickr tag recommendation based on collective knowledge. In: *Proceedings of the 17th international conference on the World Wide Web*. ACM, pp. 327–336.

Simmel, G., and Hughes, E.C. 1949. The sociology of sociability. *American Journal of Sociology*, **55**.

Simon, H.A. 1954. Bandwagon and underdog effects and the possibility of election predictions. *Public Opinion Quarterly*, **18**(3).

Simon, H.A. 1955. On a class of skew distribution functions. *Biometrika*, **42**(3/4).

Snijders, T.A.B., Steglich, C.E.G., and Schweinberger, M. 2006. Modeling the co-evolution of networks and behavior. In *Longitudinal models in the behavioral and related sciences*, Routledge.

Solomonoff, R., and Rapoport, A. 1951. Connectivity of random nets. *Bulletin of Mathematical Biology*, **13**(2).

Spaccapietra, S., Parent, C., Damiani, M.L., De Macedo, J.A., Porto, F., and Vangenot, C. 2008. A conceptual view on trajectories. *Data and Knowledge Engineering*, **65**(1), 126–146.

Stevens, S.S. *On the Theory of Scales of Measurement, Science*, **103**.

Stephen P. Borgatti and Martin G. Everett. 1993. Two algorithms for computing regular equivalence. *Social Networks*, **15**(4).

Strang, D., and Soule, S.A. 1998. Diffusion in organizations and social movements: from hybrid corn to poison pills. *Annual Review of Sociology*, **24**.

Strehl, A., Ghosh, J., and Cardie, C. 2002. Cluster ensembles-a knowledge reuse framework for combining multiple partitions. *Journal of Machine Learning Research*, **3**(3).

Su, Xiaoyuan, and Khoshgoftaar, Taghi, M. 2009. A survey of collaborative filtering techniques. *Advances in Artificial Intelligence*, **4**.

Sun, J., Faloutsos, C., Papadimitriou, S., and Yu, P.S. 2007. GraphScope: parameter-free mining of large time-evolving graphs. In: *Proceedings of the 13th ACM SIGKDD international conference on Knowledge Discovery and Data Mining*. ACM.

Tan, P.N., Steinbach, M., Kumar, V., et al. 2005. *Introduction to data mining*. Pearson Addison Wesley.

Tang, Jiliang, and Liu, Huan. 2012a. Feature Selection with Linked Data in Social Media. In: *SDM*.

Tang, Jiliang, and Liu, Huan. 2012b. Unsupervised Feature Selection for Linked Social Media Data. In: *KDD*.

Tang, Jiliang, and Liu, Huan. 2013. CoSelect: Feature Selection with Instance Selection for Social Media Data. In: *SDM*.

Tang, Jiliang, Gao, Huiji, Liu, Huan, and Sarma, Atish Das. 2012a. eTrust: understanding trust evolution in an online world. In: *KDD*.

Tang, Jiliang, Gao, Huiji, and Liu, Huan. 2012b. mTrust: discerning Multi-Faceted Trust in a Connected World. In: *WSDM*.

Tang, Jiliang, Gao, Huiji, Hu, Xia, and Liu, Huan. 2013a. Exploiting Homophily Effect for Trust Prediction. In: *WSDM*.

Tang, Jiliang, Hu, Xia, Gao, Huiji, and Liu, Huan. 2013b. Exploiting Local and Global Social Context for Recommendation. In: *IJCAI*.

Tang, L., and Liu, H. 2010. Community detection and mining in social media. *Synthesis Lectures on Data Mining and Knowledge Discovery*, **2**(1).

Tang, Lei, and Liu, Huan. 2009. Relational learning via latent social dimensions. In: *Proceedings of the 15th ACM SIGKDD international conference on Knowledge Discovery and Data Mining*. ACM, pp. 817–826.

Tang, Lei, Wang, Xufei, and Liu, Huan. 2012. Community Detection via Heterogeneous Interaction Analysis. *Data Mining and Knowledge Discovery (DMKD)*, **25**(1), 1–33.

Tarde, G. 1907. *Las leyes de la imitación: Estudio sociológico*. Daniel Jorro.

Thanh, N., and Phuong, T.M. 2007. A Gaussian Mixture Model for Mobile Location Prediction. In: *2007 IEEE international conference on Research, Innovation and Vision for the Future*, pp. 152–157.

Travers, J., and Milgram, S. 1969. An experimental study of the small world problem. *Sociometry*, **32**.

Trotter, W. 1916. *Instincts of the Herd in War and Peace.*

Ugander, Johan, Karrer, Brian, Backstrom, Lars, and Marlow, Cameron. 2011. The Anatomy of the Facebook Social Graph, arXiv preprint arXiv:1111.4503.

Valente, T.W. 1995. *Network models of the diffusion of innovations,* Hampton Press.

Valente, T.W. 1996a. Network models of the diffusion of innovations. *Computational & Mathematical Organization Theory,* **2**(2).

Valente, T.W. 1996b. Social network thresholds in the diffusion of innovations. *Social Networks,* **18**(1).

Veblen, T. 1899. *The Theory of the Leisure Class.*

Wang, F., and Huang, Q.Y. 2010. The importance of spatial-temporal issues for case-based reasoning in disaster management. In: *2010 18th international conference on Geoinformatics.* IEEE, pp. 1–5.

Wang, S.S., Moon, S.I., Kwon, K.H., Evans, C.A., and Stefanone, M.A. 2009. Face off: implications of visual cues on initiating friendship on Facebook. *Computers in Human Behavior,* **26**(2).

Wang, Xufei, Tang, Lei, Gao, Huiji, and Liu, Huan. 2010. Discovering Overlapping Groups in Social Media. In: *10th IEEE international conference on Data Mining.*

Wang, Xufei, Kumar, Shamanth, and Liu, Huan. 2011. A study of tagging behavior across social media. *SIGIR Workshop on Social Web Search and Mining (SWSM).*

Warshall, S. 1962. A theorem on boolean matrices. *Journal of the ACM (JACM),* **9**(1).

Wasserman, S., and Faust, K. 1994. Social network analysis: Methods and applications. Cambridge University Press.

Watts, D.J. 1999. Networks, dynamics, and the small-world phenomenon 1. *American Journal of Sociology,* **105**(2).

Watts, D.J. 2002. A simple model of global cascades on random networks. *Proceedings of the National Academy of Sciences,* **99**(9).

Watts, D.J. 2003. *Small worlds: the dynamics of networks between order and randomness.* Princeton University Press.

Watts, D.J., and Dodds, P.S. 2007. Influentials, networks, and public opinion formation. *Journal of Consumer Research,* **34**(4).

Watts, D.J., and Strogatz, S.H. 1997. Collective dynamics of small-world networks. *Nature,* **393**(6684).

Welch, I. 1992. Sequential sales, learning, and cascades. *Journal of Finance,* **47**.

Weng, J., Lim, E.P., Jiang, J., and He, Q. 2010. Twitterrank: finding topic-sensitive influential twitterers. In: *Proceedings of the third ACM international conference on Web Search and Data Mining.* ACM.

West, D.B. 2001. *Introduction to graph theory.* Vol. 2. Prentice-Hall.

White, D.R. 1980. Structural equivalences in social networks: concepts and measurement of role structures. In: *Research Methods in Social Network Analysis Conference,* pp. 193–234.

White, D.R. 1984. Regge: a regular graph equivalence algorithm for computing role distances prior to blockmodeling. *Unpublished manuscript, University of California, Irvine.*

Witten, I.H., Frank, E., and Hall, M.A. 2011. *Data Mining: practical machine learning tools and techniques.* Morgan Kaufmann.

Xu, R., and Wunsch, D. 2005. Survey of clustering algorithms. *IEEE Transactions on Neural Networks,* **16**(3), 645–678.

Yang, J., and Leskovec, J. 2010. Modeling information diffusion in implicit networks. In: *IEEE 10th International Conference on Data Mining.*

Young, H.P. 1988. *Individual strategy and social structure: an evolutionary theory of institutions.* Princeton University Press.

Yule, G.U. 1925. A mathematical theory of evolution, based on the conclusions of Dr. J.C. Willis, FRS. *Philosophical Transactions of the Royal Society of London. Series B, Containing Papers of a Biological Character,* **213**.

Zachary, W.W. 1977. An information flow model for conflict and fission in small groups. *Journal of Anthropological Research,* 452–473.

Zafarani, Reza, and Liu, Huan. 2009a. Connecting Corresponding Identities across Communities. In: *ICWSM.*

Zafarani, Reza, and Liu, Huan. 2009b. Social computing data repository at ASU. *School of Computing, Informatics and Decision Systems Engineering,* Arizona State University.

Zafarani, Reza, and Liu, Huan. 2013. Connecting users across social media sites: a behavioral-modeling approach. In: *Proceedings of the 19th ACM SIGKDD international conference on Knowledge Discovery and Data Mining.* KDD.

Zafarani, Reza, Cole, William D., and Liu, Huan. 2010. Sentiment propagation in social networks: a case study in LiveJournal. In: *Advances in Social Computing.* Springer, pp. 413–420.

Zhao, Zheng Alan, and Liu, Huan. 2011. *Spectral feature selection for data mining.* Chapman & Hall/CRC.

Index